T0330150

CLIMATE CHANGE, TRANSPORT AND ENVIRONMENTAL POLICY

NEW HORIZONS IN ENVIRONMENTAL ECONOMICS

General Editor: Wallace E. Oates, *Professor of Economics,*
University of Maryland

This important series is designed to make a significant contribution to the
development of the principles and practices of environmental economics. It
includes both theoretical and empirical work. International in scope, it addresses
issues of current and future concern in both East and West and in developed and
developing countries.

The main purpose of the series is to create a forum for the publication of high
quality work and to show how economic analysis can make a contribution to
understanding and resolving the environmental problems confronting the world in
the late twentieth century.

Recent titles in the series include:

Climate Change, Transport and Environmental Policy

Empirical Applications in a Federal System

Edited by

Stef Proost

Associate Professor of Economics, Catholic University of Leuven, Belgium and Research Fellow, Fund for Scientific Research, Flanders

and

John B. Braden

Professor of Environmental Economics and Director of the Water Resources Center, University of Illinois, US

NEW HORIZONS IN ENVIRONMENTAL ECONOMICS

Edward Elgar
Cheltenham, UK • Northampton, MA, USA

Published by
Edward Elgar Publishing Limited
8 Lansdown Place
Cheltenham
Glos GL50 2HU
UK

Edward Elgar Publishing, Inc.
6 Market Street
Northampton
Massachusetts 01060
US

A catalogue record for this book
is available from the British Library

Library of Congress Cataloguing in Publication Data

Climate change, transport and environmental policy: empirical
   applications in a federal system/edited by Stef Proost, John B.
   Braden.
     — (New horizons in environmental economics)
   Includes index.
   1. Environmental policy — European Union countries — Congresses.
   2. Environmental policy — United States — Congresses. 3. Climatic
     changes — Government policy — European Union countries — Congresses.
   4. Climatic changes — Government policy — United States — Congresses.
   5. Transportation and state — European Union countries — Congresses.
   6. Transportation and state — United States — Congresses.   I. Proost,
   S.   II. Braden, John B.   III. Series.
   GE190. E85C55   1998
   363.738'7456—dc21   97–29927
                                                                                                          CIP

ISBN 1 85898 599 4

Printed and bound in Great Britain by Biddles Ltd, Guildford and King's Lynn

Contents

Figures

Tables

Contributors

Braden, John B., Professor in the Department of Agricultural and Consumer Economics and Director of the Water Resources Center at the University of Illinois at Urbana-Champaign, US.

Böhringer, Christoph, Head of the Section for Energy Economy Analysis at the Institute of Energy Economics and the Rational Use of Energy, University of Stuttgart, Germany.

Capros, Pantelis, Professor at the Technical University of Athens, Greece.

Carraro, Carlo, Professor in the Department of Economics at the University of Venice, Italy, CEPR Fellow and Research Director of Fondazione Eni Enrico Mattei.

Conrad, Klaus, Professor in the Department of Economics at the University of Mannheim, Germany.

De Borger, Bruno, Professor of Economics at the University of Antwerp, Belgium.

Degraeve, Zeger, Associate Professor of Management Science at the Department of Applied Economics at the Catholic University of Leuven, Belgium.

Denis, Cécile, Directorate-General for Economics and Financial Affairs, Commission of the European Communities, Brussels, Belgium.

Ferris, Michael, Associate Professor in the Department of Computer Science at the University of Wisconsin, US.

Galeotti, Marzio, Professor in the Department of Economics at the University of Bergamo, Italy, and Fondazione Eni Enrico Mattei Fellow.

Georgakopoulos, Panayiotis, Research Officer at the Technical University of Athens, Greece.

Hall, Jane V., Professor in the Department of Economics and Associate Director of the Institute for Economic and Environmental Studies, California State University, US.

Harrington, Winston, Fellow at Resources for the Future, Washington D.C., US.

Koopman, Gert Jan, Commission of the European Communities, Brussels, Belgium.

McConnell, Virginia, Professor in the Department of Economics at the University of Maryland, Baltimore County, and Fellow at Resources for the Future, Washington D.C., US.

Ochelen, Sara, Research Officer at the Centre for Economic Studies at the Catholic University of Leuven, Belgium.

Proost, Stef, Research Fellow of the Fund for Scientific Research Flanders and Associate Professor in the Department of Economics at the Catholic University of Leuven, Belgium.

Rutherford, Thomas F., Associate Professor in the Department of Economics at the University of Colorado at Boulder, US.

Schmidt, Tobias F.N., Research Officer at Centre for European Economic Research (ZEW), Mannheim, Germany.

Swysen, Didier, Research Officer at the Centre for Social and Economic Research (SESO) of the University of Antwerp, Belgium.

Teunen, Leen, ASLK Bank, Brussels, Belgium.

Van Regemorter, Denise, Research Officer at the Centre of Economic Studies at the Catholic University of Leuven, Belgium.

Walls, Margaret, Fellow at Resources for the Future, Washington, DC, US.

Zografakis, Stavros, Research Officer at the Technical University of Athens, Greece.

Foreword

The events that culminated in 1992 in Europe, and the changing political landscape in the United States have had important effects on the way relationships are defined between the central (federal or confederal) governments and the member states. In recognition of these trends, in 1990, the US Information Agency (USIA) issued a special call for transatlantic collaboration on economic and political integration. The seeds of this book were sown in that initiative.

The USIA selected the University of Illinois at Urbana-Champaign (US), the Catholic University of Leuven (Belgium) and Wageningen Agricultural University (Netherlands) to conduct joint research on the consequences of integration for environmental policies. In an attempt to provide a forum for academic researchers from Europe and the US to reflect upon these developments, the cooperating universities organized two symposia. The first, 'Environmental Policy with Political and Economic Integration: The European Union and the United States', took place between 30 September and 2 October 1993, at the University of Illinois in Urbana-Champaign. The papers from this conference were compiled in a book by the same name, edited by John Braden, Henk Folmer and Tom Ulen, and published by Edward Elgar Publishing, Ltd. The second symposium, 'Economic Aspects of Environmental Policy Making in a Federal System', took place between 14 and 16 June 1995, at the Catholic University of Leuven, Belgium. The collection of works presented in this volume has emerged from the latter conference. It is a state-of-the-art scholarly assessment of the economic models used to select environmental governance options in a federal or confederal context. The chapters concentrate on two issues: 1. climate change policies, and 2. transportation and environmental policies. The papers included here are substantially revised versions of those originally given at the Leuven conference, the result of an effort by the contributing authors to incorporate the suggestions and comments of the participants and of reviewers since the summer of 1995. The theoretical papers presented at the conference in Leuven have been grouped in a complementary volume, [a] published by Edward Elgar Publishing, Ltd. [b] in 1997.

In addition to the scholarly symposium, several of the conferees participated in a seminar involving representatives of the European Commission, the government of Belgium, and Belgian scientific and industrial groups, held at the Catholic University of Leuven's faculty club on 16 June 1995. This seminar was extremely helpful in exploring practical applications of the ideas represented in these papers.

The editors gratefully acknowledge the following organizations, without whose support this project would not have materialized:

- Directorate-General for Science, Research and Development of the Commission of the European Communities – 'Human Dimensions of Environmental Change' Programme.
- Directorate-General for Environment, Nuclear Safety and Civil Protection of the Commission of the European Communities.
- American Cultural Centre Brussels.
- United States Information Agency – University Affiliates Program (Project No. IA–ASPS–G1190234).
- The Catholic University of Leuven.
- Centre for Economic Studies (CES).
- University of Illinois at Urbana-Champaign:
  Institute for Environmental Studies
  Illinois Agricultural Experiment Station (Project No. 05–0331).

We would also like to acknowledge the contributions of the following individuals: Jos Delbeke, Mathias Mors, and William Watts, all in the service of the European Commission, and Wim Moesen, Chairman of the Department of Economics at the Catholic University of Leuven, who were instrumental in securing the funding and cooperated greatly with the symposium; Carlo Carraro, Bruno De Borger, Zeger Degraeve, Gert Jan Koopman, Jim Shortle, Ekko Van Ierland and Denise Van Regemorter who made the symposium livelier with their discussions of the theoretical papers presented in this volume; Mathias Mors, Domenico Siniscalso and Ekko van Ierland, who also presented their work at the symposium; Camilla Myrglod and John Ries who served as technical editors for this volume, and Eva Crabbe and the other members of the secretariat of the Centre for Economic Studies, without whose able secretarial services the symposium would not have been possible.

1. Introductory chapter

Stef Proost and John B. Braden

Introduction

One of the major social trends of the late twentieth century has been
political and economic realignment. The unification of Europe, the
dissolution of the Soviet sphere, and the emergence of important new
trade alliances in the Americas and Asia are leading examples. The
political and economic shifts have presented major challenges to many
areas of public policy, including environmental policy. Who will protect
the environment, it may be asked, in a world driven by the struggle for
economic comparative advantage or by nationalistic tendencies that
de-emphasize problems which cross country borders? Can these problems
be adequately dealt with locally? By nations? Or, is there a need
for transnational authority?

There are three well-known reasons why a local approach to environmental problems may prove to be inadequate. First, many environmental
problems have impacts that extend beyond the local level. Acid rain,
ozone formation, global climate change, some forms of water pollution
and bio-diversity degradation are problems on a wider scale. Second, the
solutions to some pollution problems require coordination on a wider
scope because of scale economies in production. For example, a clean car
is easier to produce for a larger market. Finally, some environmental
policy instruments that aim to correct externalities of a local nature
can be misused to protect local industry or to export taxes. In all three
cases some coordination or regulation at a higher level of governance
would be necessary.

In the last 30 years the economics of environmental policy has developed into a well-established field. Most of the literature concentrates on
the problem of an individual government that must contend with the
polluters under its jurisdiction. In recent years this has been comple-
mented by literature on the economics of international agreements where
independent governments voluntarily agree to cooperate in solving
certain environmental problems. This literature is important in order to
understand why the Rio accords from the 1992 Earth Summit or the
regional conventions on acidification in Europe (Helsinki and Sofia
protocols) do or do not work. In fact, it turns out that many regional

1

environmental problems are dealt with in a federal state structure that is neither a monolithic government nor an assembly of independent states. Rather, realistic policies often involve a division of complementary authorities among local, national and transnational authorities.

In recent years, research has been increasing on the unique aspects of policy-making in a multi-layered government, and in particular on the analysis of environmental policy design within such a framework. In the light of these developments, two symposia were held. The first took place in 1993 at the University of Illinois at Urbana-Champaign with a multi-disciplinary approach (Braden et al. (eds) 1996). The second symposium took place in June 1995, at the Catholic University of Leuven, Belgium and focused exclusively on economic issues. Two volumes of papers have been prepared from the 1995 conference. The present volume contains the final versions of the empirical papers presented on that occasion. The theoretical papers on the same subject have been grouped in a complementary volume (Braden and Proost (eds) 1997).

The empirical case studies presented in this volume all share three characteristics. First, there are at least two levels of government considered in each of the studies. Second, they all concentrate on one of two problem domains: greenhouse gas abatement or the transportation sector. Third, they all use quantitative techniques to compare alternative solutions. This last feature is important because the theoretical prescriptions of economists are often inconclusive and depend on combinations of particular parameter values. The empirical analyses explore the implications of plausible parameter values. A quantitative approach also makes it possible to investigate the costs and benefits of a particular solution and their distribution between different groups. In fact, in the European Union, the environmental policy proposals of the European Commission must take into account the costs and benefits to the member states' public authorities (Mors 1994). Finally, a quantitative approach provides insight into the economic consequences of local versus national or federal enactments. This issue is a matter of necessity in Europe as well, where the Community is authorized to take action to protect the environment only to the extent that the objectives can be better attained at the Community level rather than at the level of the individual member states (Art. 130r(4) of the Single European Act, cited in Mors 1994). In conclusion, policy-making requires a quantitative balancing of costs and benefits of alternative policy options.

Structure of policy problems
To tackle the policy problems, models with differing degrees of complexity have been used. In theory, all the problems we deal with have a

three-level structure: there is a federal government, several local governments and many economic agents that pollute.

In Table 1.1, we have distinguished four typical problem settings.

Table 1.1 Structure of regulation problems

Federal Government	Local government	Comments
A Full information on local governments and polluters' behaviour		Federal government maximizes its welfare function; local government is administrative agent of federal government
Full set of policy instruments		
B Full information on local government and polluters' behaviour	Full information on polluters' behaviour	Both levels of government have to share policy instruments on the same polluters; central government acts as von Stackelberg leader
Partial set of policy instruments or	Partial set of policy instruments	
Sets institutions for local governments		
C Imperfect information on local government and on polluters' behaviour	Full information on polluters' behaviour	Local government has information advantage; principal – agent problem where the central government is the principal
Sets institutions	Full set of instruments within the institution	
D Imperfect information on local government and on polluters' behaviour	Imperfect information on polluters' behaviour	Two-level principal agent problem
Sets institutions	Full set of instruments within the institution	

The most tractable problem is case **A** where the federal government has
all relevant information and full control over both the local government
and the polluters. While this is formally equivalent to a typical

one-government problem, it is nonetheless a model that can be helpful in exploring the structure of the problems. Typically, the federal government can deal with environmental problems that differ strongly among regions. In the presence of scale economies in the production of abatement, or constitutional limitations on the type of instruments available (no discrimination of taxes or regulation on a geographical basis), the federal government already faces a fairly complex control problem where it has to balance the benefits and costs in different states. Alternative solutions will have different distributional consequences for the regions involved. In this model setting, the local government has no independence; the fully informed central government uses the local government as an efficient administrative agent. Although this type of information is a prerequisite for rational decision-making in countries with or without federal structures, one finds very few empirical applications. Most of the applications in this book contribute to this area of cost-effectiveness or regional distribution studies.

In case B, the local government has some independence and shares policy instruments with the federal government. As both government levels have a different objective function,[1] perfect coordination between both levels of government is not automatic. Generally, one assumes that the federal government knows the behaviour of the local government and of the polluters. One possible justification for this is that the central government policy adjusts simultaneously to the behaviour of many local governments. In this case it is difficult for the local government to infer the federal government's preferences. Another justification can be found in the political–institutional framework where the local governments give up power to the federation. The federal government becomes a 'leader' in the sense of von Stackelberg. This means that the federal government perfectly anticipates the behaviour of polluters and of the local governments. The local government and the polluters cannot anticipate the behaviour of the federal government, and they take its behaviour as given. An example of this can be found in Ochelen and Proost (1996).

When the federal government can only establish the institutions, that is, the 'rules of the game' for the local governments, but has no direct policy instrument under its control we have an extreme example of a von Stackelberg setting. The federal government will compare alternative equilibria using a welfare function. In each (non-cooperative) equilibrium, local governments use the allocated instruments to their proper advantage. In setting the institutions, the federal government acts as a leader because it anticipates all the reactions of the agents it controls. This setting requires a model where the interaction of local governments is represented. The model has been used to study environmental tax and regulatory competition among states or nations. A survey of these models can be found in Ulph (1996) and an application to tax competition with an illustrative model in Conrad (1997).

In fact, problem setting B can be helpful in analysing a particular policy problem, but it is not internally consistent. If indeed the federal government has all the information, there is no reason to devolve part of the responsibility to the local governments. Therefore case C is more realistic. In this case the central government has an information disadvantage compared to the local government, which has perfect information. Because the local government has perfect information on the local polluters, this problem is a traditional principal–agent problem where the central government is the principal and the local governments are the regulated agents that can have a diverging objective function. Ulph (1997) deals with a theoretical model of this nature. He considers two producers, located in two different states that form a duopoly. Both producers create environmental damage only in their own country. Both state governments use taxes and regulations strategically in order to limit the market share of the producer in the other country. Ulph then introduces a federal government. If that government has perfect information it can correct the equilibrium by restricting the use of certain instruments (for example, minimum standards or taxes). In general, the federal government only has imperfect damage information, meaning that its policy intervention will have some additional constraints. Segerson et al. (1997) provide another example. They model the moral-hazard problem that exists when the federal government has to provide the necessary funds to the state governments to carry out the federal environmental mandates.

Problem setting D is the most realistic but also the most difficult. It is more realistic because the polluters have no incentive to reveal all information to the local government. Baron (1985) is an example of such a model. He deals with the problem of regulating power plants in the midwestern United States that cause acid rain in the northeast states and the eastern provinces of Canada. The revenues of the power plants are regulated by public utility commissions at the state level. The emission abatement equipment of the power plants is, however, regulated by the Federal Environmental Protection Agency. Both controlling agencies have imperfect information on the efficiency of the abatement equipment. Only the firm knows this parameter. Both agencies have conflicting objectives: the local public utility commission wants low production costs and low prices for its consumers, whereas the federal agency takes into account the environmental damage and wants more costly abatement equipment to be installed. Baron shows that if both agencies cooperate they can obtain first-best type of results despite the asymmetric information. If, however, there is no cooperation among the agencies the imperfect information leads to second-best results.

Analysis of climate change policies

The nature of the problem
To combat climate change, several international conferences (Toronto 1988, Cairo 1990, Rio 1992 and Berlin 1995) have called for significant reductions in worldwide CO_2 emissions. These emissions are associated with the use of fossil fuels and are considered to be an important contributor to climate changes that have the potential to warm the globe by one to four degrees Celsius over the next century. In Rio 1992, the European Union promised to stabilize CO_2 emissions by 2000 at the level of 1990, if the other major regions (US and Japan) promised to make similar efforts. Until now, there has been no binding commitment from the other regions. Nevertheless, there is an interest from the side of the EU to reduce carbon dioxide emissions. Different instruments and different strategies have been proposed to achieve this aim. The instruments considered include a carbon-energy tax (originally proposed at a level of $10/bbl of oil equivalent), permits by country and also more diverse sets of instruments that simultaneously address other externalities. Each of these instruments can be applied to all sectors or can be targeted at only some of the polluters. The strategies proposed vary between a fully harmonized introduction of the instruments in all member states to a strategy where the initiative is left to the member states. As a policy problem, global warming raises at least two very different types of questions for a federal state. The first question has to do with the global dimension of the problem: what are the benefits and the costs for the EU or for any other individual nation or group of nations of independent action? This question requires accurate assessments of the damage caused by climate change and a good behavioural representation of the players on the world scene. The second question is internal to the EU and concerns the choice of appropriate instruments and the level of cooperation among member states that achieve the EU reduction goals. It is this second question that has been addressed by four of the chapters in this volume.

The models used
All four of the contributions on global climate change policies use applied general equilibrium models. Capros, Georgakopoulos, Zografakis, van Regemorter and Proost (Chapter 5 in this volume) and Conrad and Schmidt (Chapter 3 in this volume) use the same GEM–E3

model. Carraro and Galeotti (Chapter 4 in this volume) use the WARM model. Böhringer, Ferris and Rutherford (Chapter 2 in this volume) use a special purpose model.

The Böhringer et al. model is a static, neoclassical representation of the EU economy. It contains general equilibrium models for six European states that are linked (representing 90 per cent of the economic activity in the EU) and a 'rest of the world' representation via export and import functions. The model contains eleven sectors and 1985 is used as the benchmark equilibrium. The model does not include a representation of existing taxes.

The WARM model is a dynamic model that contains representations for twelve countries of the EU. It has two distinguishing features. It models the labour market as a segmented market with a wage bargaining game in the leading production sector. This is important because in a noncompetitive labour market, labour can absorb part of the social security reductions that are made possible by carbon taxes. Second, there is an endogenous technical change that is driven by energy prices and this is an important part of the response of economic agents to energy price changes.

The GEM–E3 model is a dynamic general equilibrium model that contains models for eleven EU countries. These countries trade among themselves and with the rest of the world. All types of environmental policy instruments are represented. The labour market can be in disequilibrium. The model contains eleven sectors and models all existing taxes in a detailed way. Conrad and Schmidt use a version where the wage and labour supply are fixed. Capros et al. use a version where labour demand and supply are both variable and are in equilibrium.

The answers provided
1. *What is the cost of emission reductions for the EU as a whole?*
   Böhringer et al. compute a welfare loss[2] of traded auctioned permits of the order of 0.4 per cent for a reduction of 20 per cent.

   Carraro and Galeotti report on the costs of implementing a $10/bbl carbon-energy tax in all EU countries. They find a reduction of GDP of the order of 0.5 per cent in the short run, accompanied by a small increase in employment. This result is obtained due to lags in the bargaining of the unions. Once they start to claim part of the lower social security contributions, employment will decrease compared to the reference situation. In the medium term there are some other perverse effects: GDP growth rates are higher than in the reference and even emissions could be higher than in the reference. This medium-term result is due to income effects.

Conrad and Schmidt report on a reduction of CO_2 emissions of 10 per cent via tradable and nontradable permits, finding that there is a small welfare loss (–0.24 per cent of GDP). Capros et al. report on the implementation of a $10/bbl carbon-energy tax. This corresponds to a decrease of emissions of some 11 per cent and, in the long run, also to a very small gain in GDP of the order of 0.2 per cent.

All in all, the welfare costs of a 10 to 20 per cent reduction in CO_2 emissions seem to be small when there is a coordinated effort at the EU level. Important assumptions to obtain this type of result are a high degree of substitutability among production factors and some market power on the export markets. If neither condition is fulfilled, the welfare costs are likely to be much higher.

2. *Burden sharing among states in the European Union.* Any CO_2 reduction programme needs to be equitable. This should hold within each country with respect to the poorer households. The idea of equitable burden-sharing should also hold with respect to the poorer countries within the Union: the poorer countries should not bear too much of the costs of such a programme.

None of the general equilibrium models discussed here have several types of households explicitly modelled and none have modelled the benefits of reducing CO_2 emissions.[3] Conrad and Schmidt and Capros et al. discuss the distribution of the burden among EU countries. Conrad and Schmidt find that with a 10 per cent reduction via nontradable permits, the largest costs per capita are borne by Denmark and the UK. The costs are never much higher than three times the EU average. Capros et al. find that for $10 a carbon-energy tax, benefits are lowest for Italy, the UK and Germany. As both these results have been produced by the same model GEM–E3, the differences obtained in burden-sharing show that the choice of the environmental policy instrument (taxes versus permits) can have an important effect.

3. *Is trading of emissions among countries important and who gains in that process?* Böhringer et al. find that trading of emissions between countries is not very important. Marginal costs diverge in the nontrading equilibrium mainly between the UK and the others. As a low-cost abater of greenhouse gases, the UK would sell emission allowances to Italy and France. The differences are small, however, so there is almost no aggregate welfare gain for the EU.

Conrad and Schmidt discuss a system of grandfathered permits that reduce the aggregate emissions of carbon dioxide by 10 per cent. When the permits are not tradable, there is an aggregate loss in welfare of 0.25 per cent of GDP. Permit prices diverge strongly between EU countries so that gains can be achieved by trading emission permits between countries. When permits are traded within the EU, the overall welfare costs of emission reduction are reduced to 0.20 per cent of GDP. This means that overall gains from trade are rather small and that the gains of coordination among EU countries would be rather small. Italy, the UK and Denmark are net buyers of permits while Germany and Belgium are important net sellers. The trading of permits among sectors of the same country is much more important than the intercountry trade. Conrad and Schmidt find that not all countries gain in this trade. This is a rather odd result that can only be explained by the incomplete character of the welfare measure used.

The results of Böhringer et al. and Conrad and Schmidt are strikingly contradictory as regards the net sellers and buyers: Böhringer et al. find that the UK is a net seller, while Conrad and Schmidt find that the UK is a net buyer. This has to be explained by different energy data sources or differences in the modelling of the electricity sector. This contrast points out the importance of assumptions and parameter values in the empirical models: slightly different starting-points can have sharply different consequences. A remaining challenge is to refine our understanding of the data and modelling assumptions that led to these conflicting results.

4. *The choice between taxes and grand-fathered permits.* Most industries would prefer grandfathered permits to taxes because they are less costly for the polluters and because they reduce the risks of carbon leakage in the carbon-intensive sectors. One can reckon that, for a reduction of 20 per cent of emissions in a particular industry, a grandfathered permit system costs industry only 10 to 15 per cent of the costs of a carbon tax system. But a grandfathered subsidy also has two disadvantages. First, it constitutes a relative subsidy for the most polluting products and this requires that overall abatement efforts (per unit of product) have to be increased. Second, it does not generate any tax revenue and therefore forgoes the possibility of reducing other more distortionary taxes.

Böhringer et al. find that grandfathering adds 50 per cent to the welfare costs of reducing emissions. The marginal cost of emission reduction doubles. The Böhringer et al. model has no existing taxes so that the 'subsidy to polluters' argument is sufficient cause to prefer taxes or auctioned permits to grandfathered permits.

5. *Are unilateral emission reductions feasible?* Recently the EU switched from a coordinated strategy (the same tax for all EU countries) to a voluntary strategy: let all member states decide for themselves about the implementation of a carbon tax in their own country. This can be interpreted as a noncoordinated strategy. A unilateral 20 per cent

reduction of carbon dioxide emissions by Germany is tested by Böhringer et al. using auctioned permits and grandfathered permits as instruments. This generates a welfare loss for Germany of the order of 0.4 per cent with auctioned permits (or taxes) and of 0.8 per cent with grandfathered permits. The leakage rate is limited to 6 per cent in the case of auctioned permits and to 1 per cent in the case of grandfathered permits. Grandfathered permits reduce the leakage rate because there is a lower cost increase for carbon-intensive industries that are also export intensive (iron and steel, and so on). The welfare loss, however, is larger with grandfathering than with taxes. To summarize the findings of Böhringer et al., it can be said that the welfare cost of unilateral reductions is not extremely high but remains much higher (more than a factor 4) than the cost of the same aggregate emission reduction effort achieved at the EU level. On the other hand, the cost for Germany of unilaterally reducing CO_2 emissions is smaller in absolute terms than the cost for Germany in a coordinated action. Finally, it should be mentioned that unilateral emission reductions require important sectoral shifts in activity (for example, the iron and steel industry reduces its output by 34 per cent).

The Böhringer et al. results were obtained with an Armington type of representation of international trade flows within the EU. They also test a specification where the Armington assumption is replaced by a homogeneous representation of trade for the intra-EU trade. This implies much higher degrees of substitution between home production and exports from other EU countries. Welfare losses for auctioned and grandfathered permits are now slightly smaller (0.3 and 0.7 per cent instead of 0.4 and 0.8 per cent) because it is easier to reduce German CO_2 emissions by substituting carbon-intensive production by imports from other EU countries. This implies very high leakage rates: 70 per cent in the case of auctioned permits and 21 per cent in the case of grandfathered permits. In the homogeneous good formulation the high leakage rates correspond to even larger sectoral shifts in activity for the carbon-intensive sectors. This illustrates the importance of carefully modelling the international trade for estimating the overall efficiency of policies.

Carraro and Galeotti also report results for a unilateral carbon tax introduced by Germany. This seems to have positive effects on GDP in the short run but negative effects on GDP and employment in the medium term. This means that international coordination is not really necessary because unilateral carbon taxes have a positive payoff in the shortrun. This result contrasts with the Böhringer et al. model result and should probably be attributed to the recycling of the tax revenue used to reduce payroll taxes in the Carraro and Galeotti model. In the Böhringer et al. model recycling was lump-sum because there are no pre-existing taxes in the model.

Capros et al. find that when Germany[4] introduces a CO_2 tax unilaterally, it will produce the same small gain in GDP for Germany as a coordinated introduction.

Research agenda

The general equilibrium models produce conflicting results on the welfare cost of CO_2 reductions. There is also no unanimity on the relative costs of carbon emission reduction in different countries and this implies that it is difficult to determine the gains of more coordinated policies. One of the major uncertainties is the intra-EU trade flows. How large are the substitution possibilities between home production and production in the other EU countries? It is this degree of substitutability that will determine what are the effects of noncoordinated policies.

The four chapters all consider a type B regulation problem (c.f. table 1.1) where there is full information and where local government behaviour is myopic, that is, it fails to take account of impacts or reactions in other jurisdictions. Progress can be made in modelling CO_2 tax games between countries and in including asymmetric information aspects.

Analysis of transportation policy issues

The nature of the problem

Mobile source emissions have been an important source of concern in the US since the 1970s and in the European Union since the 1980s. In the US, the federal government sets ambient air quality standards and uses minimum regulations for the tailpipe emissions of cars. The states can impose stronger vehicle emission standards (like California) and can set up maintenance and inspection programmes to meet the ambient standards. This raises two important policy questions. The first question is whether the economies of scale in the production of cars are compatible with locally differentiated car emission standards. The second question is whether decentralized instruments such as inspection and maintenance programmes can function effectively in the hands of the states.

The European Union faces similar problems. Until now it has worked with Union-wide tailpipe emission standards. This has been insufficient to meet the air quality objectives, and the introduction of stricter standards and tax instruments on the use of cars seems likely in the future. The tax instruments have the advantage that they can be more easily differentiated among countries or cities. In the European Union, however, the use of cars is already heavily taxed so that a proportional tax increase will not be effective to reduce pollution. Instead, a complete revision of the structure of taxes is necessary. Moreover, this new structure has to address the pollution dimension, has to raise enough government revenue and should simultaneously correct for the other externality problems that are linked to car use. The other externalities, such as congestion and accidents, might well be more important than air pollution.

The techniques used

The four contributions in this volume dealing with transportation all use partial equilibrium techniques. The focus is on the transportation markets. Interactions with the rest of the economy via the use or the distribution of the tax revenues collected in the transportation sector or via other channels are neglected. This approach is justified as a second-best modelling strategy in so far as current applied general equilibrium models are still too aggregated to address the specificities of the car pollution problem.

Harrington, McConnell and Walls (Chapter 6 in this volume) opt for a cost-benefit perspective in their discussion of California's car standards and in their appreciation of the inspection and maintenance (I&M) programmes. They compare the costs of stricter measures with the environmental benefits provided.

Hall (Chapter 8 in this volume) argues that in the case of automobile pollution, there is often not enough benefit information available to make a full cost-benefit analysis. The author prefers a multicriteria analysis as decision-making tool.

Degraeve, Koopman, Denis and Teunen (Chapter 7 in this volume) make a spatial cost-effectiveness analysis. The environmental constraint is to reach predetermined air quality levels in certain European cities and the objective function is to minimize total compliance cost by selecting the best policy mix. A great variety of policy instruments are represented including different types of standards for cars and fuels, different tax and subsidy programmes for cars, as well as public transport pricing. As policy measures interact and as standards are of a discrete nature, this becomes a complex non-linear programming problem with integer variables for which specific numerical techniques have been developed.

De Borger, Ochelen, Proost and Swysen (Chapter 9 in this volume) use a partial equilibrium model where the different transportation modes are integrated. This model takes into account all external costs, including pollution, congestion and accidents and selects the pricing instruments that maximize the welfare function. The model is solved as a non-linear maximum problem where the levels of different taxes are the control variables. The model is applied to an urban centre and a surrounding non-urban area.

The answers provided

1. *Are stricter nationwide emission standards appropriate?* Harrington et al. find that extending California's car standards to the rest of the country is not efficient. In general, the benefits of lower pollution do not match the extra costs. Because a wider adoption allows larger economies of scale, California would benefit from a wider adoption. The gains to California are much smaller than the net costs to the other states though. Even an adoption limited to the north east of the US would not generate enough benefits. Of course, California has a strong incentive to try to persuade the others to adopt their stricter standards.

   Hall finds that a federal standard can sometimes be the most appropriate instrument even if it is not the most cost-effective. The most cost-effective solution sometimes turns out to be very complex and demands important efforts from a few groups. Since such a solution is difficult to implement in an interregional negotiation framework, federal standards can be preferred.

   Degraeve et al. do not select stricter European-wide standards as the most appropriate instrument to improve air quality in the cities. They opt for a structured circulation tax on emissions that is regionally differentiated. This tax will trigger the adoption of cleaner cars only in those areas where it is necessary.

2. *The future of inspection and maintenance programmes for cars.* Inspection and maintenance (I&M) programmes are potentially very effective in reducing emissions because older cars are responsible for an important share of total car emissions. Harrington et al. find that I&M programmes that were left originally in the hands of the state did not function properly for different reasons. There was a lack of incentives and a lack of knowledge on the effectiveness of testing and repairing. The new federal regulations leave much less freedom to the states but do not guarantee better results. What is needed is a more innovative policy approach that includes tests of new instruments such as remote sensing, repair subsidies and emission fees.

3. *What new structure for car taxation?* At present, European fuel and car taxes bear no relationship to the different external costs that car use generates. De Borger et al. expect that congestion costs will be the dominant external costs followed by air pollution and accidents. In the long term, fuel taxes and car taxes should therefore be replaced by congestion levies that differentiate between peak and off-peak travel. There can remain a role for small fuel taxes (one-fifth of present European levels) that discriminate according to the pollution characteristics of the fuels. Degraeve et al. also favour the replace-

ment of fuel taxes by circulation taxes that are a function of the pollution characteristics of the car. Harrington et al. urge the US to experiment with emission taxes for automobiles.

4. *Are further emission reductions in the transport sector cost-effective?* There seems to be a tendency to overcontrol pollution from the transport sector because it is more visible than the pollution from other sectors. In the three transportation chapters in this volume there is a cost-effectiveness comparison with efforts in other sectors. Harrington et al. think that more abatement efforts in other sectors are probably more cost-effective in California than in the other states. Degraeve et al. include the stricter emission control in other sectors (residential heating and industry) as one of the policy instruments and this instrument is included in most cost-effective policy packages. Finally, De Borger et al. explicitly include the marginal damage of the pollutants in their objective function and in this way control the cost-effectiveness of the efforts in the transport sector. They also find that for pollutants such as CO_2, large efforts in the transport sector are not cost-effective. These conclusions differ between the various pollutants and the different regions considered.

Research agenda

The contributions in this volume indicate that progress has been made in two directions. First, cost-effectiveness studies now take into account the regional disparity of the pollution problem. Second, the range of instruments considered has been widened significantly and now includes more economic instruments. All the chapters considered have implicitly modelled the presence of two government levels. However, not all of them have made the precise objective functions of the different levels explicit. This means that imperfect information and incentive problems are not considered explicitly. These problems, though, may be important as witnessed by the failure of the decentralized I&M programmes in the US. The problems will also grow in importance when the car and fuel tax instruments are more differentiated according to local circumstances because they carry the risk of tax competition and tax exporting.

Notes

1. There are two sources of differences. First, a local government will not consider the welfare of non-inhabitants. Second, it is possible that differences in the political process lead to different welfare weights at the state and federal levels for the different types of inhabitants of the same state.
2. All welfare losses are measured gross, that is, without attributing any benefit specifically to the reduction of pollutants.
3. In GEM–E3 there is the possibility to represent the change in damage flows in all countries associated with a change in the air pollution emissions in one country using the

results of the EXTERN–E research programme of the European Commission (JOULE programme of the Research Directorate).
4. Capros *et al.* also report results for a unilateral action of a core group consisting of Germany, the Netherlands and Denmark.

References

Baron, D. (1985), 'Non-cooperative regulation of a nonlocalized externality', *Rand Journal of Economics*, **16** (4), 553–68.

Braden J., H. Folmer and T. Ulen (eds) (1996), *Environmental Policy with Political and Economic Integration*, Cheltenham: Edward Elgar.

Braden J. and S. Proost (eds) (1997), *The Theory of Environmental Policy in a Federal State*, Cheltenham: Edward Elgar.

Conrad, K. (1997), 'Environmental tax competition: a simulation study for non-symmetric countries', in Braden and Proost (eds), *The Theory of Environmental Policy in a Federal State*, Cheltenham: Edward Elgar.

Mors, M. (1994), 'Applying environmental economics in the European Union: the role and the potential', paper presented at the Fifth Annual Meeting of the EAERE (European Association of Environmental and Resource Economists), Dublin, 22–24 June.

Ochelen S. and S. Proost (1996), 'Internalisation of transport externalities by a local government', paper presented at the NBER (National Bureau of Economic Research) workshop on 'Public Policy and the Environment', Cambridge, 30–31 July.

Segerson K., T. Micelli and Lih-Chyi Wen (1997), 'Intergovernmental transfers in a federal system: an economic analysis of unfunded mandates', in Braden and Proost (eds), *The Theory of Environmental Policy in a Federal State*, Cheltenham: Edward Elgar.

Ulph, A. (1996), 'Strategic environmental policy, international trade and the single European Market', in Braden, Folmer and Ulen (eds), *Environmental Policy with Political and Economic Integration*, Cheltenham: Edward Elgar.

Ulph, A. (1997), 'International environmental regulation when national governments act strategically', in Braden and Proost (eds), *The Theory of Environmental Policy in a Federal State*, Cheltenham: Edward Elgar.

2. Alternative CO_2 abatement strategies for the European Union

Christoph Böhringer, Michael Ferris and Thomas F. Rutherford

Introduction

To combat global warming several international conferences (Toronto 1988, Cairo 1990, Rio 1992 and Berlin 1995) have called for significant reductions in world-wide carbon dioxide emissions associated with the combustion of fossil fuels. Because of the difficulties of identifying and implementing a 'fair' worldwide CO_2 reduction schedule for all countries, no concerted policy action has yet been undertaken. Given this situation, there is increasing political pressure for unilateral action within the European Union (EU): if any climate change policy is to be implemented, the developed countries will have to take a leading role. EU policy-makers, who fear negative impacts on international competitiveness, put EU-wide CO_2 reduction measures under the condition that other important developed economies (the US and Japan) take similar steps. This 'conditionality' clause has led groups in EU member countries to call for unilateral action at the national level in order to promote EU-wide or worldwide solutions. However, when one region or country acts unilaterally, significant efficiency losses potentially arise. 'Carbon leakage' occurs when emission reductions in one region are (partially) offset by increased emissions elsewhere. The question of how CO_2 reduction strategies within the EU or specific member countries can be implemented in order to minimize overall efficiency losses is linked to several important policy issues, such as:

- regional distribution of burdens and benefits;
- changes in comparative advantage (international competitiveness);
- distributional impacts and corresponding concessions to specific sectors (tax exemptions, grandfathered permits); and
- revenue recycling of carbon taxes and the possibility of a 'double dividend' when reducing pre-existing distortionary taxes.

Given the need for policy advice on the economic and emission implications of alternative CO_2 mitigation strategies, the main purpose of this chapter is to describe a general equilibrium model which can address important policy issues of CO$_2$ mitigation in a consistent, analytical way. The model presented incorporates a multisectoral and multiregional structure for the European Union and is based on the most recently available consistent data on bilateral trade and energy flows as well as national statistics on domestic production and consumption patterns. The potential usefulness of the model for policy advice is illustrated by simulations of several mitigation scenarios which are discussed among European policy-makers. The first set of scenarios examines the relationship between the scope of concerted action within the EU and the costs of meeting given reduction targets. The cases include (i) EU-wide abatement with tradable emission permits (uniform taxes); (ii) uniform reduction targets for all member countries without trade in national emission rights; and (iii) unilateral CO$_2$ taxes in one member country, Germany. The second set of scenarios considers the idea that freely distributing emission permits to industrial sectors on the basis of their benchmark emissions (that is, 'grandfathering') represents a cost-efficient CO$_2$ mitigation strategy which maintains international competitiveness of emission- and trade-intensive sectors and reduces carbon leakage, as has been argued by Koutstaal et al. (1994).

The results which emerge from the numerical computations are as follows:

- there are substantial efficiency gains within the EU associated with coordinated action: unilateral action by a single EU country is far more costly than EU-wide action to meet the same EU reduction target;
- accounting for general equilibrium effects and endogeneity of the permit price, there can be substantial efficiency costs associated with the grandfathering of emission permits as compared to auctioned permits;[1]
- grandfathering is justified on efficiency grounds only when leakage rates are substantial;
- it is difficult to estimate leakage rates associated with unilateral abatement by a single EU member state. The model-based result depends crucially on the formulation of international trade. In an Armington (regionally differentiated goods) model, leakage rates are low; in a Ricardo–Viner (homogeneous goods) model, leakage rates are high. At present, there is not sufficient empirical evidence to determine which of these models is closer to the truth;
- there are substantial differences in the distributional impacts of alternative CO$_2$ abatement strategies. The grandfathered permit approach is clearly beneficial to workers and capital owners in energy-intensive industries. Surprisingly, another finding is that the grandfathered permits are also beneficial to wage earners in a model with fully flexible wages. The efficiency costs of grandfathered permits work through reduction in the return to capital in other sectors.

Although the results confirm economic intuition, they are still quite preliminary. This chapter should be regarded as a progress report on ongoing research. Further sensitivity analysis on the underlying data and specific model features is required to test the robustness of concrete estimates of crucial values, such as the leakage rates associated with unilateral abatement policies.

The chapter is organized as follows. The first section motivates the choice of the scenarios by a short discussion of problems involved in the design of cost-efficient CO_2 abatement strategies. The second section provides an algebraic summary of the model structure. The third section summarizes the benchmark data sources and motivates the choice of regional and sectoral detail which is included in the empirical model. The fourth section describes the modelling experiments. The fifth section reports the numerical results and their economic interpretation. Finally, the conclusion entails a discussion of the findings.

Background: cost-efficient CO_2 reduction and unilateral action
As a main instrument of an international climate policy, some form of carbon tax has been proposed (Pearce 1991; Poterba 1991). Global cost-effectiveness suggests that a carbon tax should be uniform across countries and sectors in order to equalize the marginal cost of emission reduction across sources (Markusen 1975; Siebert et al. 1980). In spite of this proposition, no concerted action has yet been undertaken because the costs of uniform taxes may be inequitable and appropriate side-payments to make all signatory countries better off are very difficult to assess and negotiate (Burniaux et al. 1992). International CO_2 abatement could be characterized as a prisoners' dilemma where no country acting alone has an incentive to significantly cut its own emissions, given the negligible impact on the overall carbon concentrations in the atmosphere. The global nature of the CO_2 externality leads individual countries to insist on coordinated action (Commission of the European Communities 1992a).

Despite the impending economic losses, there might be reasons for single countries to take a leading role and to act unilaterally. For example, a country may decide to make short-term sacrifices in the expectation of long-run benefits from an increase in the number of signatory countries. Another motivation could be the domestic political environment where voters demand concrete environmental action.

Unilateral action to combat an international externality such as CO_2 emissions produces efficiency losses through spillover effects of carbon emission constraints on international markets. Unilateral CO_2 taxes affect international trade and the pattern of comparative advantage. One adverse consequence is that unilateral reductions may increase emissions by nonparticipating countries. This phenomenon has been referred to as carbon leakage. The problem of carbon leakage is likely to be significant for goods with a high energy content (Pezzey 1992; Rutherford 1993; Bohm 1993; Felder and Rutherford 1993). There are two basic channels through which carbon leakage can occur. First, leakage can arise when the production of CO_2-intensive goods relocates and increases the emission levels in the nonparticipating regions. Second, cutbacks of energy demands in a large region, because of CO_2 taxes, may induce a significant drop in world energy prices, which in turn could lead to an increase in demand in other regions. This again could offset part of the CO_2 reductions in the unilaterally acting region.

There are different strategies for regions acting unilaterally to avoid leakage and to increase efficiency of (global) CO_2 reduction. One approach would be to use direct trade restrictions by setting barriers to exports and imports of carbon(energy)-intensive products. In theory, this could produce a first-best optimal tax structure which involves a uniform carbon tax in concert with tariffs and subsidies on carbon embodied in imports and exports. If border adjustments through tariffs are ruled out because of trade agreements or GATT obligations, a second-best policy is to differentiate tax rates across domestic sectors (Hoel 1994). This theoretical proposition is reflected in the design of several unilateral mitigation strategies such as the EU proposal for an EU-wide combined energy and carbon tax (Commission of the European Communities 1992b) or the most recent CO_2 tax plan for Germany (Enquete-Kommission 1994), both of which exempt energy- and trade-intensive sectors from taxation. It is, however, unclear that the theoretical argument for tax differentiation justifies total exemptions. If leakage effects are of a second-order magnitude, wide-ranging exemptions will significantly increase the costs of stabilizing CO_2 emissions (Böhringer and Rutherford 1997). From a practical standpoint, there are reasons why an exemption system could be undesirable, for example high costs of administration and lobbying. Furthermore, the analytical derivation of optimal tax rates is already quite complex under very simplified assumptions (Hoel 1994). Even the definition of the 'optimal tax structure' is problematic in a world economy where trade taxes enacted for environmental objectives provide an opportunity for altering the terms of trade.

Grandfathered permits to production are an alternative remedy for adverse distributional impacts. Under arrangements such as the US SO_2 abatement programme under the 1990 Clean Air Act, emission permits are freely distributed to firms which subsequently can use the permits for their own emissions or sell the permits to others. Overall emissions may be reduced with the number of permits. In practice, grandfathered permits work as a subsidy which affects the allocation of resources. Carbon leakage provides one justification for assisting emission- and trade-intensive sectors through an appropriate design of the grandfathering system. In evaluating these programmes, it is important to evaluate the efficiency costs involved in this transfer of resources. Advocates claim that grandfathering can be used to ease the distributional effects of CO_2 mitigation on emission- and trade-intensive sectors 'without consequences for reaching the emission reduction goal and its cost efficiency' (Koutstaal et al. 1994, p. 1). Their argument is that grandfathered permits do not affect the input choice of a sector but leave the incentive to internalize the external effects of the CO_2 emissions. In this chapter it is argued that this logic overlooks potentially important   general equilibrium effects. The excess burden of grandfathered permits as compared to auctioned permits depends on the initial distribution of permits and its subsequent reduction schedule. In the simulations below, it is shown that a 'popular' grandfathering system, where permits are   allocated to industries on the basis of initial emission patterns with subsequent proportional cut-backs across sectors for given overall reduction targets can produce significant welfare costs which may not be outweighed by the decline in carbon leakage.

Model formulation

This section provides an algebraic summary of equilibrium conditions for a 'generic' static multiregional, multisectoral model in which:

1. output and factor prices are fully flexible and markets are perfectly competitive;
2. labour and capital are in fixed supply. Labour is intersectorally mobile within a region but cannot move between regions. Capital rents accrue to both sector-specific inputs and malleable capital. The latter is freely mobile across sectors and countries;
3. in international trade, goods are either differentiated by region of origin (the Armington model) or homogeneous (the Ricardo–Viner model). In the Armington model, regions are linked together through endogenous bilateral trade flows calibrated to base year values. In the Ricardo–Viner model, only base year net trade flows are replicated as goods move freely between countries. In both models, goods from countries which are not explicitly represented (rest of the world–ROW) are differentiated, and a set of export demand and import supply functions determine the trade between ROW and the countries whose production and consumption patterns are described in detail;[2]

4. government demand within each region as well as the balance of payment surplus are fixed at benchmark levels. Investment demand (savings) is determined through a constant marginal propensity to save by private households; and
5. there is one representative consumer for each region.

The model equations correspond to the three classes of conditions associated with an Arrow–Debreu general equilibrium: (i) exhaustion of product (zero-profit) conditions for constant-returns to scale producers; (ii) market clearance for all goods, factors, permits markets and trade balance with ROW; and (iii) income balance for representative agents in each of the explicitly modelled member states.[3] An equilibrium allocation determines market production, prices and incomes.

In the following algebraic exposition, the notation Π^X_{jr} is used to denote the profit function of sector j in region r; where X is the name assigned to this activity. Formally, all production sectors exhibit constant returns to scale, hence, differentiating Π^X_{jr} with respect to input and output prices provides compensated demand and supply coefficients which appear subsequently in market-clearance conditions.

Finally, it should be noted that the equations as presented in the following correspond to the Armington model with goods differentiated by region of origin. The Ricardo–Viner specification follows directly when P_{jr} is replaced by P_X, and the set of market-clearance conditions for good i in region r are replaced by a single equation for good i.

Exhaustion of product conditions
Within each region nested, separable, constant elasticity of substitution (CES) cost functions with three levels are employed to specify the substitution possibilities in domestic production between capital, labour, energy and material inputs (KLEM). The material input of good i in sector j corresponds to an Armington aggregate of non-energy inputs from domestic production and imported varieties which trade off with a constant elasticity of substitution (in equation (2.1) below, the index EG denotes the set of energy goods). At the top level, these material inputs are employed in fixed proportions with an aggregate of energy, capital (sectorally fixed and regionally mobile) and labour. A constant elasticity describes the substitution possibilities between the energy aggregate and the aggregate of labour and capital at the second level. Finally, at the third level capital and labour trade off with a unitary elasticity of substitution. On the output side good production is linked in fixed proportions (zero elasticity of transformation) to the entitlement of the producing sector with emission permits. This specification of the output side allows

for transfer payments to be made to each sector reflecting 'grand-fathering' of emission permits based on the benchmark emission patterns. The resulting zero-profit condition for the production of good j in region r is:

$$\Pi_{jr}^Y = P_{jr} + V_{jr} - \sum_{i \notin EG} a_{ijr} \left[\theta_{ijr}^M P_{ir}^{M^{1-\sigma_{DM}}} + (1-\theta_{ijr}^M) \, P_{ir}^{1-\sigma_{DM}} \right]^{\frac{1}{1-\sigma_{DM}}}$$

$$- a_{jr}^{KLE} \left[\alpha_{jr}^E \, P_{jr}^{E^{1-\alpha_{KLE}}} + (1-\alpha_{jr}^E) \left(W_r^{\beta_{jr}^L} r_{jr}^{\beta_{jr}^S} R^{\beta_{jr}^K} \right)^{1-\sigma_{KLE}} \right]^{\frac{1}{1-\sigma_{KLE}}} = 0$$

(2.1)

where:

P_{jr} is the output price of good j produced in region r,

V_{jr} is the value of emission permits per unit output of sector j in region r,

a_{ijr} is the benchmark value share of non-energy input i in sector j of region r,

θ_{ijr}^M is the import value share for sector i inputs to sector j in region r,

P_{ir}^M is the import price aggregate for good i imported to region r,

σ_{DM} is the elasticity of substitution between domestic and imported inputs or demands,

a_{jr}^{KLE} corresponds to the aggregate value share of capital, labour and energy inputs (KLE aggregate) in sector j of region r,

α_{jr}^E denotes the energy input value share of the KLE aggregate in sector j of region r,

P_{jr}^E stands for the composite price for aggregate energy inputs into sector j in region r,

σ_{KLE} represents the elasticity of substitution between the energy aggregate and the aggregate of capital and labour,

W_r is the economy-wide wage rate in region r,

r_{jr} is the rate of return for sector-specific capital inputs in sector j of region r,

R is the uniform rate of return for (interregionally and intersectorally) mobile capital,

β_{jr}^k denotes the value shares for labour ($k = L$), sector-specific capital (S) and interregionally mobile capital (K) in sector j of region r and

Y_{jr} is the associated dual variable which indicates the activity level of producing good j in region r.

Intermediate demands for fuels are split into energy throughput ('non-energetic') and energy use ('energetic') components. The first of these demands enters through the material aggregate, while the second forms the energy input aggregate. Energetic energy demands are specified by means of a two-level CES function. At the bottom level, an Armington aggregation function provides a constant elasticity of substitution between domestic and imported varieties of each energy good. The resulting Armington energy good is linked to a specific carbon emission coefficient which determines the carbon tax payment for this energy carrier. At the top level, different Armington energy goods (after accounting for carbon tax payments) trade off with a constant elasticity of substitution. The zero-profit condition for energy supply to sector j in region r is given by:

$$\Pi_{jr}^{E} = P_{jr}^{E} - \left[\sum_{i \in EG} \theta_{ijr}^{E} \left\{ \left| \theta_{ijr}^{M} P_{ir}^{M^{1-\sigma_{DM}}} + (1-\theta_{ijr}^{M}) P_{ir}^{1-\sigma_{DM}} \right|^{\frac{1}{1-\sigma_{DM}}} + \varepsilon_{ijr} PCO \right\}^{1-\sigma_{E}} \right]^{\frac{1}{1-\sigma_{E}}}$$

$$= 0 \quad (2.2)$$

where:

P_{jr}^{E} is the composite price for aggregate energy inputs into sector j in region r,

θ_{ijr}^{E} is the benchmark value share of energy good i in aggregate energy demand by sector j of region r,

σ_{E} is the elasticity of substitution between energy inputs,[4]

ε_{ijr} is the carbon emission coefficient for energy input i in sector j of region r,

PCO is the market price of carbon emission rights and

E_{jr} is the associated activity level representing aggregate energy demand for producing good j in region r.

Import supply for region r and good j is composed of a CES aggregate of imports from all other regions (including ROW). The exhaustion of product condition for these import activities is given by:

$$\Pi_{jr}^{M} = P_{jr}^{M} - \left(\sum_{r' \neq r} \theta_{jr'r}^{MM} P_{jr'}^{1-\sigma_{MM}} + \theta_{jROWr}^{MM} P_{jROWr}^{M^{1-\sigma_{MM}}} \right)^{\frac{1}{1-\sigma_{MM}}} = 0 \quad (2.3)$$

where:

$\theta_{jr'r}^{MM}$ is the benchmark value share of region r' exports in aggregate imports of good i into region r,

θ_{jROWr}^{MM} is the benchmark value share of ROW exports in aggregate imports of good i into region r,

σ_{MM} is the elasticity of substitution between imports from different foreign countries,

P_{jROWr}^{M} is the price for good j produced in ROW and

M_{jr} is the associated activity level of this constraint, meaning the level of demand in region r for the aggregate import variety of commodity j.

In each region composite investment is a Leontief aggregation of Armington inputs which are composed of domestic and imported commodities:

$$\Pi_r^I = P_r^I - \sum_i a_{ir}^I \left[\theta_{ilr}^M P_{ir}^{M^{1-\sigma_{DM}}} + (1-\theta_{ilr}^M) P_{ir}^{1-\sigma_{DM}} \right]^{\frac{1}{1-\sigma_{DM}}} = 0 \qquad (2.4)$$

where:

P_r^I stands for the composite price for investment demand in region r,

a_{ir}^I is the benchmark value share of input i in investment of region r,

θ_{ilr}^M denotes the import value share for sector i inputs into investment formation of region r and

I_r is the associated activity level, representing investment supply in region r.

Public goods and services are produced with a Cobb–Douglas aggregation of commodity inputs within which there is an Armington aggregate of domestic and imported commodities:

$$\Pi_r^G = P_r^G - \prod_i \left[\theta_{iGr}^M P_{ir}^{M^{1-\sigma_{DM}}} + (1-\theta_{iGr}^M) P_{ir}^{1-\sigma_{DM}} \right]^{\frac{\alpha_{ir}^G}{1-\sigma_{DM}}} = 0 \qquad (2.5)$$

where:

P_r^G is the composite price for government demand in region r,

θ_{iGr}^M denotes the import value share for sector i inputs into public good production of region r,

α_{ir}^G represents the value share of commodity i in public output of region r and

G_r is the level of public output in region r.

Household demand is given as a CES composite which combines consumption of an energy aggregate and a non-energy consumption bundle. Substitution patterns within the non-energy consumption bundle are Cobb–Douglas functions with an Armington aggregation of imports and domestic commodities. Non-energy Armington goods are an aggregate of domestic and imported varieties which trade off with a constant elasticity of substitution. Exhaustion of production for household demand is given by[5]:

$$\Pi_r^C = P_r^C - \left[\theta_{Cr}^E \, P_{Cr}^{E\,1-\sigma_{EC}} + (1-\theta_{Cr}^E)\right.$$

$$\left.\left\{\prod_{i\notin EG}\left[\theta_{iCr}^M \, P_{ir}^{M\,1-\sigma_{DM}} + (1-\theta_{iCr}^M)\, P_{ir}^{1-\sigma_{DM}}\right]^{\frac{\alpha_{ir}^C}{1-\sigma_{DM}}}\right\}^{1-\sigma_{EC}}\right]^{\frac{1}{1-\sigma_{EC}}} = 0 \qquad (2.6)$$

where:

P_r^C stands for the composite price for aggregate household demand in region r,

θ_{Cr}^E represents the benchmark value share of the energy aggregate in household demand of region r,

P_{Cr}^E is the composite price for aggregate energy inputs into household demand in region r,

σ_{EC} is the elasticity of substitution between the energy aggregate and the non-energy consumption bundle in household demand,

θ_{iCr}^M denotes the import value share for sector i inputs into household demand of region r,

α_{ir}^C corresponds to the value share of non-energy commodity i in household demand for non-energy consumption bundle of region r and

C_r is the associated activity level representing aggregate household consumption in region r.

Energy consumption by households is characterized in the same way as energy demand of producing sectors, with zero-profit condition being expressed as:

$$\Pi_{Cr}^E = P_{Cr}^E - \left(\sum_{i\in E}\theta_{iCr}^E \left\{\left[\theta_{iCr}^M \, P_{ir}^{M\,1-\sigma_M} + (1-\theta_{iCr}^M)\, P_{ir}^{1-\sigma_M}\right]^{1-\sigma_M}\right.\right.$$

$$\left.\left. + \varepsilon_{iCr}\, PCO\right|^{1-\sigma_E}\right]^{\frac{1}{1-\sigma_E}} = 0 \qquad (2.7)$$

where:

θ_{iCr}^E represents the benchmark value share of energy good i in aggregate energy demand by the household in region r,

ε_{iCr} corresponds to the carbon-emission coefficient for energy input i into household demand of region r[6] and

E_{Cr} is the associated activity level of household energy demand in region r.

Market clearance
In this exposition, Shepard's Lemma is used to provide a compact representation of compensated demand and supply functions. Primary

factors of production are labour, sector-specific capital for each region and interregionally mobile capital. The market-clearance conditions for labour is expressed:

$$\bar{L}_r = \sum_j Y_{jr} \frac{\partial \Pi^Y_{jr}}{\partial w_r} \tag{2.8}$$

where:

$\bar{L}_r$ is the aggregate labour endowment for region r.

The supply–demand balance for inter regionally mobile capital is expressed:

$$\sum_r \bar{K}_r = \sum_{j,r} Y_{jr} \frac{\partial \Pi^Y_{jr}}{\partial R} \tag{2.9}$$

where:

$\bar{K}_r$ denotes the aggregate endowment of interregionally mobile capital for region r.

As to sector-specific capital, market clearance corresponds to:

$$\bar{K}^S_{jr} = Y_{jr} \frac{\partial \Pi^Y_{jr}}{\partial r_{jr}} \tag{2.10}$$

where:

$\bar{K}^S_{jr}$ is the sector-specific capital for sector j in region r.

Goods produced in each region enter intermediate demand, consumer demand, government and investment demand as well as import demand from other regions including ROW. The market-clearance condition for each produced commodity is expressed:

$$Y_{ir} = \sum_j Y_{jr} \frac{\partial \Pi^Y_{jr}}{\partial P_{ir}} + C_r \frac{\partial \Pi^C_r}{\partial P_{ir}} + I_r \frac{\partial \Pi^I_r}{\partial P_{ir}} + G_r \frac{\partial \Pi^G_r}{\partial P_{ir}}$$

$$+ \sum_r M_{ir'} \frac{\partial \Pi^M_{ir}}{\partial P_{ir}} + M_{irROW} \tag{2.11}$$

where:

M_{irROW} is the aggregate export demand of ROW for good i from region r (see the foreign closure rule in equation (2.13) below).

The market for imports is analogous to the market for regional outputs. The supply–demand balance for imported goods is expressed:

$$M_{ir} = \sum_j Y_{jr} \frac{\partial \Pi^Y_{jr}}{\partial P^M_{ir}} + C_r \frac{\partial \Pi^C_r}{\partial P^M_{ir}} + I_r \frac{\partial \Pi^I_r}{\partial P^M_{ir}} + G_r \frac{\partial \Pi^G_r}{\partial P^M_{ir}} \qquad (2.12)$$

As to the trade balance of regions with respect to the ROW, a simple foreign closure rule is employed. The Armington assumption of product heterogeneity is used along with a ROW export-demand function of constant price elasticity, price-taking behaviour of countries with respect to world import (ROW) prices (perfectly elastic foreign import-supply function), and an imposed balance of payment constraint to assure trade balance between single countries and ROW:

$$\sum_{i,r} \bar{P}^X_i M_{irROW} = \sum_{i,r} \bar{P}^M_i M_{iROWr} + \sum_r \bar{B}_r \qquad (2.13)$$

where:
$\bar{B}_r$ is the net trade (balance of payment) surplus for region r,
$\bar{P}^M_i$ are the ROW prices of imports M_{iROWr} from ROW to regions r and
$\bar{P}^X_i$ are the ROW prices of exports M_{iROW} of region r to ROW.[7]

The supply-demand balance for carbon emission rights is expressed:

$$\sum_r CRTS_r = \sum_{j,r} Y_{jr} \frac{\partial \Pi^Y_{jr}}{\partial PCO} \qquad (2.14)$$

where:

$CRTS_r$ gives the carbon-emission rights endowment of region r.

Income and aggregate demand
Total income of the representative household in each region is employed in fixed fractions on household demand and savings (constant marginal propensity to save). Given aggregate price indices for consumption and investment there is:

$$C_r = \frac{(1 - mps_r)\,(w_r \bar{L}_r + R\,\bar{K}_r + \sum_j r_{jr} \bar{K}^S_{jr} + PCO\,\theta^{CO}_{Hr}\,CRTS_r - P^G_r \bar{G}_r - \bar{B}_r)}{P^C_r} \qquad (2.15)$$

$$I_r = \frac{mps_r \left(w_r \bar{L}_r + R \, \bar{K}_r + \sum_j r_{jr} \, \bar{K}^S_{jr} + PCO \, \theta^{CO}_{Hr} CRTS_r - P^G_r \bar{G}_r - \bar{B}_r \right)}{P^I_r}$$

(2.16)

where:

θ^{CO}_{Hr} is the fraction of carbon-emission permits allocated to households in region r and

mps_r is the constant marginal propensity to save in region r.

Grandfathered allowances which are produced at the same level of activity as regional outputs (see equation (2.1) above) render transfer payments to each sector which are equal to the allocated fraction of total revenues from carbon-emission permits:

$$V_{jr} \, Y_{jr} = PCO \, (1 - \theta^{CO}_{Hr}) \, CRTS_r \, \theta^{CO}_{jr}$$

(2.17)

where:

θ^{CO}_{jr} is the fraction of grandfathered permits allocated to sector j in region r.

Benchmark data and aggregation

As is customary in CGE modelling, the model is calibrated to available value shares and elasticity values. At the present state of model development, considerable work has been done to obtain percentage estimates for share parameters which provide a 'zeroth order approximation' of the underlying economy. The elasticity parameters used in the present version of the model are controversially discussed in economic literature, and the range of results presented below reflects this uncertainty (see, for example, the results emerging from different degrees of substitutability among traded goods).

The benchmark equilibrium data set for 1985 is constructed from three different sources which provide the most recent consistent data on energy and economic flows. These include the Eurostat input–output table with 59 production sectors for various EU member countries (Eurostat 1995); the CHELEM harmonized accounts on trade and world economy (WEFA 1995); and the International Energy Agency (IEA) energy balances (IEA 1994a).

Reconciliation of input–output data and trade data is the first step in constructing the base-year equilibrium. For this purpose, a nonlinear least squares procedure is employed to calibrate bilateral trade flows provided by CHELEM to the intra-EU and extra–EU trade totals provided in the Eurostat input-output tables. CHELEM does not cover all trade flows, and for the missing goods a target bilateral trade matrix representing the average overall traded goods is used.

The detailed description of production and consumption patterns within the EU includes six member countries which together account for more than 90 per cent of the overall EU trade volume and production output: Germany (DE), France (FR), United Kingdom (UK), Spain (ES), Italy (IT) and Denmark (DK).[8] All other countries are summarized to an aggregate rest of the world (ROW) whose representation is reduced to import and export flows to the EU countries.

The sectoral disaggregation is chosen on the basis of the potential for carbon leakage exhibited in the benchmark production and trade structure. The scope for CO$_2$ leakage crucially depends on the pattern of carbon intensity in the production of traded goods across different regions and the trade volumes of specific goods. To obtain the benchmark CO$_2$ emission intensities and intuition about the scope for leakage, a simple input-output calculation was performed. Let

x_{ir} denote the total (direct and indirect) CO$_2$ emissions per unit production of good i in region r (in the exposition below, r and its alias s are used as the index for the six EU member countries explicitly included in the model),

c_{ir} denote the direct CO$_2$ emission per unit production of good i in region r,

A_{jsir} denote the input of good j from region s per unit production of good i in region r where A includes both domestic ($s=r$) and imported ($s \neq r$) goods and

θ_{ir} denote the output value share of good i for region r in overall EU production.

The total CO$_2$ emissions per unit production of good i in region r are given by the following system of linear equations:

$$x_{ir} = c_{ir} + \sum_{j,s} A_{jsir} \, x_{js} \qquad (2.18)$$

and, assuming an average emission intensity of ROW production:

$$x_{iROW} = \sum_r \theta_{ir} \, x_{ir} \qquad (2.19)$$

As the total CO$_2$ emission of carbon per unit production x_{ir} crucially depends on the values of the direct CO$_2$ emissions c_{ir}, it is important to employ accurate estimates for these data. For this purpose the monetary flows of the national input–output tables are supplemented with physical flow data on the emission-relevant fossil fuel use in production sectors and final demand. The analysis of the implicit prices serves as a consistency check on the derived sector- and energy-specific CO_2 coefficients (in CO_2 units per national currency units). These reveal substantial price differences for the same fuel inputs across different sectors and countries.[9] The differences can be explained in part by price differentiation on energy markets (for example, cheap coal supply to electricity sector versus expensive coal supply to final demand) and by national regulation (for example, coal subsidies in Germany). In some cases, the implicit prices deviate significantly from official reports on market prices (for example, IEA statistics on energy prices and taxes, see IEA 1994b) without a satisfactory explanation, and these discrepancies call for further study. In short, the problem of reconciling physical energy flow data with economic input–output data is vexing yet widely ignored by economic model-builders working on carbon tax issues.

Despite the caveats on the concordance of energy and economic data, a key observation of the above input-output calculation is that carbon (emission) intensities vary considerably across the EU countries, which indicates a significant potential for leakage.[10] The variation of carbon intensities for traded goods across regions has important implications both for the design of instruments meant to reduce carbon leakage as well as for the appropriate level of sectoral disaggregation which has to be chosen in numerical simulations. For the calculations, the 59 sectors as given in the Eurostat input–output tables are ranked according to their scope of leakage and for the equilibrium model only those sectors are selected which reveal a significant potential for carbon leakage through trade in the benchmark production pattern. All other sectors are assigned to composite aggregates of food, manufacturing and services. This leads to a sectoral disaggregation with 23 sectors as given in Table 2.1.

Elasticities of substitution play an important role in equilibrium studies because they determine the sensitivity of economic aggregates to changes in policy instruments. In the case of carbon emission restrictions, lower elasticities are associated with higher carbon taxes (see Böhringer and Rutherford 1997). Welfare costs of CO_2 abatement depend on the input substitution possibilities in the production of energy- and carbon-intensive goods as well as the ease of substitution of these goods in intermediate demand and final consumption. Efficiency losses through carbon leakage are governed by the elasticity of substitution between the domestically produced good and the competing import aggregate, the latter of which is characterized through the substitution possibilities between imports from different foreign countries. In the Armington model, a common elasticity of substitution equal to four determines the

Table 2.1 Production sectors in the model

Sector	R59 Index	Description
COA	031, 033, 050	Coal (hard coal, lignite, coke)
REF	071, 073	Crude oil and refined petroleum products
GAS	075, 098	Natural gas and manufactured gases
ELE	097, 099	Electricity and steam
ORE	135	Iron ore ECSC iron and steel products
NFM	137	Non-ferrous metals
CHM	170	Chemical products
CEM	151	Cement lime and plaster
CER	155	Earthenware and ceramic products
GLS	153	Glass
OMN	157	Other mineral and derived products
PLP	471	Pulp and paper and board
TRA	570	Wholesale and retail trade
CON	530	Building and civil engineering works
AGR	010	Agricultural, forestry, fishery
AIR	633	Air transport services
INL	617	Inland waterway services
ROD	613	Road transport
TRS	631	Maritime and coastal transport services
RLW	611	Railway transport services
MAN		Manufactured products aggregate, including 095 Water, 110 Nuclear fuels, 190 Metal products, 136 Non-ECSC iron and steel products, 210 Agricultural and industrial machinery, 230 Office machines, 250 Electric goods, 270 Motor vehicles and engines, 290 Other transport equipment, 490 Rubber and plastic products, 473 Paper goods and products of printing, 410 Textiles and clothing, 430 Leather and footwear, 450 Timber and wooden furniture, 510 Other manufacturing products
FOO		Food products aggregate, including 310 Meat and meat products, 330 Milk and dairy products, 350 Other food products, 370 Beverages, 390 Tobacco products
SRV		Services aggregate, including 550 Recovery and repair services, 590 Lodging and catering services, 650 Auxiliary transport services, 670 Communications, 690 Credit and insurance, 710 Business services provided to enterprises, 730 Renting of immovable goods, 750 Market services of education and research, 770 Market services of health, 790 Other Market services, 810 General public services, 850 Nonmarket services of education and research, 890 nonmarket services of health, 930 Other nonmarket services

scope for substitution across domestic and imported varieties. In the Ricardo–Viner model, goods produced in different EU member states are perfect substitutes while imports from ROW remain differentiated with the Armington elasticity of substitution equal to four. Table 2.2 shows the assumptions on various key elasticities which are presently specified with common values across all regions. A major aspect of future research activities is to develop better estimates of these elasticities by sector and country.

Table 2.2 Key elasticities

Index	Description	Value
σ_{KLEM}	Elasticity of substitution between the Leontief material input aggregate and other inputs (capital, labour and energy)	0
σ_{KLE}	Elasticity of substitution between energy inputs and value-added	0.5
σ_{KL}	Elasticity of substitution between labour, sector-specific capital and mobile capital	1
$\sigma_{E\_ELE}{}^{*}$	Elasticity of substitution between the aggregate of electricity and different fossil inputs in the energy aggregate of sectoral production and household demand	0.3
$\sigma_{E\_FOS}{}^{*}$	Elasticity of substitution between fossil energy inputs in the aggregate of fossil energy inputs at the level of sectoral production and household demand	0.5
σ_{NC}	Elasticity of substitution between different non-energy inputs into the non-energy bundle of household demand	1
σ_{DM}	Elasticity of substitution between domestic and imported inputs or demands in the Armington model	4
σ_{MM}	Elasticity of substitution between imports from different foreign countries in the Armington model	4
σ_{XROW}	Elasticity of export demand of ROW for imports from EU countries	4

Notes: * Instead of trading off different energy aggregates of sectoral production and final demand with a uniform substitution elasticity of σ_E as in equations (2.2) and (2.7) an additional nesting is introduced to account for differences of substitution between electricity inputs and non-electric (fossil) energy inputs (see note 2 for the nesting and the elasticity values employed)

Modelling experiments

In the simulations reported below, two sets of scenarios are distinguished which reflect different assumptions regarding the scope for unified policies within the EU and on the administrative framework for CO$_2$ abatement.

The first set of scenarios refers to an EU-wide CO$_2$ reduction strategy where all member countries undertake CO$_2$ mitigation measures. Four designs of an EU-wide abatement strategy which differ in the degree of emission trading and the consideration of grandfathered permits are considered:

(EU_1) *Auctioned permits tradable across EU countries.* The use of tradable emission permits of CO$_2$ equalizes marginal costs of abatement across member countries. The EU countries are initially endowed with emission rights equal to the benchmark emission level. Subsequent reduction in emission rights to meet exogenous reduction targets is proportional across countries.

(EU_2) *Grandfathered permits tradable across EU countries.* Permits are issued to production sectors on the basis of their benchmark emissions. Permit endowments are then proportionally reduced to meet reduction targets.

(EU_3) *Auctioned region-specific permits.* A uniform percentage reduction across member countries at the level of the overall EU reduction target without trade in national emission rights will typically lead to differences in the marginal cost of abatement.

(EU_4) *Grandfathered region-specific permits.* Each region faces the same proportional reduction in carbon emission. Permits are grandfathered proportional to benchmark emissions.

All of the EU abatement scenarios are computed in an Armington model in which goods are differentiated by country of origin.

The second set of scenarios considers unilateral CO$_2$ abatement by one EU member country, Germany.[11] No reduction measures are undertaken in the rest of the EU. The choice of Germany is motivated by the current discussion among German policy-makers on a unilateral CO$_2$ tax as the basic instrument to achieve national reduction targets.[12] Policy-makers of all German parties experience increasing public pressure in favour of a unilateral carbon tax which could be embedded in an overall tax reform.[13] On the other hand, German policy-makers fear the political consequences of severe employment cutbacks in carbon- and export-intensive industries (for example, iron/steel and chemical products), because of a loss of international competitiveness, and consider subsidies to these politically influential industries. The efficiency implications and the induced leakage rates of unilateral action are assessed for two different permit schemes and alternative specifications of international trade (Armington versus Ricardo-Viner).

(DE_1)   *Auctioned permits for unilateral abatement, Armington model.*
Germany unilaterally introduces emission permits. The resulting
equilibrium is calculated in a model with goods differentiated by
country of origin.

(DE_2)   *Grandfathered permits for unilateral abatement, Armington
model.* Germany unilaterally issues grandfathered emission permits allocated proportionally to base-year sectoral emissions.
The equilibrium is calculated in a model with regionally-
differentiated goods.

(DE_3)   *Auctioned permits for unilateral abatement, Ricardo-Viner model.*
Germany unilaterally introduces emission permits. The equilib-
rium is calculated in a model where goods produced in different
EU countries are perfect substitutes.

(DE_4)   *Grandfathered permits for unilateral abatement, Ricardo-Viner
model.* Germany unilaterally adopts grandfathered emission
permits allocated proportionally to base-year sectoral emissions.
The equilibrium is calculated in a model where goods produced
in different EU countries are perfect substitutes.

Table 2.3 summarizes the key characteristics of the scenarios.

Table 2.3 Overview of scenarios

Scenario	Regional scope	Permit trade	Grandfathered permits	Economic model
EU_1	All EU countries	Yes	No	Armington
EU_2	All EU countries	Yes	Yes	Armington
EU_3	All EU countries	No	No	Armington
EU_4	All EU countries	No	Yes	Armington
DE_1	Unilateral (only Germany)	n/a	No	Armington
DE_2	Unilateral (only Germany)	n/a	Yes	Armington
DE_3	Unilateral (only Germany)	n/a	No	Ricardo–Viner
DE_4	Unilateral (only Germany)	n/a	Yes	Ricardo–Viner

All of these scenarios are computed in a static framework with fixed
labour and capital endowments. The revenues from auctioned permits are
recycled lump-sum to the representative households in each region.[14] In
the Armington model, 50 per cent of capital rents in the benchmark is
assigned to sector-specific capital and 50 per cent accrues to interregionally mobile capital. In the Ricardo–Viner model all capital inputs are
assumed to be sector specific (that is, there is no interregionally mobile
capital in the Ricardo–Viner model).

In the counterfactuals, the number of emission permits is fixed to compute equilibria for target reductions of 10, 20 and 30 per cent. These reductions are applied either to the EU as a whole, if concerted EU-wide abatement is analysed, or to the benchmark emissions of Germany in unilateral abatement scenarios. Comparisons across scenarios provide a meaningful basis for welfare comparison. In any of the scenarios, permit prices may be interpreted as carbon tax levels which would produce an equivalent outcome.

Results

Results from the eight scenarios are summarized in Tables 2.4–8, which are presented at the end of this section. The numbers reported are current central estimates of the economic impacts of carbon-emission reduction policies within the EU. Table 2.4 reports the average cost of emission restrictions calculated as percentage Hicksian-equivalent variations in income.[15] Table 2.5 reports the marginal cost of emission restrictions which may be interpreted as the implicit carbon tax. Table 2.6 reports changes in emissions for different countries across different scenarios. Table 2.7 reports leakage rates and Table 2.8 reports sectoral labour adjustments for the unilateral abatement scenarios DE_1 and DE_2.

Consider first scenarios EU_1 and EU_3, that is EU abatement with and without trade in permits. Table 2.4 indicates that, from the standpoint of aggregate welfare, these scenarios are very similar. The EU countries gain relatively little in aggregate from permit trade when they are initially endowed with emission rights equal to the benchmark emission level and subsequent reduction in emission rights to meet exogenous reduction targets is proportional across countries. This finding is reflected in the comparability of permit prices across countries. The main outlier here is the UK which has substantially lower permit prices when acting alone. In Table 2.4 it is apparent that the UK stands to gain a significant amount from trade in emission permits, but the other countries are relatively indifferent.

The most dramatic result in Table 2.4 relates to the cost of grandfathering. Whether comparing EU_1 with EU_2, EU_3 with EU_4, DE_1 with DE_2 or DE_3 with DE_4, it is apparent that grandfathering introduces a significant efficiency cost. Turning to Table 2.5, it can be seen that the differences in average cost of abatement for these pairs of scenarios are reflected in substantial differences in the marginal cost of abatement. This indicates that there is an important interaction between the distribution of permit rents and the permit price itself. In simplistic terms, money from permit sales is returned to exactly those firms who are buying permits. The subsidies for the most polluting production sectors lead to lower relative prices for carbon-intensive goods and hence higher demands for these goods. This creates a higher demand for permits and a higher permit price.

The gross welfare cost of grandfathering is even higher in the case of unilateral action, where the measured equivalent income variation (EV) cost for Germany (DE) increases by a factor of two under grandfathered permits.

Comparing DE_1 with DE_3, it can be seen that the Armington model generally produces large welfare costs of emission restrictions. This is consistent with the logic presented earlier: the lower the elasticities, the higher the cost of achieving a given emission reduction. The Armington model, which is here specified with all trade elasticities equal to four, is considerably less flexible than the Ricardo–Viner model in which many trade elasticities are infinite.

The specific patterns of permit trade can be interpreted from Table 2.6. Here the specific evidence on permit trades which is suggested by the welfare results is reported. In EU_1, for a 20 per cent abatement target, the UK abates by 30 per cent and sells the excess abatement rights to France and Italy (primarily). Comparing EU_1 with EU_2, it can be seen that grandfathering of permits tends to reduce the level of permit trading by all market participants.

Considering the DE scenarios in Table 2.6, leakage effects in the Armington models (DE_1 and DE_2) are very small, but are enormous in the Ricardo-Viner model. Table 2.7 presents the calculated leakage rates. These are on the order of 70 per cent for a wide range of targets, which is about as large a rate as is reported in the literature. The rates should be regarded with some scepticism given that they emerge from a model in which many elasticities are not empirically estimated.

Comparing Tables 2.4 and 2.6, it is possible to see that unilateral action is far more costly than coordinated action. A 30 per cent unilateral abatement by Germany (DE_1) leads to 8 per cent EU-wide carbon reduction and involves much higher welfare costs than a coordinated EU-wide cut back of 10 per cent (EU_1): the total EU welfare cost for a 10 per cent abatement in scenario EU_1 is less than 0.1 per cent, whereas the total EU welfare cost associated with a 30 per cent unilateral reduction by Germany is 0.4 per cent. These are dramatic differences in the cost of abatement.

Turning finally to Table 2.8, it can be seen that even for the rigid Armington model, the application of a significant carbon tax creates enormous adjustment effects. For example, the level of adjustment for sector ORE (iron and steel) varies from 17 to 50 per cent for unilateral targets of 10 to 30 per cent.

Scenario DE_2 shows that the grandfathering of permits can have a big impact on leakage rates (Table 2.7) and employment effects (Table 2.8). Table 2.8 indicates that grandfathering permits can lead to a perverse result, in which employment in many of the emission-intensive sectors (such as ORE) actually increases rather than decreases as a result of carbon-emission restrictions.

To this point, the issue of how to quantify the costs and benefits of grandfathered permits has not yet been addressed. Grandfathered permits increase gross economic costs, but they simultaneously reduce leakage rates. In order to perform a meaningful comparison of costs and benefits, it is necessary to do a comparison *holding aggregate EU carbon emission constant.*[16] This calculation, which is based on economic costs for Germany (as reported in Table 2.4) and EU total emissions (as reported in Table 2.6), is presented in Figure 2.1 (see end of this section). The figure demonstrates that in terms of aggregate efficiency, the use of grandfathered permits is justified in the Ricardo–Viner model but unjustified in the Armington model. In other words, there is sufficient divergence in the leakage estimates for these two models to produce a qualitatively different assessment of the net benefit of the grandfathering permit system.

Throughout this discussion, Hicksian-equivalent variations of income have been used for a hypothetical representative agent as though it represented the interest of citizens in different countries. This masks potentially important differences across different households within these countries. In a more complete general equilibrium model, one based on detailed household surveys of consumption and factor income, it would be possible to sort out the winners and losers. Within the current modelling framework, the best that can be done is to look at the relative price of various production factors and assume that consumer preferences are identical. Proceeding in this manner, the welfare costs of various emission strategies for a representative employed worker in Germany have been evaluated by looking at how many goods can be purchased with a worker's salary (neglecting the costs inflicted on workers who must change jobs as a result of structural adjustment). The results are portrayed in Figure 2.2 (see end of this section). It could have been expected that grandfathered permits represent a windfall gain to capital owners in energy-intensive industries. It is therefore surprising to find that the grandfathering scheme is also preferred by the representative worker. Given that the net benefit (in the Armington model) is negative, it can be concluded that the efficiency costs of grandfathered permits work through reduction in the return to capital in other sectors.

Table 2.4 Welfare effects of carbon emission restrictions reported as Hicksian-equivalent variations in income (% change of benchmark)

Differentiated goods (Armington model)

	EU_1: Traded auctioned permits			EU_2: Traded grandfathered permits		
	10%	*20%*	*30%*	*10%*	*20%*	*30%*
DE	−0.1	−0.6	−1.6	−0.1	−0.8	−2.3
FR		−0.3	−1.1	−0.1	−0.5	−1.6
ES		−0.3	−1.1	−0.1	−0.5	−1.7
IT		−0.4	−1.3	−0.1	−0.6	−1.9
UK	0.1		−0.2	−0.1	−0.5	−1.3
DK		−0.2	−0.9		−0.5	−1.8
EU total		−0.4	−1.2	−0.1	−0.6	−1.9

	EU_3: Auctioned permits			EU_4: Grandfathered Permits		
	10%	*20%*	*30%*	*10%*	*20%*	*30%*
DE	−0.1	−0.5	−1.6	−0.1	−0.8	−2.4
FR		−0.3	−1.0		−0.5	−1.6
ES		−0.2	−1.0	−0.1	−0.5	−1.8
IT		−0.3	−1.2		−0.6	−1.9
UK	−0.1	−0.6	−1.5	−0.2	−0.9	−2.4
DK		−0.3	−1.0	−0.5	−1.8	
EU total		−0.4	−1.3	−0.1	−0.6	−2.0

	DE_1: Auctioned permits			DE_2: Grandfathered permits		
	10%	*20%*	*30%*	*10%*	*20%*	*30%*
DE		−0.4	−1.2	−0.1	−0.8	−2.3
FR		−0.1	−0.1			
ES		−0.1	−0.1			
IT		−0.1	−0.1			
UK		−0.1	−0.1			−0.1
DK	−0.1	−0.1	−0.2			
EU total		−0.2	−0.4		−0.2	−0.7

Homogeneous goods (Ricardo–Viner model)

	DE_3: Auctioned permits			DE_4: Grandfathered permits		
	10%	*20%*	*30%*	*10%*	*20%*	*30%*
DE		−0.3	−0.8	−0.1	−0.7	−1.9
FR			0.1		0.1	0.1
ES			0.1			0.1
IT			0.1		0.1	0.1
UK			0.1		0.1	0.1
DK		0.1	0.2	0.1	0.1	0.2
EU total			−0.2		−0.2	−0.5

Table 2.5 Carbon tax rates for different targets (DM/tonne CO$_2$)*

Differentiated goods (Armington model)

	EU_1: Traded auctioned permits			EU_2: Traded grandfathered permits		
	10%	*20%*	*30%*	*10%*	*20%*	*30%*
EU	43	110	209	73	210	454

	EU_3: Auctioned permits			EU_4: Grandfathered permits		
	10%	*20%*	*30%*	*10%*	*20%*	*30%*
DE	53	130	240	89	246	469
FR	58	156	318	87	250	469
ES	52	133	260	73	206	446
IT	68	181	358	94	277	469
UK	24	60	109	45	126	265
DK	36	97	189	66	209	469

	DE_1: Auctioned permits			DE_2: Grandfathered permits		
	10%	*20%*	*30%*	*10%*	*20%*	*30%*
DE	51	125	234	90	252	490

Homogeneous goods (Ricardo–Viner model)

	DE_3: Auctioned permits			DE_4: Grandfathered permits		
	10%	*20%*	*30%*	*10%*	*20%*	*30%*
DE	25	63	123	78	213	444

Notes:* For comparison: the combined energy/carbon tax as proposed by the EU involves an initial tax rate of 0.35 DM/GJ (energy tax) and 4.72 DM/tonne CO$_2$ (carbon tax)   starting from 1996 with an annual nominal increase by 0.115 DM/GJ (energy tax) and 1.57 DM/tonne CO$_2$ (carbon tax) until 2020.

Table 2.6 *Carbon emissions reductions by country (% of benchmark emissions)*

Differentiated goods (Armington model)

	EU_1: Traded auctioned permits			EU_2: Traded grandfathered permits		
	10%	*20%*	*30%*	*10%*	*20%*	*30%*
DE	−8	−18	−28	−9	−18	−29
FR	−8	−16	−24	−9	−18	−28
ES	−9	−18	−27	−10	−20	−30
IT	−7	−14	−22	−8	−17	−27
UK	−16	−30	−43	−13	−25	−35
DK	−11	−22	−32	−11	−20	−29
EU total	−10	−20	−30	−10	−20	−30

	DE_1: Auctioned permits			DE_2: Grandfathered permits		
	10%	*20%*	*30%*	*10%*	*20%*	*30%*
DE	−10	−20	−30	−10	−20	−29
FR		1	1			
IT			1			
UK			1			
DK			1			
EU total	−3	−6	−8	−3	−6	−9

Homogeneous goods (Ricardo–Viner model)

	DE_3: Auctioned permits			DE_4: Grandfathered permits		
	10%	*20%*	*30%*	*10%*	*20%*	*30%*
DE	−10	−20	−30	−10	−20	−30
FR	8	15	18	1	2	4
ES	1	2	3		1	2
IT		1	3			1
UK	2	5	8	1	3	5
DK	2	7	14	1	2	4
EU total	−1	−2	−3	−2	−5	−7

Table 2.7 Leakage rates (%) associated with unilateral abatement by Germany

Differentiated goods (Armington model)

	DE_1: Traded auctioned permits			DE_2: Traded grandfathered permits		
	10%	*20%*	*30%*	*10%*	*20%*	*30%*
FR	2.1	2.2	2.3	0.4	0.5	0.7
ES	0.4	0.4	0.5			0.1
IT	1.1	1.2	1.3		0.1	0.3
UK	1.5	1.7	1.8	0.1	0.3	0.5
DK	0.2	0.2	0.3			0.1
Total	5.3	5.7	6.2	0.6	1.0	5.1

Homogeneous goods (Ricardo–Viner model)

	DE_3: Auctioned permits			DE_4: Grandfathered permits		
	10%	*20%*	*30%*	*10%*	*20%*	*30%*
FR	47.2	42.2	34.9	5.9	6.4	7.1
ES	2.2	2.6	3.0	1.4	1.6	1.8
IT	2.2	3.2	4.5	–0.2	0.5	1.2
UK	16.8	19.6	23.3	10.8	11.7	12.7
DK	2.2	3.0	4.3	0.8	1.0	1.3
Total	70.6	70.6	70.0	18.7	21.3	24.2

Table 2.8 Sectoral employment changes in Germany associated with unilateral abatement (in % change from benchmark)

Differentiated goods (Armington model)

Production sectors*	DE_1: Auctioned permits			DE_2: Grandfathered permits		
	10%	*20%*	*30%*	*10%*	*20%*	*30%*
AGR	–1	–2	–4			
COA	–19	–33	–45	–15	–24	–29
REF	–4	–10	–16	–7	–15	–23
ELE	–1	–2	–4	7	16	25
ORE	–17	–34	–50	7	13	17
NFM	–2	–5	–9			
CEM	–1	–3	–4	7	15	22
GLS	–2	–4	–8	1	1	
CER	–3	–7	–12	1	1	
OMN		–1	–2	1	2	3
CHM	–3	–6	–11	1	1	1
PLP	–3	–7	–13	1	1	1
CON	1	2	4	1	3	5
TRA	1	1	2			
RLW	–2	–4	–6		–1	–2
ROD	–1	–2	–4	1	2	2
INL	–5	–12	–19	1	1	
TRS	–1	–3	–6			
AIR	–4	–10	–16	2	3	3

Notes: * For key to prodution sectors, see Table 2.1, above.

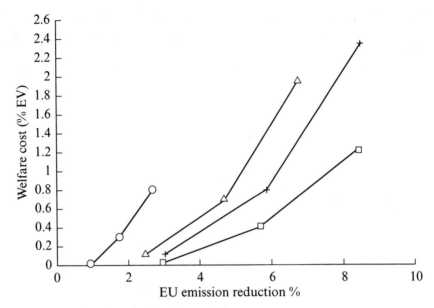

Figure 2.1 The welfare cost for a representative agent in Germany of alternative schemes for reducing EU carbon emission through unilateral action by Germany

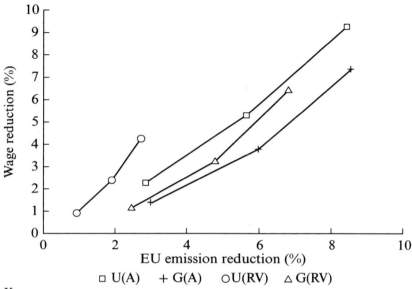

Key
☐ DE_1: Auctioned permits, Armington model.
+ DE_2: Grandfathered permits, Armington model.
○ DE_3: Auctioned permits, Ricardo–Viner model.
△ DE_4: Grandfathered permits, Ricardo–Viner model.

Figure 2.2 Welfare cost for a representative employed worker in Germany of alternative schemes for reducing EU carbon emission through unilateral action by Germany

Conclusion

This chapter has described the formulation, implementation and application of a multisectoral model for studying the effects of carbon-emission restrictions on trade and economic welfare within the European Community. The application has investigated the economic implications of coordinated and non-coordinated policies under auctioned as well as grandfathered permit systems.

The simulations provide three key insights. First, the scope for gains from permit trading within the EU is limited when EU countries are initially endowed with emission rights equal to the benchmark emission level and subsequent reduction in emission rights to meet exogenous reduction targets is proportional across countries. Carbon intensities of production computed using the Leontief inverse show some variation across countries, but no unexpected systematic differences appear.[17] The UK is an outlier in terms of carbon intensities and this difference shows up in the carbon trade scenarios. In an efficient (uniform permit price) equilibrium, the UK sells permits to the rest of the EU. Overall, this trade is relatively small and has insignificant welfare impacts. The implication of this result is that there would be relatively little efficiency loss if the EU were to contemplate emission reductions to a common abatement target across member states, provided that the member states act in unison.

The second finding is that coordinated action is essential if the EU is going to significantly reduce emissions. It is clear that when a country (here, Germany) acts unilaterally, carbon leakage can be a significant problem. The current model is unable to predict precisely how much leakage would result, but the simulations suggest that at a 20 per cent unilateral abatement by Germany, it would not be implausible that more than half of this reduction would be offset by increased emissions in other EU countries.

The final finding is that grandfathered emission permits are in most cases ill-advised. The model results indicate that these schemes can produce significant inefficiencies, either as part of an EU-wide agenda or within a unilateral abatement effort by Germany. In the Ricardo–Viner model of unilateral abatement, the use of grandfathered permits might be justified as a second-best measure to reduce leakage; but extremely high leakage rates are needed to offset the factor allocation losses induced by the implicit subsidies.

There are several issues absent from the present modelling framework which are potentially important:

- *Energy goods in the Armington model.* In the Armington model, all domestic, imported and exported varieties of every good are imperfect substitutes. This is clearly inappropriate for crude oil, coal and natural gas. At the present time, it is uncertain as to how many of the present results would carry over to a hybrid model in which some goods (oil, gas, coal, steel, aluminium and glass) are homogeneous while other goods remain imperfect substitutes.
- *Domestic energy policies.* Carbon taxes would apply amid a myriad of pre-existing domestic policies, including (but not limited to) strategic government protection of state energy sectors (for example, coal and electricity), and monopolistic competition in energy supply and distribution. Both government programmes and the realities of market structure have important implications for the effectiveness of carbon abatement policies, and these effects remain to be assessed.
- *Carbon taxes and sectoral adjustment.* In the policy debate, the application of carbon taxes is most often opposed on the basis of changes

in the pattern and level of employment. The present model adopts a flexible price formulation and frictionless labour movement between sectors within each region. It would be most interesting to examine the labour adjustment problem in a model incorporating endogenous unemployment. It is easy but unconvincing to include classical unemployment through downward rigidity of the real wage. A more intriguing approach would be to incorporate some representation of the demographic profile of workers by industry and country in order to develop an endogenous model of inter-sectoral migration with job-specific human capital. Another useful extension would be the incorporation of the role of unions which together with the employers bargain wages and employment (see, for example, Carraro and Galeotti 1994).

- *Environmental tax reform.* At present, the model entirely ignores public finance issues. It is relatively simple to incorporate taxes and public expenditure within the modelling format. The difficulty lies primarily in assembling plausible data to describe the various tax instruments.

In future research, these issues will be addressed using this model to the extent possible with available data.

Notes

1. In the auctioned permits system, the representative consumer (government) in one region is initially endowed with emission rights equal to the benchmark emission level. With grandfathered permit systems, permits are initially allocated to industries and households on the basis of specific distribution schemes (for example, distribution according to benchmark emission patterns).
2. The representation of ROW is reduced to import and export flows to these countries.
3. The model is formulated as a nonlinear system of roughly 1500 nonlinear inequalities using GAMS/MPSGE (Rutherford 1994) and solved using PATH (Dirkse and Ferris 1995).
4. Equation (2.2) as well as equation (2.7) below are minor simplifications. In the implemented model, one additional level of nesting for energy inputs is introduced, so that electric and non-electric energy first trade off (with an elasticity of 0.3), and subsequently fossil energy inputs (oil, gas and coal) enter in a lower CES nest with an elasticity of substitution equal to 0.5.
5. In a dual approach, utility-maximizing demand for consumption is represented as a cost (expenditure)-minimizing bundle of consumer goods which produces one unit of aggregate consumption utility.
6. As with industries, households have to buy emission rights (that is, pay taxes) in order to use carbon-emitting inputs within their energy consumption bundle.
7. The associated (dual) variable with this constraint indicates the real exchange rate relative to ROW (for example, 1985 ECU/1985 US$).
8. The choice of countries which are explicitly represented in the model has been made with respect to the availability of consistent data (here, Eurostat input–output tables for 1985) and the share of countries in overall EU trade volume and production output.
9. The prices for fossil fuels (oil, gas and coal) are inferred from the IEA data, based on a mapping from the IEA use sectors and the R59 branches of the Eurostat input-output tables to the following eleven sectors: AGR Agriculture, COA Coal, OIL, GAS Natural

and manufactured gases, ELE Electricity, ORE Iron and steel, CHE Chemical products, EIS Other energy-intensive sectors, EQU Equipment, CON Consumer goods, TRN Transport, SER Services including nonmarket services, and FCH Residential.

10. One example is electricity generation where France, because of the size share of nuclear and hydro power, emits a fraction of CO_2 per kWh compared to coal-based electricity production in Denmark or Germany. Given this heterogeneity among the large member states of the EU, one can only conjecture about the potential magnitude of cross country differences in production technique and the level of embodied carbon in energy-intensive goods.

11. The choice of Germany is motivated by two aspects. First, Germany is the biggest economy within the EU and has very high intra-EU trade flows in energy- and carbon-intensive commodities, suggesting significant scope for leakage. Second, the political situation in Germany is characterized by a high willingness to take a lead role in CO_2 reduction regardless as to whether other EU countries take similar steps.

12. As the main emitter of CO_2 within the EU, Germany continues to affirm its objective of reducing CO_2 emissions by 25–30 per cent by the year 2005, taking 1987 as the base year for the whole of Germany including the Five New *Länder*.

13. A popular argument for unilateral action is that CO_2 taxes used for the reduction of other distortionary taxes might allow for significant mitigation at net negative costs, that is, yield a so-called double dividend through an increase in traditional welfare and environmental quality (Greenpeace/DIW 1994, Gruppe Energie 2010, 1995). For an overview of the theoretical aspects related to the double dividend hypothesis, see Goulder (1994).

14. The current version of the model ignores other taxes in order to avoid extensive data collection and reconciliation on national tax systems. This simplification leaves doubts, however, regarding the possibility of positive or negative interactions of carbon taxes (carbon permits) with other market distortions.

15. For the accounting of carbon leakage in terms of aggregate efficiency, see the discussion of Figure 2.1, below.

16. Admittedly, it would be better to hold aggregate world emissions constant, but this is impossible within a 'subglobal' model. If it is assumed that EU, US and Japanese goods are relatively imperfect substitutes, the leakage effects outside of the EU from unilateral action by Germany may be neglected. Given the substantial share of the EU in German imports and exports, this is probably a reasonable assumption.

17. The scope for benefits of intra-EU trade of permits will change with alternative schemes for the initial distribution of permits and for the reduction patterns. Additional potential for increased benefits would also come from a wider range of variation in carbon intensities across countries with countries such as Portugal or Greece which are currently not incorporated.

References

Bohm, P. (1993), 'Incomplete international cooperation to reduce CO_2 emissions: alternative policies', *Journal of Environmental Economics and Management,* **24,** 258–71.

Böhringer, C. and T. Rutherford (1997), 'Carbon taxes with exemptions in an open economy: a general equilibrium analysis of the German tax initiative', Journal of Environmental Economics and Management, 32, 189–203.

Burniaux, J.-M., J.P. Martin, G. Nicoletti, and J.O. Martins (1992), 'The costs of reducing CO_2-emissions: evidence from GREEN', *OECD Economics and Statistics Department Working Paper*, No. 115, Paris.

Carraro, C. and D. Siniscarlo (eds) (1993), *The European Carbon Tax: An Economic Assessment*, The Fondazione Eni Enrico Mattei (FEEM) Kluwer International Series on Economics, Energy and Environment, Dordrecht: Kluwer Academic Publishers.

Carraro, C. and M. Galeotti (1994), 'Environmental fiscal reforms in a federal Europe', paper presented at the International Symposium on 'Economic Aspects of Environmental Policy Making in a Federation', Leuven.

Commission of the European Communities (1992a), COM(92) 226 final, Brussels.

Commission of the European Communities (1992b), *European Economy: The Climate Challenge – Economic Aspects of the Community's Strategy for Limiting CO₂ Emissions*, Brussels.

Copeland, B.R. (1994), 'International trade and the environment: policy reform in a polluted small open economy', *Journal of Environmental Economics and Management*, **26**, 44–65.

Dirkse, S. and M. Ferris (1995), 'The PATH solver: a non-monotone stabilization scheme for mixed complementarity problems', *Optimization Methods & Software*, **5**, 123–56.

Enquete-Kommission 'Vorsorge zum Schutz der Erdatmosphäre' des Deutschen Bundestages (1994), *Mehr Zukunft für die Erde*, Band 3, Bonn: Economica Verlag.

Eurostat (1995), 'The Input–Output Tables Database of Eurostat', Luxembourg.

Felder, S. and T. Rutherford (1993), 'Unilateral CO₂ reductions and carbon leakage: the effect of international trade in oil and basic materials', *Journal of Environmental Economics and Management*, **25**, 162–76.

Goulder, L.H. (1994), 'Environmental taxation and the double dividend: a reader's guide', *mimeo*, Stanford: Stanford University.

Greenpeace Deutsches Institut für Wirtschaftsforschung (DIW) (1994), *Wirtschaftliche Auswirkungen einer Ökologischen Steuerreform*, Berlin.

Gruppe Energie 2010 (1995), *Zukünftige Energiepolitik*, Bonn.

Hoel, M. (1994), 'Should a carbon tax be differentiated across sectors?', mimeo, Department of Economics, University of Oslo.

Institute of Economic Affairs (IEA) (1994a), 'Energy Balances of OECD countries', Paris.

Institute of Economic Affairs (IEA) (1994b), 'Energy Prices and Taxes', Paris.

Koutstaal, P., H. Vollebergh, and J. de Vries (1994), 'Hybrid carbon inventive mechanisms for the European Community', *Research Memorandum* 9406, Research Center for Economic Policy (OCFEB), Erasmus University, Rotterdam.

Markusen, J.R. (1975), 'International externalities and optimal tax structures', *Journal of International Economics*, **5**, 15–29.

Pearce, D.W. (1991), 'The role of carbon taxes in adjusting to global warming', *Economic Journal*, **101**, 935–48.

Pezzey, J. (1992), 'Analysis of unilateral CO₂ control in the European Community', *The Energy Journal*, **13**, 159–72.

Poterba, J.M. (1991), 'Tax policy to combat global warming', in R. Dornbush and J.M. Poterba (eds), *Global Warming: Economic Policy Responses*, Cambridge, MA:MIT Press, pp. 71–97.

Rauscher, M. (1991), 'Foreign trade and the environment', in H. Siebert (ed.), *Economics and The Environment: the International Dimension*, Tübingen: Mohr, pp. 17–31.

Rutherford, T. (1993), 'Welfare effects of fossil carbon restrictions', in *The Costs of Cutting Carbon Emissions: Results from Global Models*, Paris: OECD, pp. 95–106.

Rutherford, T. (1997), 'General equilibrium modelling with MPSGE as a GAMS Subsystem', *Applied Computational Economics* (forthcoming).

Siebert, H., J. Elchberger, R. Gronych, and R. Pethig (1980), *Trade and Environment – A Theoretical Inquiry*, Amsterdam.

WEFA (1995), 'Comptes Harmonisés sur les Echanges et L'Economie Mondiale', Paris.

3. National economic impacts of an EU environmental policy: an applied general equilibrium analysis

Klaus Conrad and Tobias F.N. Schmidt

Introduction

Preventive measures to protect the earth's atmosphere and the associated policies required are at the centre of international conventions concerning the environment. A large number of states have decided, or are beginning to decide, in favour of a drastic reduction of energy-related carbon dioxide (CO_2) and sulphur dioxide (SO_2) emissions. The greenhouse gas CO_2 results from the combustion of fossil carbon, therefore, a reduction of CO_2 emissions can only be achieved by reducing the use of fossil energy carriers. These sources of energy, however, are the backbone of current energy supply. Since a reduction of CO_2, SO_2 or NO_x emissions cannot be achieved by technical measures alone, the use of economic instruments such as taxes and marketable permits has also been, and still is being, taken into consideration to achieve predefined emission goals. The objective of this chapter is to quantify the economic effects of the introduction of tradable permits for CO_2 in the European Union (EU). For this purpose, linked applied general equilibrium models (AGE) are used for eleven EU member countries (EU–12 without Luxembourg). This method enables the measurement of the change in competitiveness for domestic industries, the impact on growth, employment and inflation in member countries, the cost-effectiveness of a coordinated environmental policy and the costs and benefits of a cooperative approach in adhering to an EU target of emissions of air pollutants. The results presented are the first results from the SOLVEGE/GEM–E3 Project. GEM–E3 stands for General Equilibrium Modelling for Energy–Economy–Environment, a joint undertaking of NTUA–Athens (P. Capros, P. Georgakopoulos), CES–KULeuven (S. Proost and D. Van Regemorter), University of Mannheim and ZEW (K. Conrad and T. Schmidt), GEMME-CEA (N. Ladoux), University of Strathclyde (P. MacGregor) and CORE-UCL (Y. Smeers). The data consist of national social accounting matrices, an extension of the social account by an input–output table, and of an environmental data base.

The specification of the present minimum standard model consists of unit cost functions of the nested CES type for eleven industries. There are overall CES functions in the KLEM (capital, labour, energy and material) input prices with price-diminishing (factor-augmenting) technical change and CES subcost functions. The foreign trade specification is of the Armington type. The demands for the goods are distinguished not only by types of goods (eleven) but also by place of production (eleven EU member countries and the rest of the world). The share parameters in the CES specification for a good i supplied by each of the twelve countries (eleven EU countries and rest of the world) and demanded in a country k will be calculated using a trade matrix for each of the eleven goods.

The model of consumer behaviour in each social group is based on an extended linear expenditure system. The consumers choose the optimal allocation of expenditure for nondurables and for services of durables across twelve consumption categories and savings. Consumption matrices are used to break down these categories into their origins (eleven goods). The prices of the services from durables are expressed in cost prices consisting of user costs and all cost components linked to the use of the durables (for example, a gasoline tax, a motor vehicle tax). The interest rate takes care of the closure rule. Trade in goods and services between countries will not be balanced by endogenous exchange rates but the model will present changes in the national balances of trade.

The model considers two environmental problems: global warming and acidification. As the latter is not emphasized within this chapter, the description of the model features concerning this aspect is kept very brief: for the main acidification components, that is SO_2 and NO_x, abatement cost functions have been estimated for several industries. These functions depend on the degree of abatement (set as a standard by regulation or determined by the firm as an endogenous variable) and they will increase the price or unit cost of using emission-intensive inputs. Yearly increases in real net investment in equipment for cleaner air by industry and country are used to calculate degrees of abatements in the base year. Finally, from total deposition (emissions of SO_2 and NO_x) at a receptor due to a specific source are derived (i) deposition at a receptor per unit emission from a source country (transport coefficient) and (ii) the background depositions in every country.

This chapter focuses on the problem of greenhouse gases by introducing an EU-wide system of tradable permits, free of charge and based on the present energy intensity and energy mix. If tradable permits are then depreciated 10 per cent, there will be a positive market price for permits with demand by countries where the cost of substitution is high and supply by those countries where the cost of substitution is low. The implications of reducing CO_2 by 10 per cent nation by nation via a permit system versus an

EU-wide reduction of 10 per cent will be considered. Of interest is who would gain and who would lose under a cooperative approach.

While a unilateral action taken by one country might be desirable in its pioneer role as a signal for action, higher prices and a loss in growth are to be expected. However, if the EU decided to introduce an emission tax or a system of tradable permits, losses in growth might be kept within acceptable limits, as will be investigated in this chapter.

The chapter starts with a presentation of the model specification. This includes production, foreign trade, consumption and the closure of the model. The following section elaborates on the permit system used for the simulations. The next section presents the empirical findings of our study, and the final section draws the relevant conclusions.

The specification of the standard version of the GEM–E3 model
Cost function and input coefficients for the KLEM aggregate
The technology of a cost minimizing industry is characterized by nested CES cost functions. $C(X, \overline{PKE}, \overline{PLMF})$ is the cost function at the first stage with input prices for the capital/electricity aggregate KE and the labour/material/fuel aggregate LMF. The production function is assumed to be CES in KE and LMF with factor-augmenting technical change. Hence, there is price-diminishing technical progress in the cost function in terms of effective input prices. Figure 3.1 shows the nested production structure.

Profit maximization under constant returns to scale implies revenue $PX \cdot X$ equal to cost which explains the output price PX of domestic production in terms of a CES unit cost function:

$$PX = \left(d_1 \cdot \overline{PKE}^{1-\sigma x} + d_2 \cdot \overline{PLMF}^{1-\sigma x} \right)^{\frac{1}{1-\sigma_x}} \tag{3.1}$$

where $\overline{PKE} = PKE / g_{KE}(t)$ with $g_{KE}(t) = \exp(\overline{g}_{KE} \cdot t)$ as price-diminishing technical progress. The same holds for the input aggregate LMF, that is, for $g_{LMF}(t)$ ($d_1{}^{\sigma x}$ gives the distribution parameter in the primal production function). From Shephard's Lemma, the factor demand functions are derived as variable input coefficients:

$$\frac{KE}{X} = d_1 \cdot \left(\frac{PX}{PKE} \right)^{\sigma_x} \cdot g_{KE}(t)^{\sigma_x - 1} \tag{3.2}$$

$$\frac{LMF}{X} = d_2 \cdot \left(\frac{PX}{PLMF} \right)^{\sigma_x} \cdot g_{LMF}(t)^{\sigma_x - 1} \tag{3.3}$$

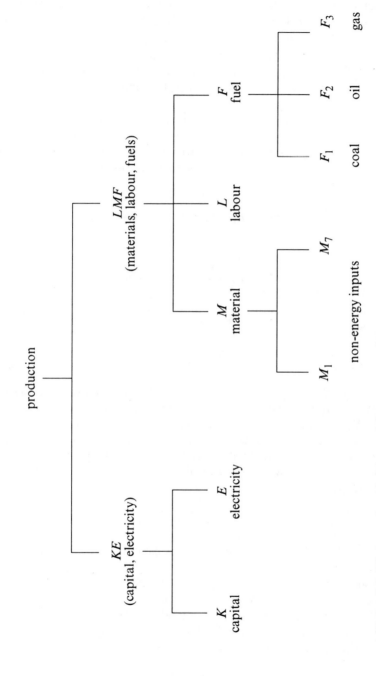

Figure 3.1 The nested production and factor price scheme

In principle, one could include all the input prices of the model in one CES unit cost function. This, however, would imply the assumption that the elasticity of substitution between all inputs is the same. Therefore, sub- cost functions are specified for the capital/electricity aggregate and for the *LMF* aggregate with different elasticities of substitution. The price function for the *KE* aggregate at that second level is:

$$PKE = \left(d_{1K} \overline{PK}^{1-\sigma_{KE}} + d_{1E} \overline{PK}^{1-\sigma_{KE}} \right)^{\frac{1}{1-\sigma_{KE}}} \tag{3.4}$$

with $\overline{PE} = PE \, / \, g_E \, (t)$, expressing electricity-augmenting (price-diminishing) technical progress. The price-dependent composition of the capital/electricity aggregate is:

$$\frac{K}{KE} = d_{1K} \cdot \left(\frac{PKE}{PK} \right)^{\sigma_{KE}} \cdot g_K(t)^{\sigma_{KE}-1} \tag{3.5}$$

and

$$\frac{E}{KE} = d_{1E} \cdot \left(\frac{PKE}{PE} \right)^{\sigma_{KE}} \cdot g_E(t)^{\sigma_{KE}-1} \tag{3.6}$$

In order to determine the capital input coefficient, one has to multiply (3.5) by (3.2):

$$a_K = \frac{K}{X} = \frac{K}{KE}(\cdot) \cdot \frac{KE}{X}(\cdot) \tag{3.7}$$

Capital input as derived from (3.7) is the desired capital stock, say K_{des} (if stocks are proportional to service flows). In the standard version of the GEM–E3 model, however, capital is treated as a quasi-fixed stock over the current year at a level from the end of the previous year, say K_{-1}. Therefore, (3.7) is used to determine an endogenous *ex post* price of capital based on a rate of return which the industry has earned *ex post*. For that purpose (3.7) is solved for PK_{post}:

$$PK_{post} = f(X, K_{-1}, PX, \overline{PE}, g_K(t), g_{KE}(t))$$

PK_{post} is the endogenous shadow price of capital which clears the market for fixed K_{-1}. It will be used to calculate capital income $PK_{post} \cdot K_{-1}$ in period t. It is easy to check that this calculation of PK_{post} is equivalent to calculating it from the zero-profit condition.[1]

If an exogenous *ex ante* price of capital is determined PK_{ante}, then (3.7) can be employed to determine the desired stock of capital K_{des}. Let this *ex ante* price be the standard user cost of capital formula:

$$PK_{ante} = PI(r + \delta)$$

where *PI* is the price of investment goods, *r* is the rate of return on risk-free government bonds (exogenous or determined by the closure rule), and δ is the rate of replacement. Then the desired capital stock is:

$$K_{des} = X \cdot d_{1K} \cdot \left(\frac{PKE}{PK_{ante}}\right)^{\sigma_{KE}} \cdot g_K(t)^{\sigma_{KE}-1} \, d_1 \cdot \left(\frac{PX}{PKE}\right)^{\sigma}{}_x \, g_{KE}(t)^{\sigma_x-1} \qquad (3.8)$$

with PK_{ante} appearing also in *PKE* as specified under (3.4). Net investment I_{net} with 'adjustment' is:

$$I_{net} = m(K_{des} - K_{-1}) \qquad (3.9)$$

Finally, capital stock for the next period is:

$$K = I_{br} + (1 - \delta)K_{-1}$$

where $I_{br} = I_{net} + \delta \cdot K_{-1}$. It should finally be conceded that a specification of a restricted cost function $C(X, K_{-1}, PKE, PLMF)$ would have been the appropriate approach to a model with a quasi-fixed capital stock. In such a case, however, the system of prices would also depend on *X* which complicates the solution process for the linked models.

If capital is mainly machinery and electrical equipment, then capital and electricity are used in fixed proportions. An alternative approach then would be to define the price of capital in terms of a cost price (Conrad 1983). A higher price of electricity increases the cost of using capital, which, in turn, may increase the demand for labour. In order to model such a relation, a partial linkage of capital and electricity is introduced.

In the cost function:

$$C(KE, PK, PE) = \min_{K, E} (PK \cdot K + PE \cdot E) \text{ s.t. } KE = f(K, E)$$

E is partitioned by $E = \alpha_E \cdot K + \tilde{E}$ where $\alpha_E \cdot K$ is the electricity demand derived from *K* and $\tilde{E}$ is the flexible electricity which can be conserved if substituted by other inputs. Inserting E in the cost definition yields:

$$C(KE, PK, PE) = \min_{K, \tilde{E}} [PK \cdot K + PE(\alpha_E \cdot K + \tilde{E})] \text{ s.t. } KE = f(K, \alpha_E \cdot K + \tilde{E})$$

or

$$C(KE, \tilde{PK}, PE) = \min_{K, \tilde{E}} [(PK + \alpha_E PE)K + PE \cdot \tilde{E}] \text{ s.t. } KE = f(K, \tilde{E})$$

where $\tilde{PK} = PK + \alpha_E PE$ is the cost price of capital. Cost prices reflect the aspect of linked inputs and provide for a different pattern of substitution. The demand for capital K and flexible energy $\tilde{E}$ can be derived by Shephard's Lemma.

A price function for the aggregate LMF must be specified next:

$$PLMF = \left(d_{2L}\,\overline{PL}^{1-\sigma_L} + d_{2M}\,PY^{1-\sigma_L} + d_{2F}\,\overline{PF}^{1-\sigma_L}\right)^{\frac{1}{1-\sigma_L}}$$

The price-dependent composition of this aggregate follows again from Shephard's Lemma:

$$\frac{input\ i}{LMF} = d_{2i}\left(\frac{PLMF}{P\,i}\right)^{\sigma_L} g_i(t)^{\sigma_L-1} \quad i = L,\,M,\,F$$

Finally, there is a unit cost function on the third level for the price of fuel (coal, gas, oil):

$$PF = \left(\sum_{i=1}^{m} \delta_{1,i} \cdot \overline{PY}_i^{1-\sigma_F}\right)^{\frac{1}{1-\sigma_F}} \tag{3.10}$$

with $\overline{PY}_i = \dfrac{PY_i}{g_{F_i}(t)}$ expressing energy-augmenting (price-diminishing) technical progress.

The price-dependent composition of the fuel aggregate is:

$$\frac{F_i}{F} = \delta_{1,i}\left(\frac{PF}{PY_i}\right)^{\sigma_F} g_{F_i}(t)^{\sigma_F-1} \quad i = 1,\,...,\,m \tag{3.11}$$

Similarly, a CES specification is chosen for the unit cost function for material:

$$PM = \left(\sum_{i=m+1}^{n} \delta_{2,i}\,P\overline{Y}_i^{1-\sigma_M}\right)^{\frac{1}{1-\sigma_M}}$$

with

$$\overline{PY}_i = \frac{PY_i}{g_{M_i}(t)} \quad i = m+1,\,...,\,n$$

The cost-minimizing allocation of material to its components follows from:

$$\frac{M_i}{M} = \delta_{2,i}\left(\frac{PM}{PY_i}\right)^{\sigma_M} \cdot g_{M_i}(t)^{\sigma_M-1} \tag{3.12}$$

If the overall input coefficient is multiplied by the sub-input coefficient, the input coefficients a_i are obtained:

$$a_i = \frac{F_i}{X} = \frac{F_i}{F}(\cdot) \cdot \frac{F}{LMF}(\cdot) \cdot \frac{LMF}{X}(\cdot) \quad i = 1, ..., m \tag{3.13}$$

$$a_i = \frac{M_i}{X} = \frac{M_i}{M}(\cdot) \cdot \frac{M}{LMF}(\cdot) \cdot \frac{LMF}{X}(\cdot) \quad i = m+1, ..., n \text{ and } \tag{3.14}$$

$$a_L = \frac{L}{X} = \frac{L}{LMF}(\cdot) \cdot \frac{LMF}{X}(\cdot)$$

The $(\cdot)$ indicates that the coefficients depend on relative prices.

The foreign trade specification
For modelling intra-industry foreign trade between the EU member countries, the Armington approach is widely accepted: domestically produced goods and imports from different countries are imperfect substitutes. The dual to a CES production function $Y_c = f(X_c, IM_c)$, giving supply Y_c in country c as an aggregate of domestic production X_c and imports IM_c, is a CES unit cost function:

$$PY_c = \left[cx \cdot PX_c^{1-\sigma_x} + (1 - cx) \, PIM_c^{1-\sigma_x} \right]^{\frac{1}{1-\sigma_x}} \tag{3.15}$$

where PY_c, PX_c, and PIM_c are the corresponding prices of Y_c, X_c, and IM_c (price of aggregated imports is in national currency of country c). Derived from this cost function are both the share of domestic production in total supply:

$$\frac{X_c}{Y_c} = cx \cdot \left(\frac{PY_c}{PX_c} \right)^{\sigma_x} \tag{3.16}$$

and the share of aggregate import in total supply:

$$\frac{IM_c}{Y_c} = (1 - cx) \cdot \left(\frac{PY_c}{PIM_c} \right)^{\sigma_x} \tag{3.17}$$

If the model determines total supply, then aggregate import demand, derived from (3.17), has to be allocated to the eleven EU member state countries and to the rest of the world which contribute to this aggregate import demand. Thus import consists, in other words, of the exports of the twelve countries in that good. Therefore, in the GEM–E3 model the demands for the eleven goods are also distinguished by place of production.

There will be French import demand of consumer goods produced in the United Kingdom and in Spain. To obtain such a trade matrix with 11×12 import demand functions by good and place of production, a CES import unit cost or price function is specified:

$$PIM_c = \left[\sum_{k=1}^{12} cm_k \left(\frac{PIM_k}{e_{k,c}} \right)^{1-\sigma_m} \right]^{\frac{1}{1-\sigma_m}} \qquad c = 1, ..., 11 \qquad (3.18)$$

where PIM_k is the price of imports as the export price by country k. As there are import taxes and duties (t_{dut}), it is $PIM_k = (1 + t_{dut}) \cdot PY_k$ (as this is distinguished by eleven goods, $PIM_{i,k} = (1 + t_{i,dut}) \cdot PY_{i,k}$ has to be written for a good i and a country k). $e_{k,c}$ is the exchange rate index in currency of country k per unit currency of country c. Given the price index PIM_{ROW} and the exchange rates $e_{ROW,c}$, the eleven prices PIM_c can be calculated. This allows the determination of PY for a certain good from (3.15) and then the shares in (3.16) and (3.17).

Again, a cost-minimizing composition of the import aggregate is the objective of the importing country. Shephard's Lemma, applied to the cost function PIM_c in (3.18), yields this composition:

$$\frac{IM_{k,c}}{IM_c} = cm_k \left(\frac{PIM_c}{PIM_k/e_{k,c}} \right)^{\sigma_m} \qquad k = 1, ..., 12 \qquad (3.19)$$

where $IM_{k,c}$ is the import by country c from country k in currency of country c. Because of $\Sigma_k \, cm_k = 1$, the adding-up condition $\Sigma_k \, (PIM_k / e_{k,c}) \cdot IM_{k,c} = PIM_c \cdot IM_c$ is automatically satisfied. If (3.19) is multiplied by IM_c, derived from equation (3.17), a trade flow matrix can be filled for each of the eleven commodities. Such a trade matrix is as follows:

Country	1 $\quad$ ...	c $\quad$ ...	12	Export
1	$\left(\dfrac{PIM_1}{e_{1,1}}\right) \cdot IM_{1,1}$	... $\vdots$	$\left(\dfrac{PIM_1}{e_{1,12}}\right) \cdot IM_{1,12}$	EX_1 . . .
k . . .	$\vdots$ . . .	$\left(\dfrac{PIM_k}{e_{k,c}}\right) \cdot IM_{k,c}$	. . . $\vdots$	EX_k . .
. 12	$\left(\dfrac{PIM_{12}}{e_{12,1}}\right) \cdot IM_{12,1}$	$\vdots$ . . .	$\left(\dfrac{PIM_{12}}{e_{12,12}}\right) \cdot IM_{12,12}$	. EX_{12}
Import	$PIM_1 \cdot IM_1$ ...	$PIM_c \cdot IM_c$ ...	$PIM_{12} \cdot IM_{12}$	See (3.20)

The column sums yield the value of import of country c in the currency of country c. The quantity elements in row k, $IM_{k,c}$ ($c = 1, ..., 12$), are in the currency of country c. Multiplied by the exchange rate $e_{k,c}$ in the currency of country k per unit of the currency of country c, they can be summed up to yield export EX_k of country k, that is:

$$EX_k = \sum_c e_{k,c} \cdot IM_{k,c} \tag{3.20}$$

EX_k in turn enters final demand in the input–output accounting system. The trade surplus (TS) (deficit if negative) for a good is:

$$TS_k = PY_k \cdot EX_k - PIM_k \cdot IM_k$$

In the standard version of the GEM–E3 model, the exchange rates are exogenous and the balances of trade are calculated as residuals.

Consumer demand and labour supply
Usually, the behaviour of consumers is assumed to perform a two-stage budgeting procedure: an intertemporal allocation of lifetime wealth endowment between present and future consumption of goods and leisure, and an intratemporal allocation of consumption into categories. The latter are then transformed into consumption by product. Figure 3.2 shows the household's allocation problem. Furthermore, if the distributional impacts

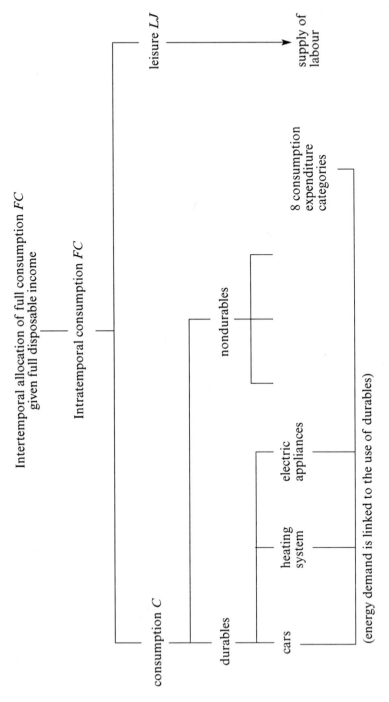

Figure 3.2 Household's allocation scheme

of policies are to be assessed, a disaggregation into several types of households is required. In the standard GEM–E3 version, a representative consumer is considered who is characterized by an expenditure function for 'full' expenditure which consists of expenditures for nondurable goods and for leisure given the stocks of consumer durables. Since environmental regulation affects the use and purchase of consumer durables such as cars, electric appliances and heating, a model of consumer behaviour should integrate demand for durables and nondurables. Demand for nondurables, such as gasoline or electricity, and demand for services from durables has to be reconciled with investment demand for modifying the stocks of durables towards their optimal levels. Therefore, a restricted expenditure function is employed with stocks of durables as quasi-fixed goods. The expenditure function is derived from the Stone–Geary utility function which underlies the linear expenditure system.

At the first stage, the household determines an allocation of its resources between present and future consumption by maximizing an intertemporal utility function subject to an intertemporal budget constraint:

$$\max_{c_t, LJ_t} \Sigma_t \, (1 + s)^{-t} \, [\beta_c \, \ln(C_t - CO) + \beta_{LJ} \, \ln \, (LJ_t - LJO)]$$

subject to

$$WT = \Sigma_t \, (1 + r)^{-t} \, (PC_t \cdot C_t + PLJ_t \cdot LJ_t)$$

where WT is total wealth. C_t is real private consumption, CO its subsistence level, LJ_t is leisure and LJO its subsistence level, s is the subjective discount rate and r is the nominal interest rate. An initial commitment for leisure could be LJO = 12 hr/day multiplied by the average working days per year. The price of leisure is $PLJ = (1-t_m) \cdot PL$ where t_m is the marginal tax rate for labour income. Under some assumptions (for example, a constant expected rate of inflation) the following demand functions for consumption and leisure can be derived:

$$C = CO + \frac{s}{r_r} \frac{\beta_C}{\beta_C + \beta_{LJ}} \frac{1}{PC} (Y_{disp} + PLJ \cdot LJ - PC \cdot CO - PLJ \cdot LJO)$$

$$(3.21)$$

$$LJ = LJO + \frac{s}{r_r} \frac{\beta_{LJ}}{\beta_C + \beta_{LJ}} \frac{1}{PLJ} (Y_{disp} + PLJ \cdot LJ - PC \cdot CO - PLJ \cdot LJO)$$

$$(3.22)$$

The last equation is implicit in LJ and has to be solved for LJ. Leisure and labour demand then add up to the yearly time endowment. The savings of households can then be determined by $S = Y_{disp} - PC \cdot C$.

Next, the expenses for durables and for the demand of energy associated with using the durables are subtracted from consumption expenditure. This gives expenditure e for nondurables. These expenditures will be allocated in the second stage of the consumer decision problem:

$$e = PC \cdot C - expenditures\ for\ durables\ and\ energy \qquad (3.23)$$

The expenditure function with three quasi-fixed durable goods (Z_1, Z_2 and Z_3 for cars, electric appliances and heating, respectively) is:

$$e(p_1, ..., p_n; u; Z_1, Z_2, Z_3) = \sum_{i=1}^{n} p_i \cdot C_{o,i} + u \cdot \prod_{j=1}^{3} (Z_j - Z_{o,j})^{-\gamma_j} \cdot \prod_{i=1}^{n} \left(\frac{p_i}{\beta_i}\right)^{\beta_i}$$

$$(3.24)$$

where $p_i = PY_i\,(1 + t_i)$ is the market price for the good, u is the utility level, $C_{o,i}$ is the minimum required quantity of good i, $Z_{o,j}$ is the minimum required quantity of a durable good j, and $\Sigma\, p_i \cdot C_{o,i}$ is 'subsistence expenditure'. The expenditure minimizing demand for nondurable goods, given utility u and the stocks of the three durables, can be derived by partial differentiation of the expenditure function with respect to the prices:

$$C_i = C_{o,i} + \frac{\beta_i}{p_i}\left(e(\cdot) - \sum_{i=1}^{n} p_i \cdot C_{o,i}\right) \qquad i = 1, ..., n \qquad (3.25)$$

Desired stocks of durables and *ex post* service prices of durables can be derived in a way analogous to that used for the restricted cost function approach. With an exogenous *ex ante* user cost of durables p_{zj}, the desired stock follows from:

$$\frac{\partial e\,(\cdot, \hat{Z}_j)}{\partial Z_j} = -p_{Z_j} \quad \text{that is,} \quad \hat{Z}_j = Z_{o,j} + \frac{\gamma_j}{P_{Z_j}}\left(e\,(\cdot) - \sum_{i=1}^{n} p_i \cdot C_{o,i}\right) \qquad (3.26)$$

Purchases of new durables under adjustment restrictions ($0 < m \leq 1$) are:

$$I_{Z_j}^{net} = m_j(\hat{Z}_j - Z_{-1,j}) \qquad j = 1, 2, 3$$

We finally obtain consumer expenditures $PCE \cdot CE$ on nondurables and on the services from durables from (3.27):

$$PCE \cdot CE = \sum_{i=1}^{n} p_i\, C_i + \sum_{j=1}^{3} p_{Z_j}\,(Z_{-1j} + I_{Z_j}^{net}) \qquad (3.27)$$

Finally, some words need to be said about the specification of the user cost of a durable, p_{Z_j}. In principle, p_Z could be set equal to $PI\,(r + \delta)$

where *PI* is the price of the durable, δ is the rate of replacement and *r* is the interest rate. In fact, the use of durables such as cars, electric appliances or heating systems requires other nondurables such as gasoline, electricity or other fuels. While a part of these requirements depends on the way of using the durable (for example, fast driving or bad maintenance of a car requires more gasoline) and is therefore disposable, there is a minimum (or average) amount which is needed for operation. Or, in algebraic terms, $C_G = \alpha_{GZ} \cdot Z + \tilde{C}_G$ where α_{GZ} is yearly gasoline consumption per unit of purchase price of the car, and $\tilde{C}_G$ is gasoline consumption from fast driving or bad maintenance of the car.[2] This implies a cost price p_z for the services of an automobile, which is the user cost of capital *PI* ($r + \delta$) plus the cost of gasoline, that is, $p_Z = PI(r + \delta) + \alpha_{GZ} \cdot p_G$. The introduction of a tax on CO_2 or NO_x will therefore increase the price of gasoline, hence the cost price of a car, and demand for new cars will decline. Under a carbon dioxide tax, for instance, the cost price of a car is $p_Z = PI(r + \delta) + \alpha_{GZ}(p_G + t_{CO_2} \cdot e_{CO_2}$ where t_{CO_2} is the tax rate and is the emission coefficient for gasoline. If, moreover, a property tax or motor vehicle tax rate τ is incorporated, then the user cost of a car is:

$$p_Z = PI[r(1 + \tau) + \delta + \tau] + \alpha_{GZ} \cdot p_G \tag{3.28}$$

For guesstimation of the parameters $C_{o,i}$, β_i and Fy_j, the properties of a linear expenditure system are made use of, that is, from guesstimates of *n* income elasticities one obtains the *n* parameters β_i and from guesstimates of *n* direct price elasticities one obtains the *n* parameters $C_{o,i}$, given the β_i's (and similarly for the parameters of the durables).

Demand, supply and the closure rule[3]
The standard system of equations for an input–output model is:

$$Y_i = \sum_{j=1}^{n} a_{ij} \cdot X_j + F_i \tag{3.29}$$

where F_i is final demand with $F_i = C_i + CG_i + I_i + IG_i + EX_i$. C_i is private consumption of good *i*, CG_i and IG_i are government consumption or investment, respectively (exogenous), and I_i is gross investment by origin.

Since the demand system used here determines consumption goods by categories, and the system of investment functions determines investment demand by destination, transition matrices are required which transform demand into deliveries from the industries. Therefore, the C_i's in final demand have to be seen as the result of the transition matrix of the type (branches × categories) multiplied by the consumption categories. Similarly, an investment matrix with fixed technical coefficients serves to compute investment demand by origin (products) from investment demand by destination (branches) as evaluated from investment behaviour in (3.7), together with investment for replacement and decay, that is, $\delta \cdot K_{-1}$. The system (3.29) can be written as a system in the unknown variables Y_i if it is rewritten as:

$$Y_i = \sum_{j=1}^{n} a_{ij} \cdot \left(\frac{X_j}{Y_j}\right) \cdot Y_j + F_i \tag{3.30}$$

with X_j / Y_j determined by (3.16).

In value terms, demand has to be equal to supply:

$$PZ_i \cdot Y_i = \sum_{j=1}^{n} PY_j \cdot X_{ij} + (1 + t_i) \cdot PY_i \cdot (F_i - EX_i) + PY_i \cdot EX_i \tag{3.31}$$

where PZ_i is the market price including indirect taxes and t_i is the indirect tax rate on final demand. The accounting identity from the input side is:

$$PY_j \cdot Y_j = \sum_{i=1}^{n} PY_i \cdot X_{ij} + PL_j \cdot L_j + PK_j \cdot K_{-1,j} + PIM_j \cdot IM_j \tag{3.32}$$

If (3.31) over i and (3.32) over j are added and then (3.32) is subtracted from (3.31), one obtains the national accounting identity asserting that the private gross domestic production from both the flow of cost approach and from the flow of product approach should be equal, that is:

$$\Sigma_j (PL_j \cdot L_j + PK_j \cdot K_{-1,j}) = \Sigma PY_i \cdot F_i - \Sigma_j PIM_j \cdot IM_j \tag{3.33}$$

However, as all variables in this accounting identity have already been determined (endogenously or exogenously – government expenditure and K_{-1}), there is no reason why this identity should have been satisfied.

The rate of return r is used, which influences the user cost of capital $PK_{ante} = PI (r + \delta)$, as the closure variable. The left hand side of (3.33) increases in r because of higher cost of capital. The right-hand side of (3.33) decreases in r because investment as a component of final demand F is falling in r (see (3.9)). Hence, an interest rate which closes the model can be expected.

Tradable CO_2 emission permits within branches and/or EU member states
According to a system of tradable CO_2 permits, an environmental agency of a country or of the EU defines desired CO_2 emission levels for a sequence of years and issues emission permits. It is assumed that CO_2 permits are first distributed free of charge on the basis of the industry's (or country's) base-year emissions. Then it is assumed that the CO_2 emissions of the base year have to be reduced by 10 per cent in that year. Thus there will be a demand for permits with a positive price for them.

Depending on the cost of substitution and avoidance, and on the level and differences in growth rates, some branches (countries) will purchase permits and some will offer them for sale. Since no retention technologies are available for CO_2 at reasonable costs, the cost of disposal corresponds to that of substitution in changing from the old least-cost solution to a new solution involving higher costs of production. The advantage of a system of tradable permits is that cost-effectiveness is achieved, that is, the marginal cost of substitution and avoidance incurred by the polluters is harmonized within firms, branches of industry and regions. The optimum procedure is to avoid emissions as long as the marginal cost of reduction is lower than the price of a permit. The amount of CO_2 produced by a firm or country can be relatively easily determined in view of the constant ratio between the carbon content of fossil fuels and the CO_2 emissions produced during their combustion. A basis for assessment is obtained by multiplying the amounts of coal, oil and natural gas by their respective emission coefficients (converted into tons of CO_2 per real fuel input in million DM). The fuel input prices will then increase by $p \cdot e_i$, with p being the permit price and e_i the emission coefficients for coal $(i = 1)$, oil $(i = 2)$, and gas $(i = 3)$.

In the simulations presented below, two types of institutional settings of the permit market are employed: a national market, where permits are traded between national agents only and an international market with EU-wide permits traded. In both cases all eleven sectors plus a representative consumer are trading partners. All market participants receive an initial allocation of permits according to their base-year emission levels. This allocation is then devaluated due to the environmental goal to be achieved.

Permits can be bought or sold according to the needs of polluters. Holding permits increases the purchaser price of an emission causing input and accordingly the costs of production. Hence, the level of the permit price affects the decision on input demand. As it is assumed that holding permits causes opportunity costs, the whole stock of permits and not only the change in the stocks (kept in the previous period) affects the cost situation of the polluter.

The receipts from the sale of these permits are treated like a rent which is – under the assumption of zero-profits – passed on to the purchasers of the good concerned by reducing the output price according to the appropriate rate, that is,

$$\tilde{PX} = PX \frac{p_{CO} \cdot \sum_{i=1}^{n} e_i^{CO} \cdot a_{i,-1} \cdot X_{-1}}{X} \tag{3.34}$$

where P_{CO} is the price of a permit.

With respect to the opportunity cost argumentation, the price PX is used to derive the intermediate demands in equations (3.2) and (3.3). That is, holding permits already bought in previous periods is costly since one could abate more CO_2 and sell these permits.

On the contrary, the reduced price $P\tilde{X}$ is used in all other formulations of the model. Hence, the receipts from permit sale do not affect decisions on the optimal structure of demand for intermediates but affect decisions on the levels of production and consumption.

The permit transactions of households are introduced in a way similar to that of a tax system, that is in each period they purchase the total amount of permits that they need and sell all that they have from the previous period. The permit price is added to the price of goods, similar to a value-added tax. Firms pass on these receipts to the bank (the government) which reimburses the cost for those permits which were already held by the households. The bank is an (temporary) 'auxiliary' account which holds the net sale or purchase of firms as well.

For a national permit system, the sum of all net transactions (sale and purchase) deposited at the bank is equal to zero if the (endogenous) permit price holds the equilibrium condition stated below.

$$Supply\ of\ Permits \equiv \sum_{j=1}^{n} \left[\sum_{i=1}^{n} (e_{i,j}^{CO} \cdot a_{ij}) \cdot X_j \right] + \sum_{i=1}^{n} e_{i,h}^{CO} \cdot C_i$$

In a permit system with multicountry trade (K countries), the constraint lies on the multicountry level, that is:

$$Supply\ of\ Permits \equiv \sum_{c=1}^{K} \left\{ \sum_{j=1}^{n} \left[\sum_{i=1}^{n} (e_{i,j}^{CO,c} \cdot a_{ij}^{c}) \cdot X_j^c \right] + \sum_{i=1}^{n} e_{i,h}^{CO,c} \cdot C_i^c \right\}$$

Again, the sum over all net transactions (sectors and countries) equals zero. To keep the consistency with the social accounts, the transactions between countries are treated as transfers from or to foreign countries.

When introducing permits free of charge, and then choosing a desired level of CO_2 which is 10 per cent below the base-year case, two offsetting sales and purchase effects occur. Figure 3.3 is based on a 20 per cent reduction of CO_2 and shows the net result of a trade in permits. MAC_i (E_i) are the marginal abatement costs (or cost of substitution and avoidance in case of CO_2) for an industry i or a country i, $i = 1, 2$. MAC has nothing to do with the abatement cost function $c(a) \cdot a$, given in the last section. MAC reflects the allocative losses in terms of substitution away from the former minimal cost combination. $MAC(E)$ is the aggregate marginal abatement cost function with $E = E_1 + E_2$.

It is assumed that the firms have emitted E_1^P and E_2^P, respectively; that is, they have been confronted with different standards. Each firm then holds tradable permits equivalent to E_i^p. Adding $E_1^P + E_2^P$ gives $\overline{E}^p$.

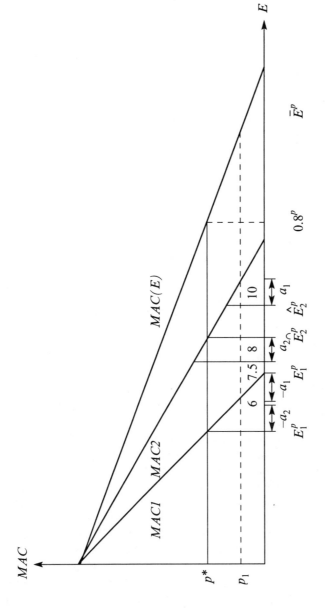

Figure 3.3 Distribution of tradable permits free of charge to firm 1 ($E_1{}^p$) and firm 2 ($E_2{}^p$) with a depreciation by 20 per cent thereafter

Immediately after the issue of permits, they are depreciated by 20 per cent. In Figure 3.3 the dotted lines refer to the costless issue of permits. Without a restrictive carbon policy, firm 2 would reduce its effort to avoid CO_2 emissions whereas firm 1 would have an incentive to avoid CO_2 emissions. It could sell these permits ($- a_1$) to firm 2 ($+ a_1$). However, given the more restrictive CO_2 policy in terms of $0.8\ \bar{E}^p$ permits, the permit price will rise to p^*. Because of the devaluation, firm 2 holds eight instead of the required ten units of permits. It avoids some CO_2 and buys the additionally needed permits ($+ a_2$) from firm 1. Firm 1 in turn holds six units instead of 7.5 units of permits after depreciation. But for firm 1 it is profitable to avoid a_2 units and to sell them to firm 2 ($+ a_2$). The optimal allocation of CO_2 avoidance requires that marginal cost of avoidance corresponds to the permit price, that is:

$$MAC_i(\hat{E}_i) = p^* \quad \text{for } i = 1, 2$$

where $\hat{E}_i$ denotes the corresponding emission. At the permit price p^* the market is cleared:

$$\hat{E}_1 + \tilde{E}_2 = \bar{E}^p \cdot 0.8$$

The net benefit of a cost–benefit calculation for industry i consists of the cost of avoidance AC_i and the cost (+) or revenue (–) resulting from the purchase or sale of permits. This yields:

$$AC_i(\hat{E}_i) + p^* (\hat{E}_i - 0.8 \cdot E_i^p)$$

If the introduction of a tradable permit system for SO_2 emissions had been considered, it also would have been possible to calculate the welfare gain from the transition to a permit system issued free of charge. This is because abatement costs per industry, consisting of expenditure for abatement activities and of investment in abatement measures were calculated. Hence, there are marginal abatement costs which differ across industries. A tradable permit system which guarantees the present air quality of SO_2 would result in a welfare gain and in a trade in permits.

The next step then could be one towards a stricter enforcement in SO_2 emissions with the effects illustrated by Figure 3.3. For CO_2, however, costs of avoiding carbon dioxide are not available. They might be zero for households and other nonregulated industries and positive for the electricity producers. Therefore, zero marginal cost of avoiding CO_2 for all industries had to be assumed, that is, a situation illustrated by points on the E-axis is the starting point. For the empirical results the assumption implies that welfare gains are underestimated and welfare losses overestimated.

The 10 per cent carbon reduction policy was first simulated country by country, that is, each country reduces its CO_2 levels by 10 per cent. The model covers:

- eleven countries: BE – Belgium, DE – Germany, DK – Denmark, FR – France, GR – Greece, IR – Ireland, IT – Italy, N – Netherlands, PO – Portugal, SP – Spain and UK – United Kingdom;
- eleven products and sectors: 1 – agriculture, 2 – coal, 3 – crude oil and refined oil products, 4 – gas, 5 – electric power, 6 – energy intensive industries, 7 – equipment goods industries, 8 – consumer goods industries, 9 – transport, 10 – services and 11 – nonmarket services.

The model considers full competitive equilibrium in all markets, excluding the labour market which is restricted by fixed labour supply and a periodically fixed wage rate. Unemployment is computed as residual. The exchange rate is kept fixed and the model allows for a free variation of the balance of payments. Concerning the CO_2-permits, the number of permits required for fossil fuel differs by the type of fuel according to different emission coefficients. Hydro and nuclear power plants therefore do not need permits.

The measure of welfare change used here is based on the Hicks measure of equivalent income variation (EV). As the economic effects of introducing CO2-permits are calculated for one single period, an intertemporal EV has not been employed. Assuming a fixed wage rate in the short term, the labour market adjusts by unemployment. In the welfare computation two types of leisure are distinguished: voluntary leisure which is fixed to the base-year value and involuntary leisure caused by unemployment. The latter is endogenous for the model and takes all changes in the labour market as residual. As it was decided not to evaluate higher unemployment as leisure, the EV is based on consumption only, that is, it follows from the expenditure function in (3.24):

$$EV = e(p^0, u^1, Z^0) - e(p^0, u^0, Z^0) \tag{3.35}$$

It gives the change in expenditure at the base-case price vector p^0 and durables Z^0, that would be equivalent to the policy-implied change in utility. The utility function which corresponds to this expenditure function is:

$$u = \prod_{i=1}^{n} (C_i - C_{0,i})^{\beta_i} \prod_{i=1}^{3} (Z_j - Z_{0,j})^{\gamma_j} \tag{3.36}$$

If EV < 0, then welfare after the policy measure is lower than in the base case. The consumer would be willing to pay the maximum amount EV at the fixed budget level $e^0 = e(p^0, u^0, Z^0)$, to avoid the decline of utility from u^0 to u^1. Similarly, if EV > 0, then the consumer would be willing to pay the maximum amount EV to see the change in environmental policy implemented.

Empirical results

The non-coordinated CO_2 reduction

Table 3.1 presents the economic impact from a 10 per cent CO_2 reduction under a noncoordinated environmental policy. The national models are linked by trade flow matrices, and a non-coordinated CO_2 policy means that each of the eleven countries reduces carbon dioxide by exactly 10 per cent.

The first column of Table 3.1 shows the equivalent variation in million ECU. Of particular interest are the signs which turn out to be negative for all countries except Portugal. Germany, for example, is willing to pay at most about 1.5 billion ECU to see that such a policy not be implemented. This is about 0.2 per cent of nominal GDP, as presented in column 3. There is, however, one country, Portugal, which has a positive EV. A Portuguese citizen is willing to pay up to 1.5 ECU for the higher standard of living under a CO_2 reduction policy. Such a result indicates that the marginal costs of avoiding CO_2 are rather low, the energy intensity in some branches is high, and the substitution of labour for energy is a significant source of higher income (see the one per cent increase in employment for Portugal).

Next, the proportionality between EV and GDP is compared to obtain a crude measure for the distributional impact of a CO_2 reduction policy. The national sacrifices can be seen by comparing the EV on a per capita basis. The cost per capita of a CO_2 reduction policy is highest in Denmark and lowest in Spain. Column 3 shows the percentage of EV in GDP as a measure of welfare gain or loss in relation to the income situation. Although EV per capita is the same for Italy and the Netherlands, the EV per GDP in column 3 expresses the real sacrifice compared to the money measures in column 2.

The figures in column 4 are the net result of changes in the components of the GDP calculation. For all countries, except Germany, Greece and the UK, a growth in real GDP can be observed. This outcome is explained by the fact that in losing countries' private consumption is lower under a CO_2 policy, as is evidenced in column 7. This is obvious, of course, because an extra constraint has been imposed on production. For the same reason, private consumption is higher for a winning country. Furthermore, gross domestic production is lower for all countries (column 6).

Table 3.1 The impact of tradable permits under a non-coordinated environmental policy (scenario: 10 per cent reduction of carbon dioxide in each country)

	EV (ECU M)	EV (ECU per capita)	EV per GDP(%)	GDP (%)	GDP deflation (%)	Production (%)	Private consumption (%)
Belgium	-60	-6.05	-0.06	0.09	0.33	-0.09	-0.09
Germany	-1449	-23.75	-0.20	-0.09	0.12	-0.24	-0.28
Denmark	-359	-70.23	-0.55	0.06	0.20	-0.17	-0.85
France	-1360	-24.72	-0.23	0.00	0.13	-0.15	-0.32
Greece	-63	-6.39	-0.08	-0.22	-0.23	-0.33	-0.10
Ireland	-62	-17.47	-0.31	0.01	0.45	-0.06	-0.42
Italy	-1424	-24.92	-0.27	0.08	0.25	-0.14	-0.41
Netherlands	-362	-24.97	-0.24	0.01	-0.13	-0.13	-0.37
Portugal	16	1.56	0.06	0.44	1.49	-0.16	0.09
Spain	-182	-4.71	-0.09	0.06	0.63	-0.22	-0.13
Great Britain	-1963	-34.66	-0.38	-0.10	-1.20	-0.54	-0.53
EU	-7268	-22.61	-0.24	-0.02	-0.05	-0.25	-0.34
Rest of world	—	—	—	—	—	—	—

	Exports (%) firms (%)	Investing (%)	Imports (%)	Employment (%)	Wage rate (%)	Permit-price ECU/ton CO_2	CO_2-reduction (%)
Belgium	-0.16	0.35	-0.26	0.15	0.00	10.64	-10.00
Germany	-0.07	-0.03	-0.35	0.05	0.00	19.97	-10.00
Denmark	-0.12	0.05	-1.27	0.31	0.00	47.28	-10.10
France	-0.09	0.05	-0.72	0.12	0.00	24.83	-10.00
Greece	-0.34	-0.18	-0.69	-0.21	0.00	10.22	-10.00
Ireland	-0.10	0.05	-0.44	0.22	0.00	19.19	-10.00
Italy	-0.13	0.10	-1.37	0.32	0.00	35.99	-10.00
Netherlands	-0.06	-0.27	-0.46	0.21	0.00	22.18	-10.00
Portugal	-0.41	1.05	-0.88	1.09	0.00	23.65	-10.00
Spain	-0.42	0.27	-1.01	0.43	0.00	20.56	-10.00
Great Britain	0.11	-1.37	-0.96	-0.29	0.00	31.12	-10.00
EU	0.01	-0.22	-1.01	0.12	—	25.10	-10.00
Rest of world	-1.01	—	0.01	—	—	—	-10.00

The variation in the rate of inflation (column 5) reflects the impact from higher energy prices, from a change in the user cost of capital, and from imported inflation. If relative prices and national GDP growth rates change, then the trade flow matrices for each of the products transmit this effect. Columns 8 and 10 show the change in national exports and imports. Imports decline in all countries. One reason is the reduction in fossil fuel imports because of higher energy prices. A second reason is the decline in private consumption. For all countries imports decline by a higher percentage than exports (for example, in Belgium, Ireland, Italy and Spain). This will have a positive net effect on the balance of trade which partly explains the measured growth in real GDP. A lower import volume for the EU implies a lower export volume for the rest of the world.

The effect of the CO_2 policy on employment is positive except for Greece and the UK. There is a substitution effect away from energy to labour which is partly offset by a negative output effect if production declines. The latter effect is highest for Greece and the UK and dominates the positive substitution effect.

Finally, column 13 shows an average permit price of 24 ECU per ton of CO_2 and a group of countries with a lower price (for example, Greece and Belgium) and a group with a higher price (for example, Denmark and Italy). The level of the permit price depends on country-specific emission coefficients, on the energy intensity, on the energy mix and on the cost of avoiding CO_2, that is, the elasticities of substitution.

To summarize, the reason for the national differences in the impacts of a CO_2 policy is the different structure of the economies in terms of different weights of the energy-intensive industries, of the service sector, of the composition of exports and imports or the difference in equipment with consumer durables. All these factors imply a different slope of the marginal cost curve of avoiding CO_2. Under the non-coordinated policy simulation the price of a permit differs considerably across countries. Since CO_2 is a global pollutant, a cost-efficient carbon reduction policy calls for a uniform CO_2 permit price for all EU countries. This policy will be introduced in the next section.

First, however, Table 3.2 indicates which sectors will buy permits and which will sell them. Sectors with a negative value offer permits because energy substitution is easier for them compared to those which demand permits. In all countries, electricity and the energy-intensive industries sell permits. Less emission-intensive industries, for instance services or industries not regulated in the past such as transport or households, are usually better off if they decide to buy permits instead of practising substitution. Since the relative price of energy increases, demand will be restructured

Table 3.2 Purchase (+) and sales of permit (−) under a non-coordinated environmental policy (in ECU m.)

	Belgium	Germany	Denmark	France	Greece	Ireland
Agriculture	1.06	13.17	-2.89	9.63	2.09	1.17
Coal	-1.22	-8.01	0.00	-10.82	-0.11	-0.01
Oil	3.39	20.36	1.36	17.61	0.48	0.06
Gas	0.01	4.43	0.94	0.57	3.04	1.29
Electricity	-4.64	-178.45	-44.87	-120.76	-12.76	-2.49
Energy-intensive industries	44.10	-286.61	-10.91	-254.54	-9.26	-15.66
Equipment goods industries	0.48	0.79	-0.73	-8.74	-0.06	-0.38
Consumer goods industries	2.93	20.50	-5.62	9.13	1.71	-0.02
Transport	3.33	29.82	5.75	34.54	2.95	0.90
Services	8.01	30.55	0.10	19.00	1.82	0.33
Non-market services	0.86	12.73	-1.01	3.51	0.93	-0.47
Households	29.88	340.71	57.88	300.85	9.18	15.26
Net EU trade volume	0.00	-0.01	0.00	0.00	-0.01	0.00

	Italy	Netherlands	Portugal	Spain	Great Britian	EU
Agriculture	1.10	-0.83	-0.13	4.17	7.42	35.94
Coal	-14.19	0.00	-0.42	-1.67	-5.68	-42.12
Oil	16.17	20.57	0.98	8.89	28.51	118.40
Gas	0.07	0.76	0.00	0.12	19.95	31.17
Electricity	-73.64	-60.22	1.02	-36.50	-216.27	-749.58
Energy-intensive industries	-305.71	-48.20	-10.20	-61.17	-147.66	-1194.02
Equipment goods industries	-5.30	-0.34	-0.15	-2.27	-22.66	-39.37
Consumer goods industries	13.62	2.11	-0.96	5.32	-30.38	18.35
Transport	45.39	9.40	2.27	23.03	51.56	208.96
Services	12.07	0.76	0.19	6.32	12.84	91.99
Non-market services	0.26	-2.05	-0.18	0.78	-1.34	14.01
Households	310.14	78.03	7.60	52.98	303.72	1506.22
Net EU trade volume	-0.01	-0.01	0.00	0.00	0.00	-0.03 *truncation error*

towards lower growth of energy-intensive products and higher growth of those industries producing less energy-intensive products. For the same reason, energy-intensive industries supply permits and growing industries, although less energy-intensive, demand permits. However, not all of the emission-intensive industries will sell permits. For example, the refineries (oil), agriculture and transport will purchase permits because this is less expensive than the substitution of labour and of non-energy for energy (see Conrad and Wang (1994) for similar results). For the other branches, purchases and sales differ country by country depending on the composition of industries making up the branch. Households buy permits but in ECU per capita their expenses are very low. A family of four persons spends 22 ECU in France and 6 ECU in Spain.

The coordinated CO_2 reduction

Finally, Table 3.3 presents the economic impact of a tradable permit system under a coordinated policy of reducing CO_2 by 10 per cent for the EU as a whole. The uniform permit price is 23 ECU, which is approximately the average of the different permit prices obtained under a non-coordinated policy. The fact that it is lower by 1 ECU (23 instead of 24.10) already reflects the welfare gain from a coordinated policy. A lower welfare cost for the EU in total is expected (–6491 ECU versus –7268 ECU for the non-coordinated case). EV in ECU per capita drops from –22.6 to –20.2. The sacrifice in the standard of living is lower if the actions are coordinated. From the perspective of a single country, not all benefit from the coordination. The EVs in Table 3.3 are more negative for Belgium, Germany, and the Netherlands. The countries which benefit are Denmark, France and Great Britain. For Italy, for example, the EV in ECU per capita is 33 per cent lower (–16.5 instead of –24.9). In principle, countries with a steeper marginal cost of avoidance curve should be better off under a coordinated CO_2 policy whereas countries with a flatter marginal cost curve should be worse off. These are the countries which had a permit price of less than 24.10 ECU in Table 3.1.

The economic variables reflect this result because the decline in production is now higher for those countries which are worse off under a coordinated policy. Although private consumption is now lower, 0.31 per cent on average compared to 0.34 in Table 3.1, only the consumers of countries with a former higher permit price benefit. Those countries now avoid less than 10 per cent of CO_2 whereas the other countries now avoid more than 10 per cent of CO_2. The revenues from selling permits to the former high-permit price countries do not compensate the consumers of the former low-permit price countries for their higher effort in avoiding CO_2 for the EU member states. When comparing the EVs of the two

Table 3.3 The impact of tradable permits under a coordinated environmental policy (scenario: 10 per cent EU-wide reduction of carbon dioxide)

	EV (ECU m.)	EV (ECU per capita)	EV per GDP(%)	GDP (%)	GDP deflation (%)	Production (%)	Private consumption (%)
Belgium	-180	-18.29	-0.18	0.13	0.76	-0.14	-0.26
Germany	-1735	-28.43	-0.24	-0.11	0.17	-0.27	-0.33
Denmark	-174	-34.07	-0.27	0.06	0.06	-0.08	-0.41
France	-1303	-23.68	-0.22	0.00	0.12	-0.15	-0.31
Greece	-50	-5.04	-0.06	-0.03	0.49	-0.17	-0.08
Ireland	-85	-24.09	-0.43	-0.01	0.54	-0.10	-0.57
Italy	-946	-16.56	-0.18	0.06	0.13	-0.11	-0.27
Netherlands	-374	-25.81	-0.25	0.01	-0.12	-0.13	-0.38
Portugal	14	1.42	0.06	0.43	1.45	-0.16	0.08
Spain	-196	-5.07	-0.10	0.08	0.75	-0.23	-0.14
Great Britain	-1461	-25.81	-0.28	-0.08	-1.05	-0.43	-0.39
EU	-6491	-20.19	-0.21	-0.02	0.00	-0.23	-0.31
Rest of world	—	—	—	—	—	—	—

	Exports (%)	Investing firms (%)	Imports (%)	Employment (%)	Wage rate (%)	Permit-price ECU/ton CO_2	CO_2-reduction (%)
Belgium	-0.18	0.66	-0.41	0.39	0.00	23.06	-17.04
Germany	-0.07	-0.03	-0.41	0.07	0.00	23.06	-11.20
Denmark	-0.08	0.02	-0.71	0.16	0.00	23.06	-5.69
France	-0.08	0.04	-0.69	0.11	0.00	23.06	-9.51
Greece	-0.35	0.57	-0.37	0.31	0.00	23.06	-17.15
Ireland	-0.11	0.05	-0.55	0.27	0.00	23.06	-11.55
Italy	-0.11	0.06	-1.00	0.20	0.00	23.06	-7.32
Netherlands	-0.06	-0.28	-0.48	0.23	0.00	23.06	-10.27
Portugal	-0.40	1.02	-0.87	1.07	0.00	23.06	-9.83
Spain	-0.43	0.32	-1.07	0.51	0.00	23.06	-10.95
Great Britain	0.04	-1.14	-0.80	-0.26	0.00	23.06	-7.89
EU	0.00	-0.16	-0.90	0.13	—	23.06	-10.00
Rest of world	-0.90	—	0.00	—	—	—	—

73

policies one expects that the absolute values of the EV in the coordinated policy are lower because every country should gain when multiregional tradable permits are introduced. Our measure of utility is, however, based on consumption of goods only. It is easy to check that all countries with a higher absolute value of the EV under the coordinated policy (Belgium, Germany, Ireland, the Netherlands and Spain) are compensated instead by a higher growth rate of employment. If one would include the reduction in involuntary leisure (unemployment) in the welfare measure, then those countries would gain. On the other side, welfare of those countries which gain according to the consumption-based EV (Denmark, France and Italy) will gain less if their lower growth rate of employment would have been taken into account in the welfare measure. Great Britain is the only country which shows a win–win effect for consumption as well as for the labour market in terms of a lower decline in unemployment under the coordinated policy. An exception is Greece, which benefits from the sale of higher-priced permits to permit demanders. The rest of the world also benefits from the economic impact of a coordinated CO_2 policy because total EU import demand declines less under such a policy (–0.9 compared to –1.01).

Table 3.4 indicates who will be an exporter or importer of permits. Countries with a permit price from the non-coordinated policy below the uniform price of 23 ECU are exporters of permits. On the permit market, electric utilities and the energy-intensive industries are the main suppliers of permits, and households and transportation the main demanders.

Conclusion
Any attempt to solve global pollution makes the linkage between energy and the environment evident. National differences in environmental concern, affectedness, per capita income and the free-rider situation delay a coordinated action. Cooperation is much easier if a good substitute for a pollutant exists as in the case of CFCs. But for fossil fuel no substitute is in sight in the near future. The simulations have shown that there is no free lunch in reaching lower CO_2 emission levels. A unilateral policy by a single country is, in economic terms, less attractive than an action by all EU member states. But the difference in costs seems to be rather low. A common EU permit market could reduce the loss in welfare, measured in terms of equivalent variation, by 10.7 per cent. If the difference in the equivalent variation under a non-coordinated policy and under a cooperative policy could be used as side-payments to agree to a cooperative CO_2 policy, then countries which should obtain side-payments as compensation for the reduction in welfare are (in million ECU): Belgium (120), Germany (286), Ireland (23), the Netherlands (12)

Table 3.4 Purchase (+) and sales of permit (−) under a coordinated environmental policy (in ECU m.)

	Belgium	Germany	Denmark	France	Greece	Ireland
Agriculture	0.11	11.25	1.06	9.90	1.44	1.05
Coal	-5.90	-11.48	0.00	-9.28	-0.49	-0.01
Oil	6.72	22.35	1.06	16.61	0.93	0.07
Gas	0.02	3.30	1.06	0.57	7.14	1.26
Electricity	-45.59	-278.44	-0.22	-102.92	-83.27	-4.46
Energy-intensive industries	-222.27	-405.19	-0.68	-217.32	-47.41	-21.89
Equipment goods industries	-1.44	-5.58	0.40	-6.53	-0.52	-0.66
Consumer goods industries	2.26	16.89	1.17	10.50	1.51	-1.89
Transport	5.62	29.93	8.25	33.46	4.69	0.85
Services	3.23	26.89	2.49	20.59	1.60	-0.04
Non-market services	-1.92	8.27	1.38	5.24	0.54	-0.93
Households	61.58	388.53	30.19	280.39	20.19	17.65
Net EU trade volume	-197.59	-193.27	46.16	41.21	-93.64	-8.99

	Italy	Netherlands	Portugal	Spain	Great Britian	EU
Agriculture	5.25	-1.52	-0.03	2.95	9.47	40.94
Coal	-6.34	0.00	-0.40	-2.17	-2.73	-38.82
Oil	13.33	20.06	0.98	9.66	22.20	113.96
Gas	0.10	0.77	0.00	0.13	36.66	51.02
Electricity	-0.47	-65.16	1.13	-54.90	-50.77	-685.08
Energy-intensive industries	-114.93	-52.12	-9.58	-82.06	-69.03	-1242.48
Equipment goods industries	2.47	-0.53	-0.13	-3.35	-8.17	-24.03
Consumer goods industries	15.85	1.75	-0.80	3.60	-7.78	43.05
Transport	42.17	9.51	2.28	23.37	46.30	206.44
Services	32.45	0.28	0.30	4.12	25.69	117.60
Non-market services	8.56	-2.64	-0.15	0.04	13.41	31.79
Households	206.44	80.81	7.42	59.14	233.66	1386.01
Net EU trade volume	204.88	-8.80	1.00	-39.48	248.92	0.40 *truncation error*

and Spain (14). Countries which gain from a cooperative policy and therefore have to pay are: Denmark (–185), France (–57), Greece (–13), Italy (–478), Portugal (–2) and Great Britain (–502). The winning countries (their total gain is 1,237) have to pay the amount of 455 million ECU to the losing countries and the amount left is the difference in the equivalent variations for the two simulations.

The objective in this chapter has been to show that the cost of a CO_2 policy can be expressed in economic magnitudes. The benefits of such a policy with respect to the greenhouse gas problem are more difficult to estimate and should be higher than the costs obtained here in order to justify a CO_2 reduction policy. Our future work will focus on this aspect using an integrated assessment framework.

Notes

1. Insert into the zero-profit condition (with K_{-1} for K) the inputs E, and LMF from (3.3) and (3.6) and solve for PK by using (3.1).
2. For more detail, see Conrad and Schröder (1991b).
3. The closure rule presented below differs from the one specified by Capros et al. (see Chapter 5). The latter approach solves the zero-profit condition explicitly, for the (short-term) price of capital services. With a fixed (long-term) interest rate, Walras's Law then holds the national accounting identity (that is, sum over all surpluses of the agents is zero).

References

Bergman, L. (1990), 'Energy and environmental constraints on growth: a CGE modeling approach', *Journal of Policy Modeling*, **12**, 671–91.

Bergman, L. (1991), 'General equilibrium effects of environmental policy: a CGE modeling approach', *Environmental and Resource Economics*, **1**, 67–85.

Capros, P., P. Karadeloglou and G. Mentzas (1990), 'An empirical assessment of macroeconometrics and CGE approaches in policy modelling', *Journal of Policy Modeling*, **12** (3), 557–85.

Conrad, K. (1983), 'Cost prices and partially fixed factor proportions in energy substitution', *European Economic Review*, **21**, 299–312.

Conrad, K. (1993), 'Applied general equilibrium modeling for environmental policy analysis', in W. Kuckshinrichs, W. Pfaffenberger and W. Ströbele (eds), *Economics of the Greenhouse Effect*, Jülich, Bd. 13, pp. 33–88.

Conrad, K., and I. Henseler-Unger (1986), 'Applied general equilibrium modelling for longterm energy policy in the Federal Republic of Germany', *Journal of Policy Modeling*, **8**, 531–49.

Conrad, K. and M. Schröder (1991a), 'The control of CO_2-emissions and its economic impact', *Environmental and Resource Economics*, **1**, 289–312.

Conrad, K., and M. Schröder (1991b), 'Demand for durable and non-durable goods, environmental policy and consumer welfare', *Journal of Applied Econometrics*, **6**, 271–86.

Conrad, K. and M. Schröder (1993), 'Choosing environmental policy instruments using general equilibrium models', *Journal of Policy Modeling*, **15** (5 and 6), 521–43.

Conrad, K. and J. Wang (1994), 'Tradable CO_2 emission permits versus CO_2 taxes: economic impacts and costs by industry – an applied general equilibrium analysis for West-Germany', in J-Fr. Hake, M. Kleeman, W. Kuckshinrics, D. Martinsen, M. Walbeck (eds), *Advances in Systems Analysis: Modelling Energy-Related Emissions on a National and Global Level*, Forschungszentrum Jülich, Bd 15, pp. 241–61.

Friedrich, R. (1990), 'Umweltpolitische Instrumente zur Luftreinhaltung – Analyse und Bewertung', unpublished PhD thesis, Stuttgart.

Jorgenson, D.W. and P.J. Wilcoxen (1990a), 'Environmental regulation and U.S. economic growth', *Rand Journal of Economics*, **21**, 314–40.

Jorgenson, D.W. and P.J. Wilcoxen (1990b), 'Intertemporal general equilibrium modeling of U.S. environmental regulation', *Journal of Policy Modeling*, **12**, 1–30.

Jorgenson, D.W. and P.J. Wilcoxen (1992), 'Reducing U.S. carbon dioxide emissions: the cost of different goals', in J. R. Moroney (ed.), *Energy, Growth and Environment: Advances in the Economics of Energy and Resources*, **7**, Greenwich, CT: JAI Press, pp. 125–58.

Jorgenson, D.W. and P.J. Wilcoxen (1993), 'Energy, the environment and economic growth', in A.V. Kneese and J.L. Sweeney (eds), *Handbook of Natural Resources and Energy Economics*, Vol. 3, Amsterdam: Elsevier, pp. 1267–349.

Manne, A.S. and R.G. Richels (1991), 'Global CO_2 emission reductions – the impact of rising energy costs', *Energy Journal*, **12**, 87–108.

Oates, W.E., P.R. Portney and A.M. McGartland (1989), 'The net benefits of incentive-based regulation: a case study of environmental standard setting', *American Economic Review*, **79** (3), 1233–42.

Welsch, H. (1995a), 'Joint vs. unilateral carbon/energy taxation in a two-region general equilibrium model for the European Community', Discussion Paper, Institute of Energy Economics, Cologne.

Welsch, H. (1995b), 'The carbon tax game: differential tax recycling in a two-region general equilibrium model of the European Community', Discussion Paper, Institute of Energy Economics, Cologne.

Whalley, J. and R. Wigle (1991), 'Cutting CO_2 emissions: the effects of alternative policy approaches', *Energy Journal*, **12**, 109–24.

4. Environmental fiscal reforms in a federal Europe

Carlo Carraro and Marzio Galeotti

Introduction

The recent debate on environmental policy in Europe has followed three main steps.

At the beginning the debate focused on which policy instrument should be implemented to protect the environment (chiefly, to reduce CO_2 emissions). In this debate the (carbon) tax was singled out as the optimal (cost-effective) economic instrument. As a consequence, research was devoted to assessing the costs of the tax, that is, the trade-off between environmental protection and economic growth (see Carraro and Siniscalco (1993a) for results concerning Europe).

Then, when it became clear that the cost of the tax was likely to be high (as well as the uncertainty on the impact of the greenhouse effect), attention of economists and policy-makers moved towards the so-called 'no regret' environmental strategies, that is, policy and economic decisions that would reduce pollution without slowing down economic growth. There is now a large consensus that these types of strategies may exist, even if they have to be carefully designed (Bovenberg 1997). The reason behind such a consensus is that the environmental tax provides two benefits: on the one hand, it helps control the exploitation of natural resources by raising their price; on the other hand, it provides the government with additional funds that can be spent either to foster economic growth (through appropriate expenditure policies), or to reduce existing distortions in the tax systems.

Finally, the above debate joined the increased preoccupation with the high rates of unemployment in Europe. As a consequence, among the possible uses of the environmental tax revenue, the one in which the revenue is redistributed in the form of a general reduction in social security payments by employers received the greatest attention (Drèze and Malinvaud 1993). Therefore, an environmental fiscal reform was strongly advocated whose main feature would be a shift of the tax burden from labour to environmental and natural resource inputs (chiefly, energy). The main objective of this reform is to achieve the so-called 'employment double dividend' (Carraro et al. 1996), that is, a decrease in both emissions and unemployment.

What are the latest achievements of economic research on the effects of an environmental fiscal reform on growth and employment? Four points seem to emerge clearly.

First, the theoretical literature on the 'employment double dividend' hypothesis has been unable to reach clearcut conclusions.[1] Noneth less, it seems to indicate that very restrictive conditions must be met for the recycling of environmental taxation to produce an increase in aggregate employment (Bovenberg 1997). Moreover, even when these conditions are met, the effects on employment of a fiscal reform which reduces distortionary taxation on the labour market and increases environmental taxation are likely to be small (Bovenberg and Goulder 1993).

Second, the above theoretical results are sometimes in contrast with the existing econometric evidence on the 'employment double dividend' issue. As discussed in Grubb *et al.* (1993), Repetto *et al.* (1992), and Denis and Koopman (1994), simulation of large econometric models, in which environment–economy interactions are accounted for, seems to suggest that higher emission taxes associated with a reduction of the tax burden on labour demand would raise employment and lower pollution (see, for example, Barker 1996 and Capros 1996 for results concerning European countries).

Third, the existing CGE or econometric models used for environmental policy analysis do not appear to address satisfactorily some fundamental aspects of environment–economy linkages (Grubb et al. 1993; Hourcade 1993). In particular, available empirical evidence increasingly appears to show that a reduction or stabilization of emissions at desired levels can hardly be attained through price-induced substitution effects (that is, along a given isoquant) (for example, carbon taxes), but rather via technological substitution and innovation (that is, through shifts of isoquants).[2] Despite this evidence, however, most empirical models assume technical progress to be exogenous, thus omitting some crucial feedbacks between environmental policy, economic growth and employment. More importantly, in order to assess the validity of the 'employment double dividend' hypothesis, it is necessary to capture the crucial features of the European labour market, which is highly centralized and in which wages are usually the outcome of a bargaining process between unions and firms (Layard et al. 1991; Holmlund and Zetterberg 1991). However, most empirical models, being designed to represent the energy sector above all, do not possess a satisfactory description of the labour market, which is often assumed to be perfectly competitive.

Finally, the political debate on a European policy towards more employment and a better environment is moving faster than the theoretical and applied economics literature. In the political agenda a new issue has recently emerged as the most controversial: which kind of institutional framework is the most appropriate to introduce an emissions tax and the revenue recycling to boost employment? More clearly, should the environmental fiscal reform be designed at the central level by the European Commission, or should such a reform be decentralized according to the subsidiarity principle?

The latter option appears to have received a large consensus among policy-makers. The difficulty in moving towards a European carbon tax is probably the explanation of this change of direction which allows each country to set its own policy mix. However, is subsidiarity really the best institutional framework through which an environmental fiscal reform can be implemented?

This chapter is a first attempt to tackle these issues. Starting from the recognition that existing empirical models are not satisfactory, a new model of the European Union (EU) is developed here which is designed to assess the impact of environmental policy on innovation, growth and employment. This model, being more general and disaggregated than theoretical models, and more accurately designed than previous European econometric models, should provide a more reliable empirical assessment of the 'employment double dividend' and related issues. In particular, the 'World Assessment of Resource Management' (WARM) model accomplishes two main goals: (i) it captures the relevant features of the European labour market by explicitly modelling the bargaining process between unions and firms, and it provides an endogenous representation of technical progress; and (ii) it describes the behaviour of European economies in an integrated framework in which each EU member country is viewed as a region belonging to the EU economic system. These features of the WARM model are described in the next section.

Given the model, this chapter proposes an empirical analysis of the effects of a European fiscal reform designed to achieve two goals: on the one hand, a better protection of the environment, for example, a stabilization of CO_2 emissions; and, on the other hand, a more efficient tax system, for example, a lower tax burden on labour to increase employment. The analysis is carried out under four alternative institutional frameworks.

First, the case of a harmonized fiscal reform is analysed in which a homogeneous emissions tax rate is imposed in all countries (thus equalizing marginal abatement costs) and in which all countries recycle the revenue by reducing the employer's payments for social security contributions. This harmonized policy reform may be the likely outcome of successful negotiations towards a cooperative environmental policy.

Second, in order to check the necessity and stability of such a cooperative agreement, the effects of unilateral policy decisions in some
European countries will be analysed.[3] In this way, it can be verified
whether countries unilaterally introducing the fiscal reform will suffer an
economic loss, that is, lower employment and economic growth, because
of the possible lower competitiveness in international markets. Here the
issue is controversial because on the one hand the tax penalizes domestic
firms, but on the other hand lower gross wages and higher net wages (as a
result of the bargaining process between unions and firms) increase both
competitiveness and domestic consumption. The net effect depends on
the functioning of the labour market and on the trade structure of each
country. It is obvious that if the net effect is positive, a country gains even
when the fiscal reform is introduced unilaterally (even if the gain may be
larger when all countries cooperate), thus providing an argument in
favour of the subsidiarity principle.

Third, the impact of the application of the subsidiarity principle is
explored, that is, it is assumed that each country sets its own tax rate
(equal to the domestic marginal damage) and uses the revenue to reduce
social security contributions paid by employers. In this case, the national
budget deficit (surplus) is assumed to remain unchanged.

Finally, the case in which Europe is a federation of countries is considered. This implies that a central authority sets the tax rates in
all countries (equal to those defined by the cooperative agreement), and
indicates the way in which the tax is recycled. The case in which
the European tax revenue is redistributed according to unemployment
levels in the different EU member states is considered. Tax revenues are
therefore centralized and then redistributed under the constraint that
the federal budget deficit (surplus), rather than each national one, must
remain unchanged.

When the decision on the design of the environmental fiscal reform is
taken at the federal level two gains should, at least in principle, be
achieved. First, free-riding behaviours in some countries may be avoided.
Second, an explicit system of transfers in favour of some member states
may take place, thus increasing the profitability of the fiscal reform at the
EU level. This chapter aims to provide some preliminary information on
the actual gains deriving from centralizing decisions concerning the environmental fiscal reform.

The structure of the chapter is the following: the first section presents
the main features of the WARM model. In particular, the endogenization
of technical progress dynamics and of the wage bargaining process are
carefully described. The reader who is interested in only the comparison
of the effects of the environmental fiscal reform may skip this section and

move to the next section, which presents the results of the simulation experiments, and compares the impacts of the environmental fiscal reform previously described under alternative institutional settings (from decentralized to federal policy schemes). Finally, the attempt to draw a few policy guidelines and to propose some directions for further research concludes the chapter.

The WARM model
The model used in this chapter, called WARM (World Assessment of Resource Management), represents the behaviour of production, household, government and foreign sectors. In this section the modelling of each sector is described. A more detailed description can be found in Carraro and Galeotti (1994a).[4]

The WARM model shares many features of top-down econometric general equilibrium models of which a prominent example is that of Jorgenson and Wilcoxen (1990). In particular, it describes the behaviour of economic agents by means of supply and demand relationships which clear the markets for goods and services. Moreover, it makes use of flexible functional forms to parametrize tastes and technologies. However, because of data availability, the model is limited to the description of real flows, and only contains a broad disaggregation of production activities.

The novel features of WARM are as follows:

1. The model describes the economic structure of twelve European countries as well as that of the (pre-1995) European Union (EU–12 hereafter) as a whole. Rather than adopting an interlinked methodology, it integrates the country-specific differences from a common European denominator within a unified and homogeneously designed framework.
2. The model devotes special attention to the issue of technical change. Its effects are incorporated in the firm's decision rules via an index of the quality of capital stock. This index is constructed using a latent variable approach where a Kalman filter technique permits the use of some relevant economic indicators (including R&D expenditure, patent imports, GDP growth) to decompose the time series of the capital stock into two components, the 'environment-friendly' and the 'polluting' one, which then yield an index of the quality of the capital stock.
3. Markets are not assumed to be perfectly competitive. In particular, the labour market is segmented. In the primary labour market, pertaining to the leading production sector, a trade union is active and plays a Nash bargaining game with the employer's representatives that yields

the equilibrium wage structure, which in turn affects the employment–wage relationships of the whole economic system. This feature is especially relevant for the European countries.

The main characteristics of each block of the model are briefly described below.

Production

Four types of production activities carried out by representative firms operating in each European country are distinguished. The manufacturing firm is involved in the production and distribution of non-agricultural non-energy outputs consisting of durables, nondurables and services.[5] The factors used are the services from labour, capital, energy and a non-energy intermediate input. The demand for this intermediate good results from the aggregation of agricultural products and imported (durable and nondurable) goods and services. The energy aggregate is made up of electricity and fossil fuels. These fuels in turn are composed of coal, gas and petroleum products (divided into products for industrial use and for transportation). Electricity is supplied by the electricity firm which uses capital, labour and energy sources as inputs. This firm also directly imports electricity from abroad to be distributed nationwide. The fossil fuel transformation firm (or energy firm for short) supplies and distributes non-electric energy sources to all other firms and to households combining primary factors along with imported fuels. Finally, the agricultural output is entirely supplied to the manufacturing sector by an agricultural firm which combines capital, labour, land and energy. The flow diagram of the manufacturing firm is shown in Figure 4.1.

Firms are run by managers who act in the best interest of their owners. Owners and managers are part of the household sector. The set of decisions made by firms is broken down into three different conceptual stages. First, given the amounts of outputs and capital stock, the cost-minimizing levels of variable inputs are determined. Through appropriately maintained assumptions about the technology, this problem is formulated as a multi-stage decision process and yields sets of interrelated input demands. Next, variable profits are maximized by selecting the optimal output levels: this process generates a set of inverse supply relationships or price functions. Finally, the optimal investment decisions are taken by the firm in such a way that total long-run profits are maximized.

The technological relationship which, at each point in time, constrains the producer's choices, is embodied in a variable cost function that allows for multi-output production. To achieve the highest level of

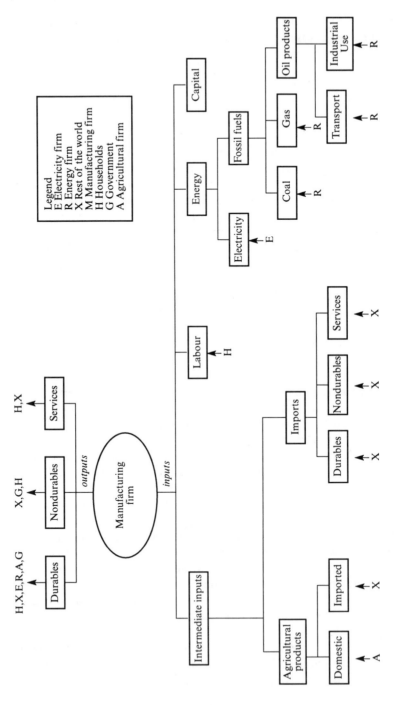

Figure 4.1 The multi-output manufacturing firm

84

disaggregation permitted by the data, the manufacturing firm is assumed to produce three distinct outputs (durables, nondurables and services), while the energy firm separately supplies outputs of coal, oil products and gas. The remaining firms of the model produce a single output. Besides variable input prices, output levels, and quasi-fixed input stocks, the variable cost function (see Lau 1976) depends upon an index of the state of the system: changes in this indicator represent technological improvements which induce outward shifts of the production isoquant over time. This is the vehicle through which technical change displays its effect on production activities.

The variable cost function is parametrized as a modified generalized Leontief flexible functional form (Morrison 1988). Application of Shephard's Lemma yields the system of demand functions for variable inputs. A maintained assumption regarding the firm's production structure is that of a homothetically separable technology, a feature shared by many econometric and applied general equilibrium models. With it, relevant simplifications in the design of the input decision process can be achieved: these choices proceed along several stages where the optimal mix within homogeneous groups of inputs is found and the aggregate input quantities, to be used in higher stages of the decision tree, are formed.

Turning now to the output supply side, on the basis of the assumed generalized Leontief technology a marginal cost function for each output produced can be computed. Then, to obtain the firm's supply relationships specific assumptions about the nature of output markets need to be made. In the model it is assumed that in general imperfect competition prevails. While it should be noted that the perfect competition hypothesis may be sustained in the case of (very) long-run analyses, entry barriers which do not vanish in the medium-term can be considered as the rationale for imperfect competition in this model. Moreover, from the European experience it is apparent that labour markets are far from competitive. Finally, in WARM some activities are noncompetitive by construction: for instance, this is the case of the electricity and energy firms which are the sole domestic suppliers of their output.

To describe the price formation process it is assumed that firms are price-makers and apply a mark-up pricing rule. In the current version of the model the price mark-up is assumed to be constant and time invariant. While this assumption can be deemed as acceptable for a medium-term model where cyclical movements in price–cost margins ought not to be quantitatively important, there is no doubt that it represents an important simplification when it comes to explaining the determinants of margins in terms of demand elasticities and strategic firm behaviour. At a second stage, producers supply their outputs to different customers according to a price discriminating strategy. Given the price function for each type of output, the price charged to each customer is chained to the corresponding output price by means of a proportionality factor. Note that the joint estimation in the model of these price functions, together with the corresponding output demand relationships originating from the other sectors, ensure that market-clearing conditions are enforced. Finally, notice that outputs are expressed at factor cost, so that the corresponding prices are net of (net) indirect taxes. These tax rates are introduced when specifying the demand price for each product.

Investment

The firm's investment decision is based on the comparison between the actual and the desired endowment of capital stock. As is well known, given the structure of the technology, the desired amount of capital input is determined from the variable cost function via the envelope condition. In the long run equilibrium, the user cost of capital must be equal to its shadow value, given by the savings in marginal variable costs allowed by an extra unit of capital.[6]

Firms are owned by households to whom the share of profits being distributed accrues. Gross profits are given by value added less labour costs, depreciation and indirect taxes (plus production subsidies). To obtain net profits, direct taxes paid by firms are subtracted and net transfers from the 'rest of the world' are added. Distributed profits are given by net profits plus capital account transfers to firms, less net investment and change in inventories.[7] Distributed profits are part of the income available to households. Note that direct taxation not only affects net profits and therefore households' available incomes, but also investment decisions via the user cost of capital.

Technical change

One of the crucial features of the WARM model is an explicit attempt at describing the mechanism through which economic variables affect technical change. The basic idea is that the dynamics of technical change cannot be observed, and that traditional approaches, in which technical change is proxied either by a time trend or by the computation of factor productivity indexes, yield biased and inconsistent estimates.[8]

Here a latent variable structural equation model is proposed which uses data on total expenditures for research from public and private sources, on imports of patents and on business-cycle indicators as cause variables for the latent technological variable (see Carraro and Galeotti 1994a for details). The latent variable approach extracts information from indicators and cause variables while being able to avoid using them as exact representations of technological change. The goal is to minimize measurement errors and thus inconsistency in the estimation procedure.

It is assumed that the capital stock is composed of two components: an energy-saving stock and an energy-consuming one. Each year a new vintage of capital becomes operational. In this way new capital is added to the two components. The characteristics of this new capital depend on a number of economic variables which affect the firm's decision of installing energy-saving capital (for example, the energy prices). More precisely, relative prices, including the price of energy, affect both the decision to carry out R&D and the composition of the capital stock (for example, higher energy prices induce firms to invest in energy-saving vintages of the capital stock).

In the model, energy-saving technical progress is measured by the ratio between the two components of the capital stock. The average growth rate of this indicator is fairly low in the developed EU countries (about 2 per cent in Germany, France and Italy, and slightly lower in the UK), whereas it is much higher in the less-developed countries (from 9 per cent in Ireland to 30 per cent in Greece). In all countries, the growth rate of the technical progress indicator becomes lower as the country grows (because the model objective is to capture the implementation of best-available technologies in the short and medium run).

The dynamics of the technical progress indicator generally affects the decision rules of all the agents in the model: not only do they affect the firm's input and output decisions, as previously shown, but also influence a household's choices, especially those pertaining to the consumption of energy sources (see below). Moreover, the dynamics of technical change concerns total private capital stock, and not only the component used as a production input by firms. Note that an important implication of the treatment of environmental technical change here is that it is a diffuse phenomenon. In fact, the technological indicator is an argument of the behavioural equations concerning the demand for inputs and the supply of outputs (via marginal costs). In particular, this is the case for the manufacturing firm. Thus, over time an increasing amount of environment-friendly capital is used in production which translates into an improvement of the production process and in turn of the quality of goods and services supplied. To the extent that these goods and services are purchased by the other firms and households, the process of endogenous technical change affects all sectors of the economy (and the rest of the world as well).

The household sector

The basic behavioural assumption that characterizes a household's decisions is the maximization of the life-cycle utility subject to a budget constraint that equates expenditures to available resources. These are given by labour income, profits distributed by firms and the return on financial wealth. In the model, financial wealth takes essentially the form of government bonds. The utility of a household is a function of leisure and overall consumption: however, for convenience, it is assumed that the utility function is separable in the two arguments, such that consumption choices can be treated independently from labour supply decisions.[9]

Consumption decisions take place in a sequential way. First, resources are intertemporally allocated, so that current and future consumption (savings) are determined.[10] At a second stage, intratemporal consumption decisions are taken. In a manner analogous to the production sector, this is a multistage decision process, each generating systems of consumer demands for homogeneous groups of goods and services. Finally, the model describes how savings are allocated between acquisition of durable consumption goods, residential buildings and financial assets. A separate section is devoted to the description of how the equilibrium wage is determined in the model.

Consumption of specific commodities Following the utility tree, the household selects the consumption of energy sources, other nondurable goods, services from durables and other services. The durables decision is predetermined relative to the other choices and is described below. It is assumed that each allocation stage is described by a rationed Almost Ideal Demand System (AIDS). The explanatory variables are the price of the *j*-th good, the technical change indicator previously described, the number of households in a given country, and the stock of durable goods and of residential buildings. Exploiting the maintained assumption of weak separability of consumer preferences, and using again the AIDS approach, the distribution of total spending on energy between transportation and residential purposes (heating and the like) is obtained. Moreover, expenditures on energy for residential use are also allocated among several energy sources.

It remains to describe the acquisition of durable goods by the household. Analogous to a firm's investment, households choose the level of the desired stock and dynamically adjust the existing stock to this target. The desired amount of durables is determined from the indirect utility function generating the AIDS system. The stock of durables affects the demand of all goods, including energy. The flow diagram of the household's decisions is shown in Figure 4.2. Savings are obtained from subtracting total current consumption from disposable income. This variable results from the sum of distributed profits and other net income from direct taxes. This includes labour income, government transfers, income from abroad and interests on the holdings of public debt.

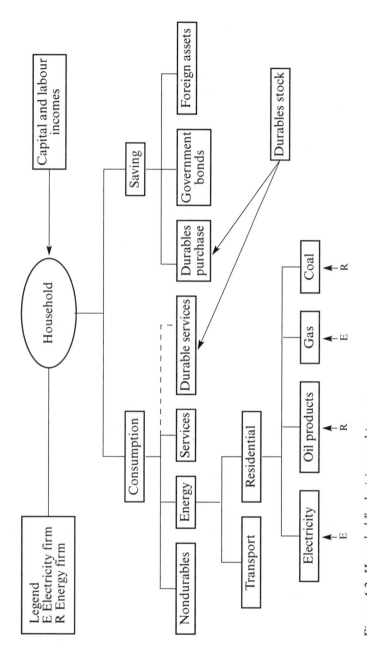

Figure 4.2 Household's decision-making process

Further, if purchases of consumption durables and new houses are subtracted, the change in a household's financial assets is obtained. Adding capital gains (assumed to be exogenous), the basis for the measure of financial wealth is obtained, which, along with real wealth (stocks of durables and housing), enters the aggregate consumption function.

Labour markets, unions and labour supplies. A distinctive feature of the WARM model is the assumed structure of the labour market, which is not competitive but segmented. In particular, a distinction is made between a primary sector and a residual sector. The former regards all production activities including the public sector, and excluding agriculture, as well as the wages and employment that are the results of a bargaining process between unions and managers. Specifically, the manufacturing multi-output firm plays a role of leadership and pattern setter for the other firms (and for the government), while both agricultural employment and unemployment have a residual role.

The institutional set-up of the European countries is such that the role of unions is more relevant than elsewhere. The union is considered to be an agent who aggregates the preferences of those who participate in the labour market and who use their bargaining power to obtain a wage above the competitive level. The presence of unions provides the rationale for involuntary unemployment which has been a typical phenomenon of European economies in the 1980s. Bargaining is a sequential process: at first, unions and representatives of the manufacturing firm agree upon the wage rate; subsequently, the other firms and the government set their wages on the basis of differentials which depend upon the union bargaining power as well as upon general and sector-specific economic conditions (see, for example, Dobson 1994). On the contrary, there are no unions in the secondary labour market (that is, agriculture) and wages are determined according to an arbitrage relative to the unemployment status.

The process leading to the determination of equilibrium wages in the economy will now be described. The manufacturing firm is the starting-point, which, as said, is pattern setter in the above process. This firm determines the level of employment on the basis of its labour demand function, taking as given the gross wage, which includes both the net wage paid to employees and the fiscal wedge (social security contributions paid by the employer plus income taxes paid by the worker). The net wage is the outcome of the bargaining process between the union and the firm. The fiscal wedge is set by the government.

For the determination of the net wage, the outcome of the bargaining process is assumed to be adequately described by the solution of a Nash bargaining optimization problem in which the equilibrium wage depends crucially upon two parameters: the union's relative bargaining power and the union's relative preference for employment. In the model, the first is endogenized as a function of the unemployment rate, unionization rate, and migration flows. Other variables influencing the equilibrium net wage are the replacement rate of manpower, the level of profits per worker, the wage elasticity of labour demand, and the fiscal wedge itself. This last variable is crucial since the size of its effect on the net wage provides a measure of the so-called wage resistance, that is, how much unions increase the net wage in response to a reduction in the fiscal wedge (specifically, a reduction of payroll taxes through recycling of environmental tax revenue).

The wage equation has been estimated as a nonlinear error correction mechanism in which the fiscal wedge affects wages both in the short and in the long run (see Brunello 1994). In the long run, the estimated effect reflects, in all EU countries, the theoretical prediction that a 1 per cent reduction of the wedge is completely offset by an increase in the net wage (the long-run elasticity is equal to –1). In the short run, the size of short-run wage resistance to changes in payroll taxes can be computed. In the short run, a 1 per cent reduction in the average payroll tax increases the net wage by 0.29 per cent at the EU level. There is, however, a large variability across EU countries, because this effect goes from 0.48 per cent in the Netherlands to 0.042 in Denmark. As far as the gross wage is concerned, a 1 per cent reduction in the average payroll tax reduces the gross wage by 0.09 per cent at the EU level (from 0.018 in Denmark to 0.14 in France). The cumulated effect is –0.22 per cent at the EU level, and ranges from –0.04 per cent in Denmark to –0.34 per cent in France. These results suggest that cuts in payroll taxes may have a limited effect on employment because unions succeed in transforming part of the tax cut into higher net wages.

Once the equilibrium wage rate of the leading sector has been determined, the wage rates of the other sectors operating in the primary labour market (electricity and energy firms and government sector) are obtained in a simple way: intersectoral wage differentials are applied.

The description of the functioning of the labour markets in the WARM model can be completed by noting that, given the wages, employment is determined by the labour demand equations (see the following section for the government's demand for labour). Given an exogenous temporal profile of the labour force, the rate of unemployment is determined residually.

The government sector
A noticeable feature of WARM is the endogenization of government behaviour. The fundamental assumption here is that its strategies can be endogenized as functions of the economic policy goals, that is, through a set of reaction functions.

The government undertakes four main activities. The first is the production of a public good *G* (public spending) using inputs from labour, fixed capital and a composite intermediate material good. This activity is formally represented by a variable Cobb-Douglas cost function which, via Shephard's Lemma, yields the demand for public employment and for materials. Both demand equations depend upon factor prices and are conditional upon a given level of output *G* and of the stock of public capital.

The second economic activity is public investment. The stock of public capital depends upon past investment. However, unlike the behaviour of the other agents, the optimal investment decision is not based on the government's variable cost function via the envelope condition. Instead, the assumption is made that public investment is one of the government's control variables used to smooth business-cycle fluctuations. It follows that public investment is endogenized through a reaction function which responds to changes in three factors: the cost of investment (as represented by variable input prices and the user cost of public capital); the cost of funds available for financing investment expenditures (as represented by the change in the degree of fiscal pressure as well as in the interest payments on public debt); and the economic policy targets (captured by the rate of change in total employment). Given the determination of public investment, the stock of public capital is again obtained by the usual perpetual inventory formula with an exogenous depreciation rate.

The production and investment activities undertaken by the public agent are subject to the usual budget constraint whereby expenditures are financed by indirect and direct tax revenues and by issue of government bonds. The items of the budget currently endogenized in the model are the revenues from direct income taxation, the interest payments on the stock of public debt outstanding, the amount of pensions paid to households, and the social security contributions due by both households and firms. The other two activities of the government are therefore the regulation of the level of business activity through appropriate fiscal and expenditure policies and the redistribution of income.

Looking now at the sources of public funds, the starting-point is that taxation serves the dual purpose of pursuing efficiency (for example, to correct externalities) and income redistribution. Indirect fiscal revenues are calculated by applying the effective tax rate and excise rate, respectively, to the value of output consumed and to the volume of goods and services consumed. Adding the revenues from each taxable basis, the overall fiscal revenue is obtained. The model accounts for eleven different VAT rates and nineteen different excise rates. The revenues from direct taxation are computed on the basis of a single time varying tax rate applied to total income.[12] The tax rate is endogenous and determined by a reaction function that depends upon the rate of inflation (to account for fiscal drag phenomena), the amount of public good supplied (public spending to be financed), and the Maastricht goals (debt to GDP ratio and budget deficit to GDP ratio, to account for the government's efforts in meeting the requirements for eligibility to the economic and monetary union.

Turning now to the uses of public funds, the nominal rate of interest on public debt is endogenized. Given the exogenous amount of existing debt, the interest rate is again treated as a control variable which depends via a reaction function upon the rate of inflation, the trade balance and the growth rate of public debt (to capture the risk premium demanded by investors in high-debt countries). The amount of pensions paid by the government is related to the number of persons over 65 relative to total population, to the average personal income, and to the distribution of income between wages and profits. Social contributions (as a share of total labour costs) depend upon the real wages, inflation rate and upon the average pension received by individuals. There is a final item, government subsidies paid to firms, which is kept exogenous in the model. This variable is used for simulation purposes, with the aim of analysing the effects of policies designed to stimulate technological innovation, export activity, and the like.[13]

The foreign sector

The model adopts a production-theoretic view of international trade flows. In fact, households cannot make direct purchases from abroad and all flows of goods and services go through the production sector (especially the manufacturing firm) which performs repackaging, distribution and similar activities.[14] Viewing imports as an input to the production process, this approach allows an integrated treatment of trade flows, in that exports are viewed as an output of the same production process (see, for instance, Kohli 1991).

The model is characterized by a precise specialization in the import–export activity of firms. The agricultural firm can sell its output to both domestic and foreign markets. The manufacturing firm is the only agent trading manufactured goods and services internationally. Imported electricity is only handled by the corresponding firm and this is also the case of other energy sources for the corresponding firm.

Import decisions take place through a two-stage allocation process. The procedure is the same as the one previously described for generic inputs: on the basis of relative prices the total import demand for each good and service is determined. Next, the aggregate price of a good being bought by the domestic firm from abroad is viewed as a unit cost function. Shephard's Lemma then yields the demand function of that good by the importing country from each selling country. Analytical tractability for a problem that involves many goods and many countries at the same time suggested the use of Cobb–Douglas unit cost functions.

On the export side, the approach used describing the behaviour of producers is followed here as well. The price of a good produced by country *i* and sold to country *j* is a constant fraction of the production price of the same good. The simple representation of trade flows just described is sufficient for describing the structure of bilateral exchanges of goods, services and energy sources among the EU–12 countries as well as the rest of the world.

Emissions

The role of the environmental module in WARM serves the purpose of assessing the impact of economic activities on the environment. This task is performed by measuring the amount of harmful emissions.[15] A series of technical coefficients provide the amount of emissions generated by the various forms of economic activity specified by the model. The attention is focused upon the following pollutants: sulphur oxide (SO_x), nitrogen oxide (NO_x), particulate matter, carbon monoxide (CO), and volatile organic components. These pollutants are to a large extent related to the use of fossil fuels in the various production and consumption activities. Moreover, fossil fuels are the most relevant anthropogenic source of CO_2 emissions, which are largely responsible for the greenhouse phenomenon. The model disaggregation across economic activities (that is, economic agents) and across energy sources allows a precise assessment of individual contributions to overall emissions.

Environmental fiscal reforms in a federal Europe: a quantitative assessment of alternative institutional settings

The model described in the previous section has been used to carry out some simulation experiments which are characterized by two complementary goals. On the one hand, to verify the existence of the so-called 'employment double dividend' under alternative institutional settings; and on the other hand, to compare the results thus obtained in order to quantify gains and losses (in terms of GDP growth, employment and emissions) deriving from decentralizing rather than from harmonizing or centralizing the decision process that leads to the implementation of the environmental fiscal reform.

To achieve these two goals, four simulation experiments have been carried out. In the four experiments, energy taxation increases in order to control carbon emissions whereas the tax revenue is recycled through a generalized reduction in payroll taxes in order to stimulate employment. In the baseline scenario, the EU economy as a whole exhibits a steady-state growth at an annual rate of 2.4 per cent, with a stable inflation rate of 1.8 per cent. It is assumed that the fiscal reform is introduced in 1995. Simulations are carried out up to the year 2010.

Harmonized tax rates with domestic revenue recycling

In this first experiment, it is assumed that all EU countries agree to introduce a harmonized environmental policy characterized by identical tax rates across countries (thus equalizing marginal abatement costs). In practice, the carbon tax is introduced according to the European Union proposal (see Official Journal of the EC 1992). In particular, the proposal specifies the tax as a mixed charge on emissions and on the energy content of different fuels and of electricity. The tax was introduced here at the highest level proposed by the European Commission (19 ECU per ton of CO_2, which corresponds to about $10 per barrel). The tax is levied on manufacturing and final energy consumption. The revenue of the tax is used to reduce payroll taxes, that is, the gross labour cost (which enters labour demand).

Notice that the tax rates are harmonized (for example, as the outcome of an environmental cooperative agreement), whereas the revenue recycling takes place in each country under the assumption that each domestic budget deficit (surplus) remains unchanged.

The impact of the harmonized fiscal reform on gross nominal wages, employment, CO_2 emissions, and real GDP growth is shown in Table 4.1 for three main EU countries (France, Germany and Italy).[16] The qualitative impact of the fiscal reform is the same in all countries. In the short run, wages are reduced and employment increases. However, in the medium run (after about ten years) wages tend to revert back to their baseline level and to increase afterwards. As a consequence, the initial increase of employment disappears in the long run. This evidence can be rationalized in terms of the modelling of the labour market here: wage bargaining implies that only in the short run are unions unable to offset the payroll tax reduction through an increase of net wages. In the long run, the fiscal change is completely absorbed by the change of net wages. Hence gross wages, other things being equal, go back to the initial level. They further increase with respect to the baseline scenario because of two feedback mechanisms: (1) the unemployment reduction achieved in the short run increases unions' bargaining power, thus inducing, through the dynamics of the bargaining equation, a counter-effect in the long run; and (2) the energy-saving R&D activity induced by the energy tax increases the growth rate of technical progress, thus increasing factor productivity and, as a consequence, firms' profits. The sharing rule which is implicit in the wage bargaining equation implies that gross wages are proportional to profits. Hence, in the long run gross wages are larger than in the baseline.

Table 4.1 Impact of a harmonized tax in the short run (after two years) and in the long run (in 2010) (percentage difference with respect to baseline)

	France		Germany		Italy	
	Short run	*Long run*	*Short run*	*Long run*	*Short run*	*Long run*
Gross nominal wages	−2.10	3.50	−3.20	5.40	−2.30	4.20
Employment	0.65	−0.25	0.41	0.02	0.25	0.20
CO$_2$ emissions	−0.41	7.00	−0.41	−0.90	−0.24	7.70
Real GDP growth rate	−0.54	0.35	−0.60	0.60	−0.63	0.18

The simulated fiscal reform can therefore achieve its main goal (employment increase) only in the short run. After that, there is no further employment gain that can be reaped by the fiscal manoeuvre.

The long-run effect on output growth is slightly above zero. In the short run, the prevailing effect is the output effect, that is, the tax change increases costs and reduces output. However, in the long run, the positive shock on employment exhibits some virtuous features, by inducing an increase in aggregate demand (through households' higher income and consumption) which increases GDP growth. This growth obviously produces negative effects on emissions. As expected, the fiscal reform reduces emissions in the short run. However, in the long run the effect on emissions tends to disappear. The transitory emission reduction can be explained by looking at the effect of the fiscal reform both on the level and the composition of aggregate demand. As previously said, unions tend to capture part of the rent given to firms by the reduction of payroll taxes. Hence, gross wages decrease less than expected, whereas net wages increase. In the long run, all the reduction in payroll taxes is transformed in net wage increase. The increase in net wages and in employment induces an increase in households' income, and then in the consumption of all goods, including energy.[17] As technical progress mainly affects production technologies, emissions per unit of output decrease, but emissions per unit of consumption do not. Therefore, the increase in energy consumption leads to higher emission levels. In some countries, this revenue effect can be larger than the emission reduction induced by higher energy prices (the substitution effect).

Summing up, the empirical analysis seems to suggest that no 'employment double dividend' can emerge in the long run. By contrast, the fiscal reform may lose the environmental dividend. There is therefore evidence in favour of the usual long-run environment–employment trade-off. However, in the short run the situation may be different, as employment increases and emissions decrease, thereby indicating the possibility of a short-run 'employment double dividend'.

Unilateral environmental fiscal reforms
In this case it is assumed that the emission tax defined in the previous case and the related revenue recycling is introduced in one country only, whereas no fiscal reform is introduced in the other eleven EU countries. Table 4.2 shows what happens to wages, employment, real GDP growth and CO_2 emissions when France, Germany or Italy is the country which introduces the fiscal reform unilaterally. Percentage differences are computed with respect to the harmonized case previously described. Even if differences are quite small, it can be seen that wages and GDP growth tend to be lower. As a consequence, emissions tend to be lower too. There are no significant differences in employment levels.

As a result, the following conclusion can be drawn. The environmental fiscal reform may reduce emissions and increase employment even when introduced unilaterally. However, gains in terms of GDP growth tend to be lower than in the case of harmonized fiscal reform, wherein no difference seems to emerge as far as employment is concerned.

This conclusion is relevant because it shows that there is no need to coordinate environmental fiscal reform for such a reform to be profitable. Hence, countries may introduce the environmental fiscal reform even unilaterally. The reason is that the negative effect of the tax, which increases costs and reduces competitiveness and output growth, is compensated by the reduction of gross wages. However, gains in terms of GDP growth are larger when the reform is introduced by all countries because of negative trade effects in the country which introduces the tax reform unilaterally.

There is, therefore, an argument in favour of an environmental tax reform introduced by all countries simultaneously. Should the tax, however, and the recycling policy be harmonized?

Table 4.2 Impact of a unilateral tax in the short run (after two years) and in the long run (in 2010) (percentage difference with respect to harmonized case)

	France		Germany		Italy	
	Short run	Long run	Short run	Long run	Short run	Long run
Gross nominal wages	0.30	3.30	0.30	3.20	0.30	3.20
Employment	−0.40	−0.07	0.01	−0.06	0.02	−0.06
CO_2 emissions	0.11	0.02	0.05	−1.02	0.06	−1.02
Real GDP growth rate	0.17	−0.55	0.14	−0.58	0.17	−0.58

Decentralized tax rates and revenue recycling: an assessment of the subsidiarity principle

To further explore this issue, the case in which the reform is introduced in all twelve EU member states considered in this chapter will be analysed, but where both the tax rate and the revenue recycling are set independently by each domestic government. In this case, each government is assumed to set a tax rate lower than the harmonized one described in the first subsection above, if the emission/output ratio is lower than the European average ratio (vice versa if the emission/output ratio is larger than the average one). The emission/output ratio is taken as a rough proxy of the technological characteristics of each country which summarizes information that should come from the environmental damage function. Even if this is just an approximation, the idea is that countries with a lower emission/output ratio perceive lower environmental damage which leads them to set a lower tax rate.

The revenue recycling takes place at the national level, that is, each government uses the tax revenue to reduce employers' payments for social security contributions under the constraint that the domestic budget surplus (deficit) remains unchanged.

The results are shown in Table 4.3. It can be seen that Germany introduces a tax rate larger than average, whereas Italy and France introduce one lower than average (the European average is 19 ECU per ton of CO_2). As a consequence, in the short run Germany suffers from a small additional output reduction, but further increases employment because of the gross wage reduction permitted by the tax recycling (comparisons are again made with respect to the harmonized case described earlier). Conversely, in France and Italy, the output growth is larger, but there is no additional employment gain.

In the long run, employment and growth are not affected by decentralizing the decision about tax rates, whereas emissions are slightly lower in Italy and France (and stable in Germany).

Table 4.3 Impact of a decentralized tax in the short run (after two years) and in the long run (in 2010) (precentage difference with respect to harmonized case)

	France		Germany		Italy	
	Short run	Long run	Short run	Long run	Short run	Long run
Tax rate (per cent)	15	14	21	20	16	18
Gross nominal wages	0.20	0.13	−0.28	0.21	0.36	−0.05
Employment	−0.08	−0.058	0.06	−0.022	−0.07	−0.040
CO_2 emissions	0.39	−0.42	−0.40	0.08	0.40	1.40
Real GDP growth rate	0.03	0.042	−0.02	0.015	0.07	−0.070

Therefore, the main differences with respect to the harmonized case concern mainly the short run. From this analysis it can be concluded that decentralizing the decision about tax rates may lead some countries to set rates too low, thus reducing the effect of the reform on employment levels. In fact, the benefits of the environmental fiscal reform come mainly from revenue recycling, that is, from higher employment levels. However, if tax rates are too low, the revenue to be recycled is not large enough to induce significant changes of employment.

An environmental fiscal reform with federal revenue recycling
The last question to which a preliminary answer is proposed is the following: can additional gains be achieved if both the tax and the expenditure policy are centralized? In particular, what happens if revenue recycling is carried out by a federal authority which takes into account the different unemployment levels in different EU countries?

To answer this question it is assumed that tax rates and expenditure policy are perfectly coordinated. As a consequence, the tax rate is homogeneous across countries (to equalize marginal abatement costs), whereas the tax revenue is recycled by giving proportionally more resources to those countries with higher unemployment levels (the federal budget surplus or deficit remains unchanged). Therefore, the reduction of payroll taxes is larger in these countries.

From Table 4.4 it can be seen that resources (tax revenues) go from Germany to Italy (also to France in the long run). As a consequence, gross wages are lower in Italy, which implies higher gains in terms of employment in the short run. Moreover, in the long run there is a small increase of employment in all countries, even if no gains in terms of either GDP growth or emissions seem to emerge.

Table 4.4 Impact of a federal tax in the short run (after two years) and in the long run (in 2010) (percentage difference with respect to harmonized case)

	France		Germany		Italy	
	Short run	Long run	Short run	Long run	Short run	Long run
Net revenue (ECU m.)	−500	6200	−5000	−800	5800	8700
Gross nominal wages	0.05	−0.62	0.35	0.06	−0.65	−0.55
Employment	−0.04	0.17	−0.19	0.03	0.28	0.05
CO_2 emissions	0.00	0.02	−0.05	0.03	−0.05	−0.03
Real GDP growth rate	−0.02	−0.02	−0.20	0.28	0.10	−0.03

These results can be explained by the fact that France, Germany and Italy are countries with similar economic structures. More relevant differences emerge when comparing all EU countries (for example, large employment gains could be achieved in Spain). Hence, the advantages of a federal environmental fiscal reform concern employment above all. On the one hand, the reform redistributes employment in the short run; on the other hand, it helps to increase employment in the long run. By contrast, no significant change in terms of emissions or GDP growth seems to appear.

Conclusion

How can these results be interpreted? What kind of policy guidelines do they provide?

It should be emphasized that these results are very preliminary. Their main goal is to initiate a theoretical and empirical debate. In fact, the simulation experiments that were carried out have some drawbacks. For example, a more accurate definition of decentralized and federal policy should be analysed with the model; gains and losses should be evaluated by estimating a welfare function in each country; and environmental damages should be calibrated in order to determine the optimal non-cooperative and cooperative tax rates.

However, even with these limitations, these simulation experiments provide some useful indications.

First, it is clear that the effects of an environmental fiscal reform essentially depends upon the functioning of the labour market. If more employment has to be achieved, then the appropriate instrument has to be found. Given the centralized wage bargaining characterizing many EU labour markets, it is unclear whether wage subsidies (that is, reductions in payroll taxes) are the appropriate instruments. On the other hand, there is evidence that a more competitive labour market, in which union bargaining power is lower, can strengthen the effects of the environmental fiscal reform (see Carraro et al. 1996).

Second, the change of the institutional setting does not modify the qualitative features which define the effects of the fiscal reform and only slightly modify its quantitative effects. However, if the main goal is employment relief, rather than emission reduction, the results suggest that a federal policy in which both tax rates and wage subsidies are harmonized is the best institutional setting. Tax rates have to be harmonized because decentralization would lead to low rates which provide fewer resources to be recycled to boost employment. Wage subsidies have to be coordinated because revenue recycling produces the largest increase of EU employment when the tax revenue is used chiefly in those countries with high unemployment levels.

Third, the small effects on employment by environmental fiscal reform suggest that restricting the reform to emission charges and wage subsidies is probably inefficient. The idea of reforming the fiscal system by correcting externalities and by lowering distortionary taxes should be considered in more general terms, by proposing an overall change of the tax system. A comprehensive, well-designed reform is likely to provide larger gains in all countries.

Finally, it seems that the environmental fiscal reform analysed in this chapter can provide significant benefits only in the short run. How to achieve permanent gains in employment and GDP growth remains an open question. An answer may be provided by policies which stimulate both human and physical capital accumulation (for example, R&D and innovation policies).[18]

More research, both theoretical and empirical, is still necessary to better understand qualitative and quantitative aspects of the policy issues discussed in this chapter.

Notes

1. Among the papers which have addressed this issue are Pearce (1991), Oates (1991), and Bovenberg and Van der Ploeg (1992, 1993a, 1993b, 1994). A collection of papers on the 'employment double dividend' is contained in Carraro and Siniscalco (1996).
2. Empirical evidence in favour of this argument can be found in Baldwin (1995), and Grossman (1995). A more general discussion is provided in Carraro and Siniscalco (1994). A theoretical analysis of the interactions between environmental taxation and innovation in a dynamic model can be found in Carraro and Topa (1994, 1995).
3. Definition and analysis of stability of international environmental agreements can be found in Carraro and Siniscalco (1993b).
4. The WARM model is the outcome of a large research project funded by the European Commission, DGXII–E1, and by the Fondazione ENI Enrico Mattei (see Carraro and Galeotti 1994a).
5. This firm carries out economic activities which go beyond manufacturing *strictu sensu*, as it also provides services. For the sake of brevity, it is denoted as 'manufacturing' here.
6. This is the first-order condition for the problem of minimizing total short-run costs, given by the sum of minimized variable costs and expenditures in fixed (that is, capital) inputs (see, for instance, Galeotti 1994).
7. The change in inventories in the model is endogenized by simply linking it to the total demand for each output produced by the firm.
8. The idea of treating technical change as an unobserved or latent variable is shared by the partial equilibrium approaches of Slade (1989) and Gao (1994), and by the general equilibrium model of Boone et al. (1992).
9. Although the WARM model includes endogenous labour supply decisions, the simulations reported above assumed an exogenous labour supply.
10. The role of expectations is accounted for by the dynamic structure of the aggregate consumption function (error correction mechanism).
11. The efficiency wages hypothesis provides an alternative rationale for the existence of involuntary unemployment. However, this theoretical option appears to be ill-suited for the European experience, as it is based upon the idea that the wage rate is unilaterally set to a level decided by the firm (see Blanchard and Fischer 1989).
12. Taxes on households and taxes on firms are not distinguished.
13. All the equations pertaining to items of the government budget constraint are estimated using partial adjustment mechanisms.

14. An important remark concerns the primary factors of production and their international mobility. The demand for labour generated by firms and by the government matches households' labour supply. Thus, the labour market is a national one and this input is internationally immobile. No migration flows are present in the model, because of the paucity of the necessary data. As far as capital is concerned, there is only one type of durable good which is either demanded by households (consumer durables) or by firms (investment goods). Capital is a partly mobile input in the following sense. While durable goods, including capital goods, can be traded internationally, once in place owing to the firm's investment activity, they become perfectly immobile. As already clarified, financial capital flows are not explicitly modelled.

15. The current version of the model does not incorporate a full-blown analysis of the environmental impact of the economic activity. In particular, the model lacks a description of the feedbacks from the environment on to the behaviour of the economic agents through households 'welfare and firms' cost-benefit analysis. There is, however, an indirect feedback via the government's reaction functions (for instance, if polluting emissions increase, energy tax rates can be raised).

16. The choice of focusing on the results concerning these three countries has been made only to provide a clearer presentation of the economic mechanisms which explain the results. The interested reader can write to the authors to receive the tables concerning all twelve EU countries.

17. The long-run increase in aggregate consumption can be assessed by looking at the consumption/GDP ratio. The increase of this ratio ranges from +0.5 per cent in Spain and the Netherlands to +2.4 per cent in the UK. The increase in consumption is partially offset by a relative reduction of government expenditure in most countries (the ratio G/GDP decreases). In the UK there is also a worsening of the trade balance.

18. On this issue, see Carraro and Galeotti (1994b).

References

Baldwin, R. (1995), 'Does sustainability require growth', in I. Goldin and A. Winters (eds), *The Economics of Sustainable Development*, Cambridge: Cambridge University Press, pp. 51–76.

Barker, T. (1996), 'Taxing pollution instead of jobs: towards more employment without more Inflation through fiscal reform in the UK', in C. Carraro and D. Siniscalco (eds), *Environmental Fiscal Reform and Unemployment*, Dordrecht: Kluwer Academic, pp. 229–72.

Blanchard, O. and S. Fischer (1989), *Lectures on Macroeconomics*, Cambridge, MA: MIT Press.

Boone, L., S. Hall, and D. Kemball-Cook (1992), 'Endogenous technical progress in fossil fuel demand: the case of France', Center for Economic Studies Discussion Paper No. 21–93.

Bovenberg, L. (1997), 'Environmental policy, distortionary labour taxation and employment: pollution taxes and the double dividend', in C. Carraro and D. Siniscalco (eds), *New Directions in the Economic Theory of the Environment*, Cambridge: Cambridge University Press, pp. 181–205.

Bovenberg, L. and L. Goulder (1993), 'Integrating environmental and distortionary taxes: general equilibrium analysis', paper presented at the Conference on 'Market Approaches to Environmental Protection', Stanford University, 3–4 December, 1993.

Bovenberg, L. and R. Van der Ploeg (1992), 'Environmental policy, public finance and the labour market in a second-best world', Center for Economic Policy Research Discussion Paper No. 745.

Bovenberg, L. and R. Van der Ploeg (1993a), 'Green policies in a small open economy', Center for Economic Policy Research Discussion Paper No. 785.

Bovenberg, L. and R. Van der Ploeg (1993b), 'Does a tougher environmental policy raise unemployment? Optimal taxation, public goods and environmental policy with rationing of labour supply', Center for Economic Policy Research Discussion Paper No. 869.

Bovenberg, L. and R. Van der Ploeg (1994), 'Optimal taxation, public goods and environmental policy with involuntary unemployment', paper presented at the NBER–University of Turin–FEEM Conference on 'Market Failures and Public Policy', Turin, 19-21 May.

Brunello, G. (1996), 'Labour market institutions and the double dividend hypothesis: an application of the WARM model', in C. Carraro and D. Siniscalco (eds), *Environmental Fiscal Reform and Unemployment*, Dordrecht: Kluwer Academic, pp. 139–70.

Capros, P. (1996), 'Double dividend analysis: first results of a general equilibrium model linking the EU–12 Countries', in C. Carraro and D. Siniscalco (eds), *Environmental Fiscal Reform and Unemployment*, Dordrecht: Kluwer Academic, pp. 193–228.

Carraro, C. and M. Galeotti (1994a), 'WARM (World Assessment of Resource Management)', Technical Report No. 94–01, GRETA Econometrics, Venice.

Carraro, C. and M. Galeotti (1994b), 'Endogenous technical progress and emission control: some experiments with the WARM model', paper presented at the Advanced Research Workshop on 'The Economics of Atmospheric Pollution', Wageningen (NL), 16–18 November.

Carraro, C., M. Galeotti, and M. Gallo (1996), 'Environmental taxation and unemployment: some evidence on the double dividend hypothesis in Europe', *Journal of Public Economics*, **62**, 141–81.

Carraro, C. and D. Siniscalco (1993a), *The European Carbon Tax: An Economic Assessment*, Dordrecht: Kluwer Academic.

Carraro, C. and D. Siniscalco (1993b), 'Strategies for the international protection of the environment', *Journal of Public Economics*, **59**, 323–32.

Carraro, C. and D. Siniscalco (1994), 'Environmental policy re-considered: the role of technological innovation', *European Economic Review*, **38**, 545–54.

Carraro, C. and D. Siniscalco (eds) (1996), *Environmental Fiscal Reform and Unemployment*, Dordrecht: Kluwer Academic.

Carraro, C. and G. Topa (1994), 'Should environmental innovation policy be internationally coordinated?', in C. Carraro (ed.), *Trade, Innovation, Environment*, Dordrecht: Kluwer Academic, pp. 167–204.

Carraro, C. and G. Topa (1995), 'Taxation and environmental innovation', in C. Carraro and J. Filar (eds), *Control and Game-Theoretic Models of the Environment*, Boston: Birckauser, pp. 109–40.

Denis, C. and G.J. Koopman (1994), 'Differential treatment of sectors and energy products in the design of a CO_2 energy tax: consequences for employment, economic welfare and CO_2 emissions', presented at the FEEM Conference on 'Environmental Taxation, Revenue Recycling and Unemployment, Milan, 16–17 December.

Dobson, A. (1994), 'Multifirm unions and the incentive to adopt pattern bargaining in Oligopoly', *European Economic Review*, **38**, 87–100.

Drèze, J.H. and E. Malinvaud (1993), 'Growth and employment: the scope of a European initiative', mimeo, CORE, Louvain.

Galeotti, M. (1994), 'The intertemporal dimension of neoclassical production theory: a survey', *Journal of Economic Surveys*, **10**, pp. 1–40.

Gao, X.M. (1994), 'Measuring technological change using a latent variable approach', *European Review of Agricultural Economics*, **21**, 113–29.

Grossman, G. (1995), 'Pollution and growth: what do we know?', in I. Goldin and A. Winters (eds), *The Economics of Sustainable Development'*, Cambridge: Cambridge University Press, pp. 19–47.

Grubb, M., J. Edmonds, P. ten Brink, and M. Morrison (1993), 'The costs of limiting fossil-fuel CO_2 emissions', *Annual Review of Energy and Environment*, **18**, 397–478.

Holmlund, B. and J. Zetterberg (1991), 'Insider effects in wage determination', *European Economic Review*, **35**, 1009–34.

Hourcade. J.C. (1993), 'Modelling long-run scenarios: methodology lessons from a prospective study on a low CO_2 intensive country', *Energy Policy*, **21**, 87–98.

Jorgenson, D.W. and P.J. Wilcoxen (1990), 'Intertemporal general equilibrium modelling of U.S. environmental regulation', *Journal of Policy Modeling*, **12**, 715–44.

Kohli, U. (1991), *Technology, Duality, and Foreign Trade*, Hemel Hempstead: Harvester Wheatsheaf.

Lau, L.J. (1976), 'A characterization of the normalized restricted profit function', *Journal of Economic Theory*, **12**, 131–63.

Layard R., R. Jackman, and S. Nickell (1991), *Unemployment*, Oxford: Blackwell.

Morrison, C.J. (1988), 'Quasi-fixed Inputs in U.S. and Japanese manufacturing: a generalized Leontief restricted cost function approach', *Review of Economics and Statistics*, **LXX**, 275–87.

Oates, W. (1991), 'Pollution charges as a source of public revenues', Resources for the Future, Discussion Paper QE92–05, Washington, DC.

Official Journal of the EC (1992), *Journal officiel des Communautés européennes*, No. C 196/1, 3 August.

Pearce, D.W. (1991), 'The role of carbon taxes in adjusting to global warming', *Economic Journal*, **101**, 938–48.

Repetto, R., R. Dower, R. Jenkins, and J. Geoghegan (1992), 'Green fees: How a tax shift can work for the environment and the economy', World Resource Institute, New York.

Slade, M.E. (1989), 'Modeling stochastic and cyclical components of technical change: an application of the Kalman filter', *Journal of Econometrics*, **41**, 363–83.

5. Coordinated versus non-coordinated European energy/carbon tax solutions analysed with GEM–E3[1] linking the EU–12 countries

Pantelis Capros, Panayiotis Georgakopoulos, Stavros Zografakis, Denise Van Regemorter and Stef Proost

Introduction

Policy analysis for CO_2 emission reduction has accumulated a rich background, worldwide. Although controversial, the analysis has concluded with the advantage of using market-oriented policy instruments, especially taxation. However, it has also demonstrated the adverse implications for economic growth, employment and competitiveness.

The European Union (EU) considers carbon taxes to be an important instrument to achieve its objective of stabilizing CO_2 emissions. Since the initial proposal of May 1992 to use a $10/barrel energy/carbon tax, the different member states have not achieved the necessary unanimity to introduce this tax. In December 1994, a new proposal (Com (92) 226 final) was advanced that allows the different member states to install an energy/carbon tax, unilaterally or jointly. In the new proposal there are two other important changes: the tax is no longer made conditional on the efforts of the rest of the Organization for Economic Cooperation and Development (OECD) and each country can make special provisions for its energy-intensive industries. It can grant them partial exemptions and the governments are encouraged to use the revenues of the tax to reduce social charges on labour as recommended in the Commission's White Paper on Growth, Competitiveness and Employment.

The aim of this chapter is to examine the economic and welfare effects of the two energy/carbon proposals. The 1992 proposal will be called a coordinated tax, and the 1994 proposal a non-coordinated energy/carbon tax. In both scenarios the tax revenues will be recycled through a reduction of the social security contributions paid by employers in view of reducing the negative employment effects.[2]

There are several reasons why such an analysis is of interest. The 1994 proposal is new and has not yet been evaluated in economic terms. The 1992 proposal has been the object of numerous studies that have looked at different aspects of this proposal but none of them has delivered sufficient information. Almost all studies have used individual country models that rendered it difficult to control for the actions of the other member countries. Moreover, on the whole, traditional macroeconometric models were used which are not well suited to analyse the effects of important shifts in the tax system.

The chapter starts with a brief presentation of the GEM–E3 model, a computable general equilibrium model with a full linkage of the EU–12 member states. Then the model's results for the above issue are presented.

The GEM-E3 model

Introduction

GEM–E3 is a computable general equilibrium model, for the European Union member states, which provides details on the macroeconomy and its interaction with the environment and the energy system. It is an empirical, large-scale model, written entirely in structural form. The model computes the equilibrium prices of goods, services, labour and capital that simultaneously clear all markets under the Walras law. In brief, the model can be characterized as follows:

- it is a multicountry model, treating each EU–12 member state separately and linking them through the endogenous trade of goods and services;
- it includes multiple industrial sectors and economic agents, allowing a consistent evaluation of the distributional effects of policies; and
- it is a multiperiod model, involving the dynamics of capital accumulation and technological progress, stock and flow relationships and backward-looking expectations.

In addition, the model covers the major aspects of public finance including all substantial taxes, social policy subsidies, public expenditures and deficit financing, as well as policy instruments specific for the environment/energy system.

The model simultaneously determines the optimizing behaviour of agents and the fulfilment of the overall equilibrium conditions on all markets. The model also contains a representation of the energy markets, of the different environmental policy instruments and of part of the environmental damages. In this sense, the model analyses the interactions between the economy, the energy and the environment systems.

The results of the model include projections of full input–output tables by country, national accounts, employment, capital, monetary and financial flows, balance of payments, public finance and revenues, household consumption, energy use and supply, and atmospheric emissions. The computation of equilibrium is simultaneous for all the domestic markets of all the EU–12 countries and the foreign trade links. In supporting policy analysis, a major aim of the model is the consistent evaluation of distributional effects, across countries, economic sectors and agents. The burden-sharing aspects of energy supply and environmental protection are fully analysed, while ensuring that all markets clear.

Model design principles
The GEM–E3 model includes a detailed representation of production structures and consumption patterns, with fully flexible coefficients, as in the D.W. Jorgenson tradition (see Jorgenson et al. 1989; Bergman 1990; and De Melo 1988). It also integrates energy and environment within production costs and the input–output structure.

The model is largely inspired by the computable general equilibrium models that are extended with an IS–LM closure (see, for example, Bourguignon et al. 1989 and Capros et al. 1991). The model implements the so-called macro/micro approach that combines a microeconomic representation of demand and supply behaviour with a macroeconomic consistent framework. In addition, it formulates an endogenous international trade and a detailed treatment of taxation, as in other trade-oriented general equilibrium models (see, for example, Shoven and Whalley 1984).

The model is based on a social accounting matrix (SAM) framework and is calibrated for a base year, as in World Bank models (see, for example, De Melo 1988). The model runs dynamically by solving a system of simultaneous nonlinear equations in each period.

Model components
Appendix 5A3 provides a stylized (and simplified) presentation of the equations of the GEM–E3 model. Appendix 5AI describes the model's nomenclature.

Domestic production is defined by the sector following the sectoral decomposition of the input–output table. It is assumed that each sector produces a single good, following a constant returns of scale technology. It is also assumed that perfect competition conditions prevail in all markets for goods. The sectoral firm decides, under profit maximization, its supply of goods or services given its selling price and the prices of production inputs. The firm can change its stock of capital only in the following year, by investing in the current year. Since the stock of capital is fixed within the current year, the supply curve of domestic goods is upward sloping and exhibits decreasing returns of scale. All production inputs are considered to be production factors. The firm flexibly adjusts the entire mix of production inputs.

The desired stock of capital for the following year is derived from profit maximization seeking to achieve an optimal level of long-run rate of return of capital, given expectations about future users' cost of capital. The optimal long-run rate of return of capital is derived according to the Ando–Modigliani formula (see Ando et al. 1974) involving the real interest rate augmented by the depreciation rate. Sectoral investment is obtained through partial adjustment of current to desired stock of capital.

The behaviour of the representative household is derived from an intertemporal model (see Lluch 1973). The model has to determine a household's decisions regarding its labour supply and the allocation of its revenue into consumption and savings. This decision is conceived for given wage rates (derived from the labour market), interest and discount rates. Labour supply depends on the allocation of fixed-time resources of households into leisure and work. A rather high labour supply elasticity is assumed in these simulations to reflect an availability of labour. Given households' total consumption, the model determines the derived demand for goods and services. The allocation mechanism is flexible, price dependent and considers durable and nondurable goods. Nondurable goods are associated with consumption purposes (food, culture, and so on). Durable goods include cars, heating systems and electrical appliances, and their use involves demand for nondurable goods, for example, energy (see Conrad and Schröder 1991).

Government behaviour is largely exogenous. The government demands consumption goods and services and requires capital goods to form public investment. Following the SAM definitions, the model distinguishes between several categories of public revenues, covering a variety of taxes and other policy instruments. Public transfers to economic agents are also represented according to the SAM definitions. For example, the government allocates transfers for social policy and receives social security contributions.

The demand for products by the consumers, the producers and the public sector (for consumption and investment) constitutes total domestic demand. This domestic demand is allocated between domestic products and imported products, following the Armington specification (see Armington 1969). In this specification, sectors and consumers use, under cost minimization, a composite commodity which combines domestically produced goods and imported goods, which are considered to be imperfect substitutes. The minimum unit cost of the composite good determines its selling price. This is formulated through a CES unit cost function, involving the selling price of the domestic good, which is determined by goods market equilibrium, and the price of imported goods, which is taken as an average over countries of origin. By applying Shephard's Lemma (see Shephard 1953), we derive the total demand for domestically produced goods and for imported goods. In GEM–E3, imports are further allocated by the country of origin, depending on their relative export prices. Dual unit-cost formulation is used throughout.

The supplier of domestically produced goods faces two markets: the domestic and the foreign. We assume that, in order to maximize one's profits, one can apply different prices according to the nature of these two markets. We introduce an export supply function to reflect the producer's decision on the optimal mix of goods offered to the domestic market and goods offered to the world market, following a constant elasticity of transformation (CET) function operating under profit maximization.

The model does not cover the whole planet and thus the behaviour of the rest of the world (ROW) is left exogenous: imports demanded by the ROW depend on export prices set up by the EU countries, while exports from the ROW to the EU are sold at an exogenous price. The imports demanded by the ROW are flexibly satisfied by exports originating from the EU countries. The latter consider the profitability of exporting to the ROW, exporting to other EU countries or selling the goods to their domestic markets. Via these profitability considerations, the EU countries set their export prices, as mentioned above. Within the EU, exports are considered homogeneous. This means that the producer sets a single export price for EU countries and another export price for the ROW. Imports demanded by the EU countries from the ROW are supplied by the latter flexibly. However, the EU countries consider the optimal allocation of their total imports over the countries of origin, according to the relative import prices. Each country buys imports at the prices set by the supplying countries following their export supply behaviour. Of course, the supplying countries may gain or lose market shares according to their price setting. When importing, the EU countries compute an index of mean import price according to their optimal allocation by country of origin. This mean import price is then compared to the domestic prices in order to allocate demand between imports and domestic production (this corresponds to the Armington assumption).

The model ensures analytically that the balance of the trade matrix in value and the global Walras law are verified in all cases. A trade flow from one country to another matches, by construction, the inverse flow. The model ensures this symmetry in volume, value and deflator.

Income flows between agents, following the SAM definitions as mentioned above, and the market equilibrium conditions complete the model. The equilibrium conditions in the markets of goods determine domestic production prices.

For the labour market it is postulated that wage flexibility ensures full employment. On the demand side we have the labour demanded by firms (as derived from their production behaviour), while on the supply side we have the total available time resources of the households minus the households' desire for leisure (which is derived from the maximization of their utility function). The equilibrium condition serves to compute the wage rate.

At the equilibrium point, the economic agents either achieve maximum profit (equal to zero) or completely use their budget constraint. The model then verifies the Walras law at the global level.

The model evaluates the energy-related emissions of CO_2, NO_x and SO_2 as a function of the energy consumption and the abatement level per sector. For SO_2 and NO_x we specify abatement costs which will increase the cost of using pollution-intensive inputs. The cost of energy, as considered in the optimizing behaviour of producers and consumers, consists of the cost of acquiring energy inputs, the costs of abatement equipment and the costs (or revenues) from transacting CO_2 emission permits. Therefore, environmental decisions of economic agents (regarding energy, abatement and pollution permits) are considered simultaneously with non-environmental (that is economic) decisions.

The policy scenarios
As mentioned in the introduction, this chapter focuses on the impact of a coordinated versus a non-coordinated energy/carbon tax policy within the EU. Three alternatives for the imposition of a tax are examined:

1. the imposition of an energy/carbon tax in all EU–12 member states;
2. the imposition of an energy/carbon tax in a core group of countries consisting of Denmark, Germany and the Netherlands; and
3. the imposition of an energy/carbon tax in Germany alone.

In all three scenarios the tax revenues are completely compensated *ex post* by a reduction of the rate of social security contributions of employers. This reduction operates uniformly in all sectors. The energy/carbon tax follows the 1992 proposal set by the European Commission. The tax is a 50–50 per cent mix of carbon and energy tax, globally at the level of $10/barrel of oil equivalent. Thus, the imposition differs by fuel according to the related CO_2 emissions only partially. There is a specific tax on electricity and the electricity sector has to pay only the carbon share of the tax on the fossil fuels burned. The tax is imposed gradually over three model periods ($3.3/barrel, $6.6/barrel and $10/barrel), and kept constant for the rest of the model simulation period. It takes the form of an excise tax, added to the existing taxes.

In all simulations we assume that the trade balance of each country and of the EU as a whole is not necessarily balanced.

The scenarios results

Scenario 1: introduction of the tax in all EU countries

Environmental and macroeconomic impacts. The implementation of the tax, associated with the recycling strategy, has a positive impact on the environment and, in most countries, a positive impact on the macroeconomic aggregates as well. The emissions of pollutants are reduced by 11 per cent for CO_2, 7 per cent for NO_x and 15 per cent for SO_2 (see Table 5.1). This decrease is largely due to the decrease of energy consumption and to fuel switching away from solid fuels.

Per country, the reduction of CO_2 emissions ranges from 18 per cent in Greece, 15 per cent in Belgium, 13 per cent in Germany and the Netherlands to about 10 per cent in Denmark, Italy, Ireland and the UK after 10 years. The increase in GDP ranges from 0.5 per cent in countries such as Belgium, the Netherlands and Portugal to 0.3 per cent or less for the UK, Spain, Germany, France, Ireland and Italy. It is only negative for Greece. In most countries the impact on private consumption is slightly higher with the exception of Greece, Italy and the UK where, on the contrary, the impact is smaller. The positive impact on domestic income through the increase in labour and real wages more than compensates for the negative impact of the policy measure on the costs and prices and hence on demand. Exports, however, decrease in nearly all countries (see Table 5.2).

Labour market and production structure. The tax and the associated decrease in the social security contribution changes the relative prices of the production factors, resulting in substitutions in favour of labour and

Table 5.1 Total emissions for the European Union as a whole

	Period 1	Period 2	Period 3	Period 6	Period 10
CO_2	−7.5	−10.2	−11.2	−11.2	−11.3
NO_x	−4.9	−6.6	−7.3	−7.4	−7.4
SO_2	−9.8	−13.2	−14.6	−14.6	−14.7

Table 5.2 Economic impact in the long run (% change from baseline)

	GDP	Private consumption	Private investment	Exports
Belgium	0.6	1.2	0.5	−0.7
Germany	0.2	0.2	−0.5	−0.2
Denmark	0.3	0.7	0.2	−0.5
France	0.1	0.3	−0.1	−0.6
Greece	−0.2	−0.5	−0.6	0.0
Ireland	0.1	0.9	0.0	−0.7
Italy	0.1	0.0	−0.2	−0.4
Netherlands	0.4	0.5	0.0	−0.3
Portugal	0.5	0.6	0.1	−0.7
Spain	0.3	0.7	0.1	−0.7
UK	0.3	0.1	−0.3	0.0

away from energy. Moreover, as labour becomes more competitive with respect to the other production factors such as capital, it implies a slow-down of investment, which in some countries is compensated for by the demand effect.

In all countries, the final impact on labour is positive, although it remains rather small, especially in countries such as Greece and Ireland where substitution possibilities are more limited (see Table 5.3).

Table 5.3 Changes in employment (absolute difference in thousand employed persons)

	Period 1	Period 2	Period 3	Period 6	Period 10
Belgium	12	22	35	35	34
Germany	47	89	142	141	139
Denmark	5	9	15	15	15
France	21	39	62	62	61
Greece	2	3	4	3	4
Ireland	1	2	4	4	4
Italy	19	37	58	57	55
Netherlands	15	28	44	44	44
Portugal	13	25	40	40	41
Spain	32	57	90	92	93
UK	47	90	142	138	137
EU Total	213	403	637	629	626

This substitution towards labour leads to a slight revaluation of the real wage by approximately 0.8 per cent, which induces an increase in the income of households and hence a positive effect on private consumption. The positive impact occurs, provided that the degree of labour supply flexibility is significant; when the labour supply elasticity (assumed to be rather high in these simulations) is decreased, the increase in employment is also reduced. A less competitive labour market, with real wage stickiness, could also lead to more negative employment results (see Proost and Van Regemorter 1995).

To provide an order of magnitude of the importance of the tax revenues and of the reduction in the social security rate, Table 5.4 reproduces the total revenue from the energy/carbon tax as a percentage of GDP and the *ex post* reduction in the social security rate for the different countries.

The substitution of energy in production induces a decrease in industrial energy consumption, which is reinforced by the shift of the demand from energy-intensive goods to consumer goods and services (see Table 5.5).

External trade. Trade competitiveness deteriorates in all EU countries: there is a decrease of exports ranging from 0.7 per cent in countries such as Belgium, France, Ireland, Portugal and Spain to 0.1 per cent in Germany, Greece and the UK (see Table 5.6). This loss in competitiveness is, however,

Table 5.4 Tax revenues and change in the social security rate

	Revenues from the tax (as % of GDP) (absolute difference)	Ex post reduction in social security rate (in % points)
Belgium	1.7	4.2
Germany	1.4	3.6
Denmark	1.3	4.0
France	0.9	1.5
Greece	0.8	0.9
Ireland	1.6	3.2
Italy	1.1	1.4
Netherlands	1.4	3.7
Portugal	1.6	4.7
Spain	1.2	2.9
UK	1.6	3.4

Table 5.5 Energy consumption (% change from baseline)

	Period 1	Period 2	Period 3	Period 6	Period 10
Belgium	−1.2	−2.2	−3.4	−3.5	−3.6
Germany	−1.7	−3.2	−4.9	−5.0	−5.1
Denmark	−1.1	−2.1	−3.3	−3.4	−3.4
France	−1.0	−1.9	−3.0	−3.0	−3.1
Greece	−1.2	−2.4	−3.8	−3.9	−3.8
Ireland	−1.4	−2.6	−4.1	−4.1	−4.2
Italy	−1.1	−2.1	−3.3	−3.4	−3.4
Netherlands	−1.2	−2.3	−3.8	−3.9	−4.0
Portugal	−1.8	−3.4	−5.4	−5.4	−5.5
Spain	−1.2	−1.8	−2.9	−2.9	−3.0
UK	−0.9	−1.9	−3.0	−3.1	−3.2

Table 5.6 External trade impact in the long run

	Current account (% GDP) (absolute difference)	Terms of trade (% difference)
Belgium	0.4	0.9
Germany	0.2	0.1
Denmark	0.3	0.8
France	0.1	0.8
Greece	0.1	−0.4
Ireland	0.5	1.1
Italy	0.2	0.4
Netherlands	0.2	0.0
Portugal	0.5	1.0
Spain	0.2	1.0
UK	0.1	−0.4

partly compensated by the improvement in the terms of trade. The trade balance also benefits from the decrease in energy consumption which is mainly imported in most EU countries. Therefore the change in the current account in terms of GDP is positive, although small. If a more competitive export market is assumed (by increasing the price sensitivity of exports), the exports and employment effects will be reduced. Moreover, in these simulations, the behaviour of the ROW is assumed to be exogenous, without reaction on their side to the policy implemented in the EU.

The sectoral impacts. The change in the relative cost structure produces a shift in demand from energy-intensive products to consumer goods and private services, as illustrated by the change in production reproduced in Table 5.7. The decrease in the production of the energy-intensive sectors is higher than the decrease in domestic demand, indicating that carbon leakage towards the ROW also contributes to the reduction of CO_2 emissions in the EU.

This simulation with GEM–E3 shows that implementing an energy/carbon tax, as proposed by the EU in 1992, with the recycling of the tax revenue through a decrease of the employers' social security contribution, can have a positive impact on the environment without too much adverse effect on the economy. There is a loss in competitiveness but partly compensated by the improvement of terms of trade.

Non-coordinated scenarios: introduction of the tax in a core group of countries, Denmark, Germany and the Netherlands, or in Germany alone.
The impact of the tax on the economy and the environment of the countries involved is rather similar to that of the previous scenario for the countries involved: positive on the environment, with a reduction of approximately 10 per cent in the CO_2 emissions, and on employment with an average increase of 0.6 per cent, with only small adverse effects on other variables. The impact on the non-involved EU countries is negligible: they do not gain from the unilaterally imposed energy/carbon tax (see Table 5.8).

Table 5.7 Sectoral production in volume in the long run (% change from baseline)

	Agriculture	Energy-intensive industries	Equipment goods	Consumer goods	Transport and communications	Private services
Belgium	−0.2	−0.7	−0.1	0.2	−0.2	0.8
Germany	−0.3	−0.8	−0.2	0.0	−0.1	0.0
Denmark	−0.2	−0.5	0.0	0.0	−0.4	0.3
France	−0.1	−0.7	−0.3	0.0	−0.4	0.1
Greece	−0.3	−0.7	−0.7	−0.3	−0.5	−0.5
Ireland	−0.3	−0.6	−0.2	−0.3	−0.4	0.3
Italy	−0.2	−0.7	−0.2	−0.1	−0.4	−0.1
Netherlands	−0.2	−0.5	0.0	0.1	−0.7	0.4
Portugal	−0.1	−0.9	−0.1	0.1	−1.0	0.3
Spain	−0.1	−0.9	−0.2	0.1	−0.5	0.4
UK	−0.1	−0.5	−0.2	0.0	−0.2	0.0

Table 5.8 Economic impact in the long run (% change from baseline)

	GD		Private consumption		Private investment		Exports	
	Core	Germany	Core	Germany	Core	Germany	Core	Germany
Belgium	0.0	0.0	0.0	0.0	0.0	0.0	−0.1	0.0
Germany	0.2	0.2	0.3	0.5	−0.4	−0.3	−0.2	−0.4
Denmark	0.3	0.0	0.7	0.0	0.2	0.0	−0.5	0.0
France	0.0	0.0	0.0	0.0	0.0	0.0	0.0	0.0
Greece	0.0	0.0	0.0	0.0	0.0	0.0	0.0	0.0
Ireland	0.0	0.0	0.0	0.0	0.0	0.0	0.0	0.0
Italy	0.0	0.0	0.0	0.0	0.0	0.0	0.0	0.0
Netherlands	0.5	0.0	0.8	0.0	0.1	0.0	−0.3	0.0
Portugal	0.0	0.0	0.0	0.0	0.0	0.0	0.0	0.0
Spain	0.0	0.0	0.0	0.0	0.0	0.0	0.0	0.0
UK	0.0	0.0	0.0	0.0	0.0	0.0	0.0	0.0

There is a slightly greater deterioration of the trade competitiveness of the countries, especially when Germany alone implements the tax, but this is compensated for by a further improvement of the terms of trade. The revenue from the tax remains of the same order of magnitude, allowing a similar reduction in the social security rate in all scenarios (see Table 5.9). This, associated with the rather low competitiveness in the export market, is the main explanation for the similarity of results between the three scenarios.

Table 5.9 Tax revenues and change in the social security rate

	Revenues from the tax (as % of GDP) (absolute difference)		Ex post reduction in social security rate (in % points)	
	Core countries	Germany	Core countries	Germany
Belgium	0.0	0.0	0.0	0.0
Germany	1.4	1.2	3.7	3.3
Denmark	1.3	0.0	4.0	0.0
France	0.0	0.0	0.0	0.0
Greece	0.0	0.0	0.0	0.0
Ireland	0.0	0.0	0.0	0.0
Italy	0.0	0.0	0.0	0.0
Netherlands	1.4	0.0	3.9	0.0
Portugal	0.0	0.0	0.0	0.0
Spain	0.0	0.0	0.0	0.0
UK	0.0	0.0	0.0	0.0

Conclusion

Comparing the effect of an energy/carbon tax when implemented in the whole EU, in a core group of countries or in a single country (Germany), it appears that the gains for the environment and for employment remain largely unaffected. The non-coordinated implementation of the energy/carbon tax does not deteriorate the country position compared to the coordinated case. However, these results are dependent on the assumptions regarding the flexibility of the labour supply, the functioning of the labour market and the competitiveness in the external market. These assumptions must, therefore, be more fully examined. Moreover, the GEM–E3 model is under continuous development. These results must be considered to be very preliminary and will be subject to further evaluation.

Notes

1   The GEM–E3 model was built under the auspices of the European Commission (DG–XII, coordinator P. Valette), by a consortium involving NTUA (coordinator), KULeuven, Mannheim University, CORE, Strathclyde University and CEA.
2   For a more detailed discussion of the 'double dividend' policy issue, see Bovenberg and Van der Ploeg (1994), Goulder (1995), Proost and Van Regemorter (1995) and Capros et al. (1996).

References

Ando, A., F. Modigliani, R. Rasche and S. Turnofsky (1974), 'On the role of expectations of price and technological change in investment function', *International Economic Review*, **15** (2), June, 384–414.
Armington, P.S. (1969), 'A theory of demand for products distinguished by place of production', *International Monetary Fund Staff Papers*, IMF, Washington, DC.
Bergman, L. (1990), 'General equilibrium effects of environmental policy: a CGE-approach', Discussion Paper, Stockholm School of Economics, Stockholm.
Bourguignon, F., W.H. Branson and J. De Melo (1989), 'Macroeconomic adjustment and income distribution: a macro–micro simulation model', Working Paper, appeared also as 'Adjustment and income distribution', Working Paper, World Bank, May.
Bovenberg, L., and F. Van der Ploeg (1994), 'Environmental policy, public finance and the labour market in a second best world', *Journal of Public Economics*, **55**, 349–90.
Capros, P., T. Georgakopoulos, S Zografakis, S. Proost, D. Van Regemorter, K. Conrad, T. Schmidt and Y. Smeers (1996), 'Double dividend analysis: first results of a general equilibrium model (GEM–E3) linking the EU–12 countries', in C. Carraro and D. Siniscalco (eds), *Environmental fiscal reform and Unemployment*, Boston, MA: Kluwer Academic Publishers, pp. 193–228.
Capros, P., P. Karadeloglou and G. Mentzas (1991), 'Market imperfections in a general equilibrium framework: an empirical analysis', *Economic Modelling*, January, **8** (1), 116–28.
Conrad, K. and M. Schröder (1991), 'Demand for durable and nondurable goods, environmental policy and consumer welfare', *Journal of Applied Econometrics*, **6**, 271–86.
De Melo, J. (1988), 'Computable general equilibrium models for trade policy analysis in developing countries: a survey', *Journal of Policy Modeling*, **10** (4), 469–503.
Goulder, L.H. (1995), 'Environmental taxation and the double dividend: a reader's guide', *International Tax and Public Finance*, **2** (2), 157–84.
Jorgenson, D.W. and P.J. Wilcoxen (1990), 'Environmental regulations and U.S. economic growth', *Rand Journal of Economics*, Summer, **21** (2), 314–40.
Lluch, C. (1973), 'The extended linear expenditure system', *European Economic Review*, **4**, 21–31.

Proost, S. and D. Van Regemorter (1995), 'The double dividend and the role of inequality aversion and macroeconomic regimes', *International Tax and Public Finance*, **2** (2), 207–20.

Shephard, R.W. (1953), 'Cost and production functions', Lecture Notes in Economics and Mathematical Systems, Berlin, New York: Springer-Verlag.

Shoven, J.B. and J. Whalley (1984), 'Applied general equilibrium models of taxation and international trade: an introduction and survey', *Journal of Economic Literature*, **22**, September, 1007–51.

Appendix 5A1: Nomenclature GEM–E3

a. All European Union countries, separately and linked.

b. Eleven products and sectors:
  - agriculture;
  - four energy branches (electricity, oil, gas and coal);
  - three industrial branches (energy-intensive, equipment goods and consumer goods industries);
  - transport;
  - two services, namely market and public services.

c. Four economic agents: households; firms; government; foreign sector.

d. Several government revenue and income flow categories:
  - direct taxation, indirect and VAT taxation;
  - energy and environmental taxation;
  - property taxes, capital taxes;
  - social security, social benefits;
  - subsidies (production and exports);
  - import duties and foreign sector transfers;
  - revenues from government enterprises.

e. Thirteen household expenditure categories:
  - nine nondurable consumption categories (food, culture, health, electricity, gas, motor fuels, other fuels, transport, house);
  - three durable consumption categories (cars, heating systems, electrical appliances);
  - investment in dwellings.

f. Two primary production factors: labour; capital.

g. Three pollutants: CO_2, SO_2, NO_x.

Appendix 5A2: Results from GEM–E3

- Dynamic annual projections in volume, value and deflators of national accounts by country.
- Full input–output tables by country and for EU–12 as a whole, for the eleven sectors.
- Distribution of income and transfers in the form of a social accounting matrix by country.
- Employment, capital, investment by country and sector.
- Atmospheric emissions, pollution abatement capital, purchase of pollution permits and damages.
- Consumption matrix by product and investment matrix by ownership branch.
- Public finance, tax incidence and revenues by country.
- Full trade matrix for EU–12 and the ROW.

The current version of GEM–E3 evaluates about 38 000 simultaneous equations per year, and follows a time-forward path.

The solution algorithm uses a combination of Gauss–Seidel and Newton Successive Over-Relaxation methods.

The model uses the SOLVER/NTUA modelling software (version 1.9) and operates in MS–WINDOWS.

Appendix 5A3: GEM–E3 model equations: a simplified presentation

Domestic supply of goods and services

$$XD_i = CES(XI_i^j, K_{i,t}, L_i, e^{it}) \tag{5A3.1}$$

where XD_i is domestic supply of good i by sector i, XI_i^j is intermediate consumption of good j by sector i, $K_{i,t}$ is capital stock (fixed within the current period t), L_i is labour force, e^{it} denotes technical progress which is separately embedded in each production factor and CES is a constant elasticity of substitution functional form;

$$P_i \frac{\partial XD_i}{\partial XI_i^j} = PI_i^j \text{ computing } XI_i^j \tag{5A3.2}$$

where P_i is the selling price of good i and PI_i^j is the purchasing price of good j used as intermediate consumption by sector i;

$$P_i \frac{\partial XD_i}{\partial L_i} = PL_i \text{ computing } L_i \tag{5A3.3}$$

where PL_i is the unit cost of labour force used by sector i;

$$P_i XD_i = \sum_j PI_i^j XI_i^j + PL_i L_i + PK_i K_i \text{ computing } PK_i \tag{5A3.4}$$

where PK_i is the effective rate of return of capital of sector i.

Sectoral investment

$$K_{i,t} = \text{fixed from previous period} \tag{5A3.5}$$

$$\overline{K_{i,t}} \text{ derived from } P_i \frac{\partial XD_i}{\partial K_{i,t}} = PINV_i(r + \delta_i) \tag{5A3.6}$$

where $\overline{K_{i,t}}$ is the desired stock of capital, $PINV_i$ is the unit cost of investment of sector i, r is the market interest rate and δ_i is the replacement rate of capital stock in sector i;

$$INVV_i = \mu(\overline{K_{i,t}} - K_{i,t}) = \mu K_{i,t} \cdot f\left(\frac{PK_i}{PINV_i(r + \delta_i)}\right) \tag{5A3.7}$$

where $INVV_i$ denotes investment of sector i;

$$K_{i,t+1} = K_{i,t}(1 - \delta_i) + INVV_i \tag{5A3.8}$$

where $K_{i,t+1}$ denotes capital stock available in the next period;

$$INVF_i^j = tcf_i^j INVV_i \tag{5A3.9}$$

where $INVF_i^j$ denotes the purchases of good j to be used in the formation of the investment of sector i and tcf_i^j is a technical coefficient (investment matrix).

Behaviour of households

$$\max U = \sum_t (1 + \rho)^{-t} LES(HCT, LJ)$$

$$\text{s.t. } \sum_t (1 + r)^{-t} (PC \cdot HCT + PJ \cdot LJ) = \tag{5A3.10}$$

$$\sum_t (1 + r)^{-t} [HTRA + PJ \cdot LH \cdot (1 - \tau i)]$$

where U denotes intertemporal utility of households, r is the subjective rate of time preferences, *LES* denotes a functional form of linear expenditure system, *HCT* is total consumption of households, *LJ* denotes leisure of households, *PC* is the deflator of households' consumption, *PJ* is the unit value of leisure (equal to net wage rate), *HTRA* denotes income transfers from government to households (for example social benefits), *LH* denotes total time resources of households (defined for example as the product of total population by the number of working hours per year) and τi is the rate of direct income taxation; in this equation, $HTRA + PJ \cdot LH \cdot (1 - \tau i)$ represents total potential income inclusive of the valuation of leisure at a labour market rate.

Households' demand and leisure

$$PC \cdot HCT = f\left[\tfrac{\bar{r}}{\rho}, HTRA + PJ \cdot LH(1 - \tau_{zi})\right] \text{ computing } HCT \tag{5A3.11}$$

$$PC \cdot LJ = f\left[\tfrac{r}{\rho}, HTRA + PJ \cdot LH(1 - \tau i)\right] \text{ computing } LJ \tag{5A3.12}$$

where $f(\ )$ are the demand functions derived from the mathematical programming problem expressed in (5A3.10).

Allocation of households' wealth

$$Savings = HTRA + PJ \cdot (LH - LJ) \cdot (1 - \tau i) - PC \cdot HCT \tag{5A3.13}$$

where *Savings* denotes gross savings of households; in this equation,
$[HTRA + PJ \cdot (LH - LJ) \cdot (1 - \tau i)]$
represents total available income without including the valuation of leisure;

$$Wealth_t = Wealth_{t-1} + Savings \tag{5A3.14}$$

where $Wealth_t$ denotes the stock of tangible and intangible assets held by households in current period;

$$House = f\left(Wealth_t, \frac{PHOUS}{r^\alpha}\right) \tag{5A3.15}$$

where *House* is the desired stock of dwellings, *PHOUS* is the unit cost of dwellings and r^α is the anticipated mean rate of return from monetary assets;

$$INVHT = \Delta (House) \tag{5A3.16}$$

where *INVHT* is investment in dwellings and Δ denotes change in the stock of dwellings including replacement;

$$INVH_i = tch_i \cdot INVHT \tag{5A3.17}$$

where $INVH_i$ denotes purchasing of good *i* used to form investment in dwellings and tch_i is a technical coefficient.

Households' consumption allocation

$$HC_i = LES \left(HCT, \frac{PHC_i}{PC} \right) \tag{5A3.18}$$

where HC_i stands for consumption of good *i* purchased by households at a price PHC_i;

$$PC = \frac{\sum_i PHC_i HC_i}{\sum_i HC_i} \tag{5A3.19}$$

Supply of labour force

$$L\_Supply = LH - LJ \tag{5A3.20}$$

where *L_Supply* denotes supply of labour force;

$$PJ = PL \cdot (1 - \tau s) \tag{5A3.21}$$

where τs is the rate of social security contribution and *PL* is the wage rate of equilibrium;

$$PL_i = PL. \tag{5A3.22}$$

Government behaviour

$$HTRA = \alpha \cdot Pop \tag{5A3.23}$$

social benefits depend on total population

$$GC_i = tcgc_i \cdot GCT \tag{5A3.24}$$

where GC_i denotes consumption of good *i* within total public consumption *GCT* (exogenous), and $tcgc_i$ is a technical coeffificient;

$$INVG_i = tcg_i \cdot INVGT \tag{5A3.25}$$

where $INVG_i$ denotes purchasing of good i to form public investment $INVGT$ (exogenous) and tcg_i is a technical coefficient.

Absorption, domestic demand and imports

$$Y_i = \sum_i Xi_j^i + HC_i + GC_i + \sum_j INVF_j^i + INVH_i + INVG_i \qquad (5A3.26)$$

where Y_i denotes total domestic consumption of good i;

$$PY_i = CES(PXD_i, PIMPT_i) \qquad (5A3.27)$$

where PY_i stands for the absorption price of good i in domestic demand, PXD_i is the price of good i addressed by domestic firm of sector i to domestic demand and $PIMPT_i$ is the price of importing good i computed as an average over all trading partners (other countries);

$$\frac{XXD_i}{Y_i} = \frac{\partial PY_i}{\partial PXD_i} \quad \text{computing } XXD_i \qquad (5A3.28)$$

where XXD_i, standing for domestically produced good i for domestic use, is evaluated by applying Shephard's Lemma to unit cost function (5A3.27);

$$\frac{IMPT_i}{Y_i} = \frac{\partial PY_i}{\partial PIMPT_i} \quad \text{computing } IMPT_i \qquad (5A3.29)$$

where $IMPT_i$, standing for total imports of good i, is evaluated by applying Shephard's Lemma to unit cost function (5A3.27).

Demand for domestic goods and export supply

$$XD_i\_Demand = CET(XXD_i, EXPT_i) \qquad (5A3.30)$$

where XD_i_Demand stands for demand for good i addressed to domestic production, $EXPT_i$ stands for total exports of good i and CET denotes a constant elasticity of transformation functional form;

$$P_i \frac{\partial XD_i}{\partial XXD_i} = PXD_i \text{ computing } PXD_i \qquad (5A3.31)$$

$$P_i \frac{\partial XD_i}{\partial EXPT_i} = PEX_i \text{ computing } PEX_i \qquad (5A3.32)$$

where PEX_i denotes domestic supply price of good i addressed to exports.

Foreign trade

In equation below, μ and v denote the countries. Index μ refers to EU countries, while index v also includes the ROW.

$$PIMPT_i^\mu = CES\,(PIMP_i^{\mu,v}, \forall v) \qquad (5A3.33)$$

where $PIMPT_i^\mu$ denotes price of total imports of good i demanded by country μ, $PIMP_i^{\mu,v}$ denotes price of good i of country μ originating from country v; $PIMPT_i^\mu$ is the same as $PIMPT_i$ used in other equations;

$$\frac{IMP_i^{\mu,v}}{IMPT_i^\mu} = \frac{\partial PIMPT_i^\mu}{\partial PIMP_i^{\mu,v}} \quad \forall v \neq RW \qquad \text{computing } IMP_i^{\mu,v} \qquad (5A3.34)$$

where $IMPT_i^\mu$ denotes imports of good i demanded by country μ, $IMP_i^{\mu,v}$ denotes imports of good i of country μ originated from country v; $IMPT_i^\mu$ is the same as $IMPT_i$ used in other equations;

$$IMP_i^{RW,\mu} = f\left(\frac{PRW_i}{PEX_i^{\mu,RW}}\right) \qquad (5A3.35)$$

where $IMP_i^{RW,\mu}$ denotes imports of good i of the ROW originating from country μ, PRW_i is the exogenous price of good i set by the ROW and $PEX_i^{\mu,RW}$ is the export price of good i set by country μ for exports to the ROW;

$$EXP_i^{\mu,v} \cdot PEX_i^{\mu,v} \cdot Ex^\mu \cdot (1 + \tau d_i^{v,\mu}) = IMP_i^{v,\mu} \cdot PIMP_i^{v,\mu} \cdot Ex^v \text{ computing } EXP_i^{\mu,v} \qquad (5A3.36)$$

where Ex^μ is the nominal exchange rate of country μ converting national currency to an international one (for example, ECU) and $\tau d_i^{v,\mu}$ is the rate of custom duties applied to imports;

$$EXPT_i^\mu = \sum_v EXP_i^{\mu,v} \qquad (5A3.37)$$

where $EXPT_i^\mu$ is total exports of good i from country μ (same as $EXPT_i$ used in other equations) and $EXP_i^{\mu,v}$ denote exports of good i from country μ to country v;

$$PIMP_i^{\mu,v} = PEX_i^{\mu,v} (1 + \tau d_i^{v,\mu}) Ex^\mu / Ex^v \qquad (5A3.38)$$

$$PEX_i^{\mu,v} = PEX_i^\mu \qquad (5A3.39)$$

indicating that a country μ applies a uniform setting of export prices, independently of country of destination.

Consumption prices and indirect taxation

$$PI_j^i = PY_i + \tau_i \qquad (5A3.40)$$

where τ^i is a rate of indirect taxation (excise tax) imposed on good i;

$$PHC_i = (PY_i + \tau_i) \cdot (1 + vat_i) \tag{5A3.41}$$

where vat_i is a rate of value added tax imposed on good i;

$$PINVP_i = PY_i + \tau_i \tag{5A3.42}$$

$$PINV_j = \Sigma_i tcf^i_j PINVP_i \tag{5A3.43}$$

$$PINVH_i = (PY_i + \tau_i) \cdot (1 + vat_i) \tag{5A3.44}$$

$$PHOUS = \Sigma_i tch_i \cdot PINVH_i \tag{5A3.45}$$

$$PGC_i = PY_i + \tau_i \tag{5A3.46}$$

Surplus or deficit of agents

$$
\begin{aligned}
SURPLUS_G = & \\
\Sigma_i \tau_i \cdot & \left[\begin{array}{l} \Sigma_j XI^i_j + HC_i + GC_i + \\[4pt] \Sigma_j tcf^i_j \cdot INVV_j + INVH_i + INVG_i \end{array} \right] \\
+ & \ \Sigma_i vat_i \cdot \left[(PY_i + \tau_i) \cdot HC_i + (PINVH_i + \tau_i) \cdot INVH_i \right] \\
+ & \ \Sigma_\mu \tau d^\mu_v \cdot PIMPT^{v,\mu}_i \cdot IMP^{v,\mu}_i \\
+ & \ \tau s \cdot \Sigma_i PL_i \cdot Li + \tau i \cdot PJ \cdot (LH - LJ) \\
- & \ HTRA - \Sigma_i (PGC_i \cdot GC_i + PINVP_i \cdot INVG_i) \tag{5A3.47}
\end{aligned}
$$

where $SURPLUS_h$, $\forall h = G, H, F, W$ denote surplus or deficit of, respectively, government, households, firms and foreign sector; it can be verified that the algebraic sum of $SURPLUS_h$ over h is equal to zero;

$$
\begin{aligned}
SURPLUS_H = & \ HTRA + PJ \cdot (LH - LJ) \cdot (1 - \tau i) - PC \cdot \\
& \ HCT - PHOUS \cdot INVHT \tag{5A3.48}
\end{aligned}
$$

$$SURPLUS_F = \Sigma_i PK_i \cdot K_i - \Sigma_i PINV_i \cdot INVV_i \tag{5A3.49}$$

$$SURPLUS_W = \Sigma_i PIMPT_i \cdot IMPT_i - \Sigma_i PEX_i \cdot EXPT_i \tag{5A3.50}$$

Equilibrium of the real side of the model

$$XD_i = XD_i\_Demand \tag{5A3.51}$$

used to evaluate domestic selling prices P_i

$$L\_Supply = \Sigma_i L_i \tag{5A3.52}$$

used to evaluate the wage rate of equilibrium PL.

Expenditures

	Sectors	Factors	Agents	Investment and Stocks	Total expenditure
Goods from Sectors	Intermediate consumption	0	Demand for goods for comsumption and exports	Demand for goods for investment	Total demand for goods
Factors (labour and capital)	Rewarding of factors from value added by sector	0	Income transfer from foreign sources	0	Total factor revenues
Agents	Indirect taxes, VAT, subsidies, duties and imports	Factor payments to agents according to ownership	Income transfers between agents	0	Total income of agents
Gross Savings	0	0	Total revenues minus investment and stocks	0	
Total Revenues	Total supply of goods	Total payments of factors	Total spending of agents	0	

(left margin label: Revenues)

Surplus or Deficit	0	0	Lending (+ or –) capacity by sector (sum = 0)	0

Figure 5A4.1 The social accounting matrix

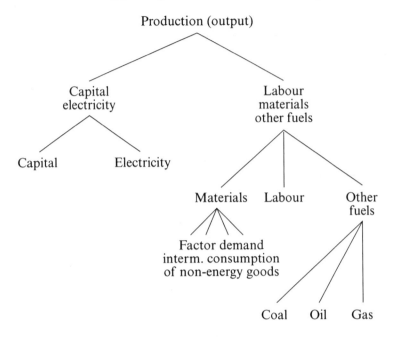

Figure 5A4.2 Domestic production scheme

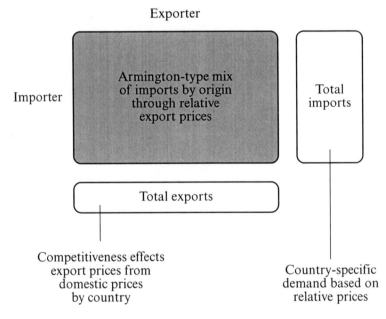

Figure 5A4.3 Trade matrix for the EU and the ROW

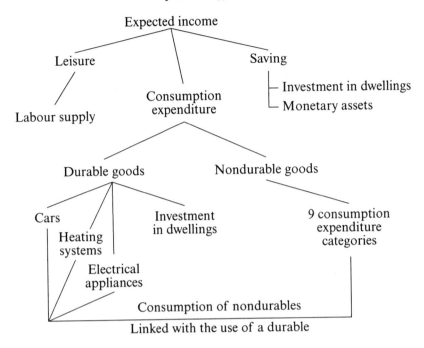

Figure 5A4.4 Household's final consumption

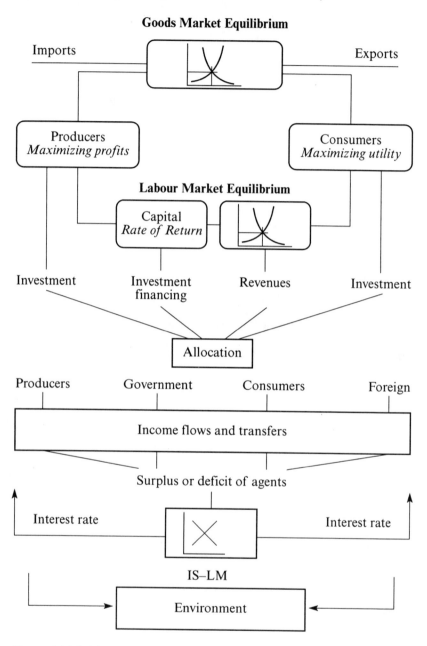

Figure 5A4.5 The general scheme of the model

6. Who's in the driver's seat? Mobile source policy in the US federal system

Winston Harrington, Virginia McConnell and Margaret Walls

Introduction

In the United States, scholars, policy-makers and the American people have debated the appropriate assignment of responsibilities among the multiple layers of government since the time of the Founding Fathers. In theory, the federal system of government should create the opportunity to reach more efficient outcomes than would a unitary system. Local and state governments can make policy decisions that are in the interests of their own citizens without imposing harm on the rest of the country. And when clear national objectives exist, the central government has the power to impose laws or regulations that apply to all citizens. In practice, however, this ideal outcome may not always be achieved.

This chapter describes the assignment of responsibilities for control of motor vehicle emissions and ambient ozone policy among the states and the central government. First, a historical overview of policy-making in the US from the 1970 Clean Air Act to the 1990 Clean Air Act Amendments (CAAA) is presented. The 1970 law introduced a strong federal role in air pollution policy by establishing national air quality goals, but, for the most part, granted states a great deal of latitude in meeting those goals. The 1990 CAAA, in response to the lack of progress towards air quality goals, particularly the ambient ozone goal, took a more prescriptive centralized approach in several important ways. Arguments for and against a centralized approach to ozone policy are presented and some key provisions of the 1990 law are evaluated.

Particular attention is paid to new car emissions standards and motor vehicle inspection and maintenance (I&M) programmes. With the exception of California, which is allowed to have its own (stricter) set of standards, new car standards have always been established at the national level. One of the main arguments for such a centralized approach has been that economies of scale in car production would lead to very high costs in the event of multiple standards. This chapter evaluates this economies of scale argument in the context of current and proposed regulations in the US. The welfare implications of a provision in the CAAA that allows states for the first time to adopt California's stringent standards are assessed. I&M programmes were only suggested by the 1970 law but very rigid I&M requirements were laid out in the 1990 CAAA and subsequently by the US Environmental Protection Agency (EPA). The reasons for this and the efficacy of such an approach are examined. Finally, some conclusions are offered and lessons drawn from the US experience.

Background on federalism and clean air policy in the United States

Those who study the history of the US government find that federalism has taken various forms over the course of the country's existence. Mason (1972) views the period up to 1861 as a period of 'dual federalism', a time when states and the central government each had their own particular responsibilities and acted independently of each other. From 1861 to the New Deal, a gradual centralization occurred. The New Deal then ushered in a new era with central government programmes and regulations growing sharply. At this point, 'intergovernmental relations', or cooperation between the central government and the states, emerged as the new federalism.

As concern about air pollution grew throughout the 1950s and 1960s, it was perhaps no surprise that the federal government took such a strong role in establishing the 1970 Clean Air Act. The Act gave the central government the broad power to set national uniform air quality standards which the states would enforce. States were required to formulate 'State Implementation Plans' (SIPs) that laid out policies they would use to attain those standards. In theory, at least, this approach leaves the door open for states to try many different approaches to reach the standards.[1] There was one exception to this, however: only California was allowed to set its own new car emissions standards; other states had to abide by one set of standards that were written into the law itself.

The approach taken by the CAA of 1970 seemed to work for particulates, sulphur dioxide and carbon monoxide, but not for ozone. Ozone is not emitted directly from motor vehicles and stationary sources but rather is created in the atmosphere by the reaction of volatile organic compounds (VOCs) and nitrogen oxides (NO_x stubbornly high over the 1970s and 1980s despite apparent reductions in VOC and NO_x emissions.[2] With a large portion of VOCs and NO_x in non-attainment areas coming from motor vehicles, Congress focused on those sources in revisions to the 1990 CAAA. New car tailpipe emissions standards were tightened and a host of requirements were imposed on ozone non-attainment areas. These requirements included implementing so-called 'enhanced' I&M programmes, selling reformulated gasoline, instituting 'employee trip reduction' (ETR) programmes, and requiring the use of alternative fuels such as methanol and natural gas in fleet vehicles. The requirements varied across areas by the degree of non-attainment, but the CAAA allowed areas not subject to some of the requirements to 'opt-in' to those requirements.[3] For the first time, it also allowed the most polluted states to adopt California new car emissions standards. These standards are very stringent and are scheduled to become more so in the future with some portion of vehicle sales in each year required to be electric vehicles.[4] In a controversial move, the Ozone Transport Commission (OTC), which governs air quality in the northeastern states, voted in 1994 to request that EPA approve the adoption of the Californian standards in twelve northeastern states and the District of Columbia. EPA gave their approval in December 1994 but also left the door open for an industry-proposed alternative, the so-called '49-state car'. Negotiations between the industry and the northeastern states are continuing.[5]

The 1970 Act and its subsequent amendments were supposed to build a new partnership between the states and central government in which the central government sets standards and the states met and enforced those standards. However, the language of the Act itself in establishing the targets for ambient air quality standards may have set up a conflict between state and central levels of government. The Act requires that ambient air quality standards be set to protect the most sensitive individuals in the population with a margin of safety. This meant that national air quality standards had to be set which would ignore the regional costs of attaining those standards. The national standard is, therefore, not likely to be the standard each of the states would have chosen for itself. Subsequent national regulations including the Clean Water Act of 1972 and the Coastal Zone Management Act did attempt to account for the costs of control or of 'consistency' between national actions and state wishes in establishing regulations. But the Clean Air Act has left itself open to serious enforcement issues as states face national requirements that clearly result in costs exceeding benefits.

The 1994 elections, in which Republicans gained control of both the US Senate and the House of Representatives, may lead to dramatic changes in clean air policy. The rallying cry of the states, which now appears to be falling on sympathetic ears in Congress, is 'no unfunded mandates' from the central government. This movement, along with disastrous starts for enhanced I&M programmes in many states, seems likely to lead to significant environmental policy changes. Whether or not a move towards assignment of more responsibilities to the states and fewer to the central government is a good idea and if so, what those responsibilities should be, is discussed in the following section.

Economic efficiency arguments

Decentralized control

There are many compelling reasons for assigning ozone policy to state and local governments. First, the costs and benefits of clean air can vary geographically for a number of reasons. The costs of reducing ozone in the Los Angeles (LA) area, for example, are very high because the meteorology and topography there create unique conditions conducive to ozone formation. A reduction in emissions in LA does not go as far towards reducing ozone concentrations as does that same reduction elsewhere. This forces LA towards greater reductions at higher marginal costs. The benefits of clean air can vary as well. One obvious way they vary is with population, since a given reduction in ozone in a heavily populated area will generate greater benefits than that same reduction in a less populated area. Moreover, if clean air is a normal good, then the benefits of ozone reduction may be higher in areas with higher levels of income. Since local jurisdictions are best able to judge the costs and benefits of policies to reduce ozone pollution in their own regions, assuming no spillovers (Oates and Schwab 1988), policies should be set at the local level.

Second, society can benefit from having a diversity of public goods available, including varying levels of clean air. Because individuals have different preferences for both public and private goods, when a mix of public goods is available across communities, individuals will choose to live in communities that offer the combination of public goods best suited to their tastes and income (Tiebout 1956). The more diversity there is across communities, the better chance individuals have of finding a community that is right for them.

In principle, it is possible for the national government to account for differences in costs and benefits across regions and establish geographically different policies and regulations. In practice, however, this tends not to occur. Because it is difficult to gather and process information about benefits and costs in many different areas and because the central government is more removed from the problem, regulations from the central government tend towards uniformity. Moreover, in the 1970 Clean Air Act, Congress had a clear national objective in mind: to protect the health of the most sensitive individuals in the population. This led to uniform ambient air quality standards, ruling out consideration of variations in benefits across regions.

Even with a national objective applied to all areas, though, there is still the issue of assigning responsibility for determining appropriate control strategies and for implementing those strategies. Again, the central government can, in principle, account for differences in costs across regions and determine cost-effective strategies. The 1990 CAAA attempted to account for some regional differences in costs by designating regions within broad ozone categories, and then requiring additional and often stricter policies in the more polluted regions. For example, 'enhanced I&M' is only required in areas that are designated as 'serious' ozone non-attainment areas or worse. However, the costs to the national government of determining the most cost-effective regulations for each region, then monitoring and enforcing those regulations, may be quite high. Even though enhanced I&M is required only in the most polluted regions, what is considered enhanced I&M by the EPA was established uniformly for all those regions, in part because of the difficulty in monitoring many different types of programmes.

This leads to a third reason why a decentralized approach may be preferred. Not only are states thought to have better information about their own costs and about what approaches work within their borders, but they are often thought to be more innovative and flexible in finding solutions to problems than the national government. Supreme Court Justice Louis Brandeis stated that: 'it is one of the happy incidents of the federal system that a single courageous State may, if its citizens choose, serve as a laboratory; and try novel social and economic experiments without risk to the rest of the country'.[6] California, and Los Angeles in particular, has served as a laboratory for ozone policy for a number of years. Because of its large size and severe air quality problems, it has been in the interest of Californians to experiment with approaches that the central government (or other smaller states) probably would not have tried. As a result, some of the approaches pioneered by California in the 1980s (for example, ETR programmes and alternative fuels provisions), became part of the broader regulations of the 1990 CAAA. California now seems to be considering more economic incentive approaches such as higher vehicle registration fees and vehicle scrappage programmes. It will be interesting to note to what extent these less costly and more efficient alternatives (see Harrington et al. 1995) end up being adopted by other states or by the central government.[7]

Centralized control

In spite of the arguments suggested above, there are a number of reasons why the central government could play a role in environmental policy to reduce ozone pollution. Most of the arguments for a strong central government role in ozone policy revolve around the issues of spillovers and economies of scale. In the case of ozone control, there is the additional issue that the social welfare goal of the central government may be different from the goal or goals chosen by the state governments. Each of these is discussed below.

Spillovers. First, if VOC and NO_x emissions in one state contribute to ozone in another state, the first state acting alone would fail to account for the spillovers and would not do enough to curb its emissions. In the US, ozone spillovers occur to a significant degree in the northeast corridor and in the Chicago–Milwaukee–Great Lakes region. The importance of spillovers in the northeast led Congress to identify this as a separate region. The CAAA initiated the Ozone Transport Commission (OTC), which now coordinates policy decisions in twelve northeastern states and the District of Columbia.

Second, positive spillovers can be generated from policies themselves and states acting alone will fail to take this into account. It was mentioned above that California has undertaken numerous actions on its own which have eventually been adopted by the central government and by other states. It is widely agreed, for example, that California's stringent new car emissions standards (the ZEV (zero emission vehicle) standard, in particular) are responsible for a rash of new research on electric motors and other alternative propulsion systems and fuels. Although California is evidently large enough to reap positive benefits from acting alone, it is probably doing less than it would if it accounted for policy spillovers. Moreover, smaller states considering these same actions would almost certainly face costs far in excess of benefits unless other states adopt similar policies. This suggests that there may be serious free-rider problems necessitating a role for the central government.

Economies of scale. A related concern about decentralized policy-making has focused on administrative economies of scale. The cost to 50 state governments of gathering information about the costs and effectiveness of different control strategies, then deciding on the exact form that these strategies should take, and finally, implementing, monitoring and enforcing these control strategies could be high, much higher than if some of that effort was expended by the central government and shared with all states. This contrasts with the observation above that state and local governments may be better able to estimate costs and effectiveness of different control strategies since they are closer to the problem than the central government. Both effects could be at work; which one dominates depends on the control strategies being considered.

Production economies of scale have been used as one of the major arguments for central government control, particularly in the area of new car emissions standards. When California and New York established separate sets of standards for emissions in the 1960s, the auto companies argued that it would be very costly to produce vehicles to meet many different standards. They convinced Congress of this point of view and ended up with one set of national uniform emissions standards with the exception of California, which was allowed to have its own more stringent standards (Elliott et al. 1985). In the 1990 CAAA, other states were permitted to adopt the California standards for the first time.

The existence of production economies of scale does not alone justify uniform standards set by the central government. Scale economies imply only that costs will be lower with a uniform standard compared to the case of regionally differentiated standards. Centralized regulation is needed only if it reduces the transactions cost of reaching a uniform standard, or if it permits a different and more socially beneficial uniform standard to be reached than would occur if the states or firms were acting independently.

The problem can be illustrated by assuming that there are two regions, A and B, and one or more manufacturers supplying automobiles to consumers in both markets. If region A sets a strict new car standard, the manufacturers must decide whether to produce separate cars for regions A and B or to produce the cleaner car in both regions. That decision will depend on industry structure, but if there are competitive conditions, price will be equal to average cost, and the firm will have zero-profit in either case and will be indifferent to producing a single car or different cars in the two regions.[8] It is assumed here that rivals will keep prices close to the competitive level, but monopoly pricing is also possible and leads to different conclusions. (The monopoly case is shown in Appendix 6AI.)

Even though firms are indifferent about producing one car or two, the interests of the consumers in the two regions may be divergent. When region A unilaterally decides to raise its emission reduction requirements, and the firm decides to offer a single car for sale in both regions, consumers in region A will clearly be better off as economies of scale make their vehicles less expensive than they otherwise would be. However, if the firm raises the price in region B to recover its average production cost everywhere, it becomes vulnerable to an entrant that will produce cheap, dirty cars for sale there. Fear of entry may thus keep the firm producing two cars for the separate markets, an action which ensures that consumers in B pay the lowest possible prices for vehicles, and no uniform standard by the central government is required.

None the less, the two-car, separate market outcome may be suboptimal once air quality benefits are examined. This possibility is illustrated in Figure 6.1, which shows the demand for vehicles, the costs of vehicle production, and environmental damage from vehicles in region B, the region that did not initiate the clean car. The three cost curves represent the cost per vehicle of the original dirtier car, AC_D, the cost of the cleaner car when both regions A and B adopt it, AC_C^{A+B}, and

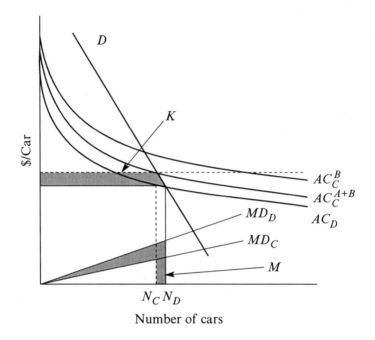

Key

AC_C^B	average cost of producing clean vehicles in region B.
AC_C^{A+B}	average cost of producing clean vehicles in region A+B.
AC_D	average cost of producing dirty vehicles in region B.
MD_C	marginal damage from clean vehicles in region B.
MD_D	marginal damage from dirty vehicles in region B.
N_C	number of cars if clean car adopted.
N_D	number of cars if clean car not adopted.
D	demand for vehicle use.

Figure 6.1 Costs and benefits of additional new car controls

the cost when only region B adopts it, AC_C^B. If clean cars are produced in
both regions, region B faces costs of AC_C^{A+B} and area K represents the loss
in consumer surplus because the region pays higher prices for a cleaner
car compared to the original dirty car. If the loss in consumer surplus is
less than the reduced damages from driving cleaner cars (area M), then
the citizens in region B would be better off with the clean vehicle.

However, there are a number of reasons why region B may not adopt
the stricter standard even though social welfare would be greater if it did.
First, the costs to B will depend on whether region A or other regions are

adopting the standards and that information may be difficult to obtain. From Figure 6.1, regional environmental authorities in region B may not know whether they are facing costs for the clean car of AC_C^{A+B} or AC_C^B. Hence, regions may not adopt, because they do not know who else will adopt, or if they do adopt first, they may try to convince other regions to adopt in order to lower their own costs.[9] Both regions might be better off if the central government stepped in and either made cost information available or set a uniform standard.

A second possibility is the case in which region A adopts the stricter standard first, and region B, based on its own costs and benefits, elects not to adopt. However, region A benefits from lower costs when B adopts. If region A can compensate region B, it becomes efficient for B to adopt. Again, there may be a role for the central government in facilitating side-payments or differential taxes, or even in setting a uniform standard.

The case of monopoly in the car market yields slightly different results (see Appendix 6A1). It appears that regardless of the industry structure, it is difficult and perhaps impossible to come up with simple rules for determining when central government intervention is justified on the basis of production economies of scale. One conclusion is clear: the simple existence of production economies is not *sufficient* to warrant central government involvement. Below, the welfare impacts of adoption of the California new car standards in the rest of the US are considered.

What role for the central government?

Even if it is determined that spillovers and/or economies of scale are significant, it remains to be seen what the central government's role should be. Would it design and implement policies, simply provide information to the states, or give states financial or other incentives to incorporate spillovers? What should be its role with respect to monitoring and enforcement activities?

The existence of spillovers or economies of scale does not mean that a strong decentralized approach must be abandoned in favour of uniform national requirements. For emissions spillovers, it may mean that the central government simply needs to facilitate cooperation and bargaining solutions – such as supporting the OTC's activities in the northeast. It may mean that it goes a step further and sets non-uniform emissions targets that account for spillovers, but it could then leave the design and implementation of control strategies up to states.[10]

Another possibility is the use of selective 'matching grants' from the central government to the states (see Oates 1993). If the central government knows the magnitude of the externality imposed on New York from emissions in Maryland, it can compensate New Yorkers to put up with the externality or, equivalently, it can subsidize Marylanders for increased emissions reductions.

Several provisions of the 1990 CAAA offer opportunity for changes in the role of the central and state governments. We shall examine several of these as examples of current federal issues in the US. First, the Act allows for states other than California to adopt the strict California new car standards. Using estimates of economies of scale in production of the new technology vehicles, the welfare implications when different states or regions adopt the standards can be determined. The appropriate role of the federal government will be examined. We then turn to a brief analysis of the controversy in the US between the federal government and the states over autonomy for vehicle inspection and maintenance programmes.

Federalism, economies of scale and new car emissions standards in the US. New car emissions standards in the US provide an interesting application of the impact of scale economies on the appropriate level of government regulation. The 1990 Amendments to the Clean Air Act required several new rounds of national new car standards and California established its own stricter standards. Table 6.1 summarizes these standards for hydrocarbons (HC) and for nitrogen oxides (NO_x). The federal Tier 1 standards are to be phased in during the mid-1990s and the Tier 2 standards will be required in 2003 if the EPA determines that they are necessary to meet air quality goals.

Table 6.1 National and California new car standards

	Hydrocarbons (g/mile)	Nitrogen Oxides (g/mile)
Federal		
1993 vehicle	0.4	1.0
Tier 1	0.25	0.4
Tier 2 (if necessary)	0.125	0.2
California		
1993 vehicle	0.25	0.4
TLEV	0.125	0.4
LEV	0.075	0.2
ULEV	0.04	0.2
ZEV	0.0	0.0

California's 'low emission vehicle' (LEV) programme, established in 1990, sets an HC standard that becomes stricter in successive years, starting with the 1994 model year (CARB 1990). To be in compliance, each manufacturer must sell vehicles so that average emissions across the fleet (weighted by sales) achieve the specified standards. Manufacturers can produce and certify vehicles with different emission levels: 'transitional low emission vehicles (TLEVs),[6] low emission vehicles' (LEVs), 'ultra low emission vehicles' (ULEVs) and 'zero emission vehicles' (ZEVs),[11] each of whose emission standards are shown in Table 6.1. These vehicles, in combination with new cars meeting the federal standards, can be produced in any combination to meet the average California HC standards. Table 6.2 shows estimates of how manufacturers may choose to achieve these standards to the year 2003. The last column of this table shows the actual California standards.

The 1990 CAAA took a different approach from the earlier legislation and allowed other states or regions to adopt the California standards. The Ozone Transport Commission in the northeastern US has been given approval by EPA to adopt the California standards. In this section, the resulting changes in consumer and producer surplus in California and in the northeast Ozone Transport Region (OTR) from the northeastern states' adoption of the California package are estimated.

Table 6.2 California standards and possible vehicle distribution to meet them (Hydrocarbon emissions %)

| | | | Vehicle certification (grams/mile) | | | | |
| | | | TLEV | LEV | ULEV | ZEV | Average |
Model Year	0.39	0.25	0.125	0.075	0.04	0.00	standard
1994	10	80	10				0.250
1995		85	15				0.231
1996		80	20				0.225
1997		73		25	2		0.202
1998		48		48	2	2	0.157
1999		23		73	2	2	0.113
2000				96	2	2	0.073
2001				90	5	5	0.070
2002				85	10	5	0.068
2003				75	15	10	0.062

Source: Sierra Research, Inc., 'The Cost-Effectiveness of Further Regulating Mobile Source Emissions', Report No. SR94–02–04, 28 February 1994.

As shown above in Figure 6.1, the costs of imposing stricter new car standards in any region will be the resulting change in consumer surplus, which depends on the difference in average costs between new cars with the stricter standards and with existing standards, and the elasticity of demand for new cars. The former depends on the number of other regions adopting the standard. For this analysis, it is assumed that the cost of a new car varies with volume (scale economies) and by type of car. It is also assumed that cars are produced under competitive conditions,[12] and that cars are driven in the region in which they are purchased. Cross-border car sales have not been a serious problem in California to date, because in order to register a car in California, it must comply with California emission standards.

The per vehicle costs of meeting either the national or California standards are uncertain, and there are a wide range of estimated costs.[13] For this analysis, cost estimates from Sierra Research, Inc. (SRI 1994) are used, which are based on data from surveys of car manufacturers. The SRI cost estimates include the equipment, redesign and operating costs required to meet the standards, as well as any additional manufacturer research and development (R&D), overhead and selling costs. The SRI analysis makes the assumption that there will be substantial learning as new technologies are developed, resulting in declining manufacturing costs for any vehicle type over time.[14] The SRI estimates of the average costs over the life of a vehicle in 1993 dollars are shown in Table 6.3.[15]

Table 6.3 Costs and emissions reductions of California new car standards relative to meeting the 1993 national standards

	Emissions Reductions* (lbs over vehicle life)		Costs/vehicle		
	HC	*NO$_x$*	*California only*	*Nationwide*	*California and northeast Ozone Transport Region*
Tier 1	27.17	64.29	284	142	253
TLEV	41.61	65.20	463	344	408
LEV	49.53	86.08	1,019	775	894
ULEV	55.79	86.08	1,116	979	980
ZEV	200.08	247.65	21,034	12,588	12,824

Note: * relative to baseline federal vehicle (per vehicle).

Source: Sierra Research, Inc., 'The Cost-Effectiveness of Further Regulating Mobile Source Emissions', Report No. SR94–02–04, 28 February 1994.

Benefits in any region depend on the emissions reductions from the new car policy, and the value of any resulting air quality improvement. It will be assumed that the marginal emissions reductions over the baseline federal vehicle are the same for each technology type for each pollutant across regions, as shown in Table 6.3. However, the dollar value of any emissions reductions will depend on the type of pollutant and the region, since the link between emissions and air quality varies greatly across regions and times of the year. In regions that are NO_x limited, reductions in VOCs will have little or no impact on ambient ozone, and the benefits of VOC reductions are close to zero. In addition, recent evidence suggests that vehicle emissions of VOC and NO_x may also combine to form aerosol particulates which are more damaging to human health than increased levels of ambient ozone (Hall et al. 1995).

Estimates of the benefits of reduction in car emissions vary over a wide range. The estimates used in this study are drawn from the literature (see Table 6.4). Small and Kazimi (1995) summarize the existing studies and provide average estimates of benefits for California. Sierra Research (1994) also uses estimates from the literature for benefit estimates for the nation as a whole and for various regions. The estimate used for California, $10/pound or $20,000/ton of HC, is a little greater than the average from the Small and Kazimi study and is close to that suggested by Sierra Research. The OTR and rest of the nation benefits estimates are from Sierra Research (1994). These benefits estimates all are high, because they include substantial particulate mortality benefits for NO_x reductions about which there is substantial controversy. Other benefits estimates are much lower (Krupnick and Portney 1991).

To examine the welfare implications of allowing states or groups of states to adopt the California standards, the costs and benefits must be aggregated across all cars in the region.[16] The aggregate costs and benefits of the increasingly tight standards are considered by looking at each year separately.[17] Table 6.5 shows the calculations of the costs and benefits as depicted in Figure 6.1[18] for California and for the nation as a whole for adopting the successively stricter fleet average standards

Table 6.4 Benefits assumptions

Region	Benefit of HC reduction	Source
California	$10/lb	Small and Kazimi (1995) and Sierra Research (1994)
OTR	$3/lb	Sierra Research (1994)
Nation	$1/lb	Sierra Research (1994)

Table 6.5 Costs and benefits of adopting California new car tailpipe standards (relative to 1993 federal vehicle, millions of 1993 dollars)

	California			Entire US	
	Costs if only California adopts	*Costs if entire US adopts*	*Benefits*	*Costs*	*Benefits*
1994	233	126	220	1260	221
1995	265	147	250	1467	250
1996	272	155	256	1554	256
1997	583	420	276	4200	276
1998	909	605	316	6084	314
1999	1066	740	364	7408	362
2000	1209	864	408	8649	406

shown in the last column of Table 6.2. For California acting on its own, the costs and benefits are very close in early years when only a small share of the relatively inexpensive TLEVs are needed to meet the standards. In 1997, when LEVs and ULEVs are introduced, the costs rise dramatically. However, if the entire country were to adopt the stricter standards, California's costs would fall as production economies are realized. The savings are large for California, and for the early years through 1996 during which TLEVs are sold, the benefits exceed costs for California if the clean cars are produced everywhere.

However, if the country as a whole adopts the California standards, even in the early years, the costs outside of California far exceed the benefits. Even if California could make some kind of side-payment to the rest of the country, the net costs to the rest of the country would still be quite high. It is important to note here, as discussed above, that the national ambient air quality standards reflect a health standard, not an efficiency standard. So it is not surprising that the costs may exceed the benefits. It is also not surprising, given these estimates, that many states might not implement these standards unless required to do so.

We now turn to another debate over new car standards in the US, which is the issue of whether the states in the northeast should adopt the California standards. Table 6.6 shows the results of estimates of the welfare impacts of the California new car standards in California and the Ozone Transport Region (OTR) of the northeastern US. The size of the OTR new car market is about two to three times the size of the California market, so extending the California standards to the OTR provides substantial savings from economies of scale. It is again clear that California

Table 6.6 Costs and benefits of adopting California new car tailpipe standards in California and the Ozone Transport Region (millions of 1993 dollars)

	California			OTR			
	Costs		Benefits	Costs		Benefits	
Year	Only CA adopts	CA and OTR adopt		Only OTR adopts	CA and OTR adopt	No payment from CA	With side-payment
1994	233	183	220	569	447	162	211
1995	265	209	250	646	510	183	239
1996	272	216	256	665	527	187	244
1997	583	480	276	1425	1174	202	305
1998	909	661	316	2221	1620	231	479
1999	1066	791	364	2603	1932	266	540
2000	1209	911	408	2955	2225	298	596

has a strong incentive to try to persuade the OTR to adopt the California standards, since there would be substantial savings to them if the OTR does adopt. According to the estimates, however, costs exceed benefits for the OTR, *even if California were to make a side-payment to the OTR.*

It is striking how costly the standards in the later years are estimated to be when ULEVs and ZEVs must be included in the fleet. The results are even more conclusive, because the benefit estimates used for this analysis are at the high end of current estimates. However, given the way the central government sets ambient air quality standards, to protect the most sensitive individuals, it is not surprising that the costs of policies such as the new car standards are high and often exceed benefits. The most that can be hoped for is that states or regions adopt policies that are *cost-effective* in reaching the air quality goal.

The cost-effectiveness of the California standards in the northeastern OTR, measured as the cost per ton of HC emissions reduced, is $16 500 in the early years (with TLEVs and a few LEVs) without a side-payment from California, and $14 000 with a side-payment. In the later years, when more LEVs and ULEVs are sold, the costs rise to $40 000 to $60 000 per ton of HC reduced.[19] These estimates are higher than the costs of many alternative measures that the OTR could adopt. For example, Krupnick et al. (1993) estimate that a small gasoline tax increase would cost slightly less than $5000 per ton of HC reduced. Alberini et al. (1994) estimate a cost-effectiveness for accelerated vehicle scrappage programmes of less than $6000 per ton. Emissions-based vehicle registration fees look even more promising, with preliminary cost-effectiveness estimates as low as $1650 per ton (Energy and Environmental Analysis 1993).

Public acceptance of such approaches may be difficult, however, and many of the other relatively low-cost options available for reducing emissions, for example, reformulated gasoline and enhanced I&M, are already in place in the northeastern states. More strict fuel reformulation requirements, such as those in California, or requirements for alternative fuel vehicles, could result in very high costs, higher than the $14,000 per ton for the early phases of the California standards. However, currently the OTR cannot adopt only the first phases of the California package. They must adopt the *entire* California package or none of it. This inflexibility means that the OTR will probably not adopt the California standards since taken as a whole they are not cost-effective.[20]

It can be concluded that the policy of allowing California to set separate stricter new car standards is reasonable, since there appears to be evidence that the benefits of emissions reductions in California are high. For TLEVs and LEVs, the benefits are greater than or approximately equal to the costs.[21]

If California adopts first, other states have reasonably good information (given existing technology) about their own costs and benefits for adopting the same standards. Allowing the states the possibility of adoption is a good idea in theory since it merely adds another potential control strategy to their list of available options. In practice, the fact that states must adopt the entire California package is a big drawback. Moreover, allowing a mechanism for side-payments from California to other states is critical. The central government could play an important role in facilitating these payments. Finally, it should be emphasized that new car standards themselves may not be the most cost-effective way to improve air quality. Incentive-based programmes such as gasoline taxes or emissions taxes may give the same result (cleaner new cars) but in a more efficient way.

Inspection and maintenance programmes. Vehicle inspection and maintenance (I&M) programmes provide another interesting case study of the promise and problems of sharing power and responsibility between central and state governments in the US. In the 1977 Clean Air Act Amendments, I&M programmes were required by regions not in compliance with national air quality standards, but their implementation was left entirely to the states. Dissatisfaction with the results of state programmes during the 1980s led Congress and the Environmental Protection Agency to subject the programmes to rigorous design standards as part of the 1990 Amendments to the Clean Air Act. The EPA issued regulations implementing the new I&M policy in late 1992.

Attempts to implement the new regulations have been disastrous. In Maine, Illinois and most recently Maryland, motorists have been subjected to long waits in lines, errors in emissions measurements, and even damage to their vehicles as new I&M programmes were begun before states had worked out how to run them. In other states, including California, Virginia and Pennsylvania, the requirement for a new I&M programme has become a major political issue and a focal point of discontent. The furor has forced the EPA to back off on further implementation, at least temporarily, and to agree to allow the states more flexibility and perhaps more time in the design of I&M programmes.

First-generation I&M programmes. When I&M programmes were first introduced in the US in the late 1970s, under the 1977 Clean Air Amendments, Congress was reacting to the emergence of information indicating a pronounced divergence between new vehicle emission certification and actual in-use emissions. At the time, legislators envisioned emission inspection to be a straightforward extension of state vehicle safety inspection programmes which had also been mandated by federal legislation. Many states, in fact, responded by tacking the I&M test on to the existing safety inspection.

By design or default then, Congress was allowing a quite decentralized approach to I&M. States were given almost no requirements and indeed no direction in the design and implementation of I&M programmes. I&M was allowed to become a laboratory of state innovation and experimentation. There was, however, this important difference: the states were allowed freedom in their choice of means to achieve a set of goals established by the central government, namely, the achievement of ambient air quality standards. The air quality standard set by the central government was probably stricter than many of the states would have chosen. Some states were simply not as committed to air quality goals, especially when it meant they had to implement a programme with highly visible costs. The issue posed by I&M is actually a very common one in the American federal system. It is a principal–agent problem, with the states in the role of agents for the federal government.

The states responded by establishing programmes that varied greatly in their effectiveness and in enforcement. Two types of I&M programmes emerged in the early 1980s: 'centralized' ('test-only') programmes, where inspections were conducted at a relatively small number of large specialized facilities operated by the state or by its franchisee; and 'decentralized' ('test-and-repair') programmes, in which motorists took their vehicles to any of a large number of privately-owned repair shops, garages and auto dealerships certified to conduct emission inspections.

By the late 1980s it had become clear that many of the initial state programmes, on which the EPA had placed such high expectations, were not very effective. The EPA concluded that certain features of state programmes were causing some state programmes to fail and advised Congress to make it difficult for states to continue those features. The lesson drawn by the EPA and Congress from these failures was that it had been a mistake to allow the states such broad flexibility in programme design. When the Clean Air Act was amended in 1990, Congress drastically centralized the programme, directing the EPA to determine where state programmes had failed and to draw up stringent programme guidelines for avoiding or overcoming these failures in the most polluted regions. The new 'enhanced I&M' regulations were to apply to the most polluted non-attainment areas and had to be in place within eighteen months.

Working under this tight deadline, the EPA's 'Office of Mobile Sources' hurriedly cobbled together new regulations. These regulations removed much of the flexibility states had for establishing their own programmes, and substituted uniform requirements on waiver limits, and on the test procedure and the type of test (*Federal Register* 1992).

Waiver limits existed in most states to mitigate the financial impact of I&M on individual motorists. Most state programmes had a maximum limit on the amount (typically $50 to $75) that would have to be spent to bring a vehicle into compliance. In response to a specific provision of the 1990 CAAA, the new regulations required this waiver limit to be at least $450.[22]

To deal with the apparent inadequacy of emission tests, the EPA developed a technically sophisticated emission test protocol that included use of expensive automatic analysers and a dynamometer. It seems likely however that EPA vastly overestimated the importance of the test protocol on I&M programme performance. The EPA 'IM240' test was more accurate than tests then in use in the states, but dynamic simulation of emissions in a fleet of vehicles subject to I&M showed that such an increase in accuracy made remarkably little difference.[23] Simulation results based on EPA assumptions showed far better performance than any state programme was currently experiencing, suggesting that test accuracy was not the critical factor. Even unsophisticated emission tests can identify extremely high emitters, which is where cost-effective emission reductions are found.[24]

Finally, the EPA concluded that decentralized test-and-repair programmes were less effective than centralized, test-only programmes. The new regulations therefore included a provision limiting the emission credits granted a decentralized, test-and-repair programme to 50 per cent of the credits available to a centralized programme. This was by far the most controversial aspect of the new regulations, because in the states with decentralized programmes there were many in the auto repair industry who had become accustomed to and even dependent on the income from those programmes and who became a strong and vocal constituency against EPA attempts at centralization.

The EPA reasoning was that mechanics in test-and-repair stations may have incentives that differ from those of the motorist and those of the enforcement agency. On the one hand, they may have an incentive to fail clean vehicles to make repairs that are not really needed. On the other hand, the mechanics may have incentives to pass vehicles that should fail, as a way of ingratiating themselves to customers and assuring repeat business.[25]

Since 1990 a large number of studies have been carried out that examine more relevant measures of I&M performance and other aspects of on-road emissions. These studies have also begun to suggest why I&M programmes may be more difficult to implement than originally thought. First, the pattern of vehicle emissions is much more complicated. While it is well-known that vehicle emission rates vary substantially at different conditions of speed and acceleration, it also turns out that emissions of some vehicles vary substantially at different times even at the same stage in the driving cycle (Bishop and Stedman 1994). This makes it more difficult to determine whether vehicles are consistent violators in a scheduled lane test, and in particular it makes it difficult to determine whether a gross-emitting vehicle has been repaired. Second, vehicle emissions are concentrated in a small number of gross emitters (Walsh et al. 1994; Lawson et al. 1990; and Lyons and Stedman 1991), such that conventional lane testing of every vehicle inevitably means that most of the vehicles tested are in compliance or nearly so. Third, really gross-emitting vehicles – the tail of the emission distribution – tend to be those that are not well maintained by their owners (Beaton 1995). There is a correlation between emissions and age, but probably because older vehicles are not as well maintained as newer ones. Fourth, vehicle repair is often costly and fails to bring vehicles completely into compliance (Cebula 1994; and Lodder and Livo 1994). Furthermore, there appears to be very little relationship between vehicle repair costs and the emission reductions achieved (California I&M Review Committee 1993). Finally, problem cars belong disproportionately to low-income households, for whom emission repair is difficult (Aroesty et al. 1994).

After nearly 15 years, there is little evidence that I&M programmes have been effective at reducing vehicle emissions. Nonetheless, studies continue to show that I&M programmes have enormous *potential* for substantial and cost-effective emission reductions. The gap between the potential and the performance is what keeps I&M an object of keen interest among policy-makers.

The US experience with I&M suggests that repetition of the policies that have been tried in the past will not produce effective programmes. It is quite clear now what does not work; unfortunately, however, there is much less certainty about what will work. Any successful I&M policy will be one that is largely untested. This means that it is important for the EPA to structure a flexible programme and one which gives states the incentives to experiment with new approaches. Recent research does suggest some policy designs that may deserve further consideration.

1. *Remote sensing.* The fact that excess emissions are highly concentrated in a small number of vehicles suggests that it is costly to subject all vehicles to a periodic lane test. The high variability of vehicle emissions, plus the fact that motorist ingenuity has defeated every periodic test so far, suggest that exclusive reliance on more sophisticated lane tests may not be a useful approach. Remote sensing, which can provide test results that are both inexpensive (on a per-test basis) and unscheduled, may be a way of dealing with these problems. Remote sensing programmes can be designed in a variety of ways, including combining them with more traditional lane tests.
2. *Repair subsidies.* The high cost of repair, coupled with the concentration of polluting vehicles in households that can least afford to repair them, suggest that some public assistance for emission repair might be effective. Subsidy policies are always risky, of course, since they can lead to large giveaways of public money and, once established, are hard to eliminate. Emission repair subsidies have been opposed in the past for these reasons and also because they could be subject to improper targeting. But no one knows how inaccurate the targeting would be. Old car scrap programmes are an alternative to repair subsidies. They can be targeted to the purchase of only the dirty cars by linking them to I&M programmes, but they may provide the wrong incentives to car owners.[26] It is possible that the programme could suffer some inefficiency and still represent an improvement over current approaches.
3. *Emission fees.* High and variable repair costs also suggest some form of emission fee. Under a command-and-control approach, vehicles with the same level of emissions are treated equally: if in violation, both must be fixed, even if the cost of emission reduction is much higher on one vehicle than on the other. Emission fees provide the proper incentive so that only one of the vehicles would be repaired. The main practical objection to emission fees has been its demands for accurate quantitative monitoring information, but the better lane tests and the promise of remote sensing may overcome this problem.

Although each of these ideas has promise, they remain untested. No state will try them as long as it will be punished by the EPA for failure. And yet, any state that does try them will be generating information useful to other states. There is a clear role for the central government here, but it is more concerned with encouraging and evaluating experiments than setting rigid standards.

Conclusions

The strong role of the central government results in more uniform policies, which is a particular problem for ambient ozone where regional variations in ambient ozone are so important. To achieve cost-effective outcomes, allowing flexibility in control strategies is critical. For example, allowing other states to adopt the Californian new car standards as part of the CAAA of 1990 was a step in the right direction. However, the fact that states or regions must adopt the entire package, which includes extremely tight standards in the future, is a serious drawback. Allowing states the flexibility to adopt only parts of the package may be preferred. For example, only TLEVs may be cost-effective outside of California.

In some cases, allowing flexibility is not enough. It must be encouraged. The I&M programme is a good example. Since it is not clear what an effective I&M programme looks like, experimentation by the states could have significant payoffs. It can be strongly argued that the EPA should encourage such experimentation by backing off from some of the strict, uniform I&M requirements.

This raises one of the most important roles for the central government: devising incentives for states to achieve the desired outcomes. This means that there must be some generally accepted way of measuring performance on the basis of empirical results. It also means that in some cases the central government should give states incentives to experiment in order to gather information about what does and does not work. In other cases, matching grants could be used to reward states for achieving emission reduction targets or air quality goals. Finally, the central government should continue to facilitate cooperation between states when there are spillovers. This could include designing a mechanism for side-payments between winners and losers.

Notes

1. Portney (1990) has argued that EPA enforcement of environmental regulations has not given much real flexibility to the states, since if they do not require the EPA 'suggested' technology, they will not get full credit for the emissions reductions. More is said about this with respect to mobile source policy, below.
2. There is some debate about whether VOCs fell by as much as the EPA's emissions models suggest. Many scientists believe, for example, that inventory model estimates of evaporative VOCs were grossly underestimated (Calvert et al. 1993).

3. For example, many areas have chosen to adopt the reformulated gasoline requirement.
4. States that have 'serious', 'severe' or 'extreme' ozone non-attainment areas can petition the EPA to adopt these standards. The standards, described in more detail below, are fleetwide average new car standards that become progressively more stringent over time beginning with the 1996 model year. Manufacturers can meet the fleetwide average with a combination of vehicles meeting so-called 'low emission vehicle' (LEV), 'ultra low emission vehicle' (ULEV) and 'zero emission vehicle' (ZEV) standards. By the year 2003, 70% of vehicles must be ZEVs.
5. The '49-state car' will meet a California LEV emission standard (less than 0.07 grams per mile HC); however, since cars in the rest of the country will use a different gasoline than California, in-use HC emissions are predicted to be about 30 per cent higher. The industry has agreed to sell the cars nationwide beginning in 2001, with some being sold earlier in the northeastern states.
6. *New State Ice Company v. Liebmann*, 285 US 262, 311 (1932).
7. Rose-Ackerman (1981) shows that a single state that imposes a tighter-than-average regulation has an incentive to lobby other states to pass similar regulations. By effecting such regulations, it lowers its own costs.
8. In this simple model it is assumed that rivals can enter the market instantaneously by simply paying the cost of entry. This abstracts from the more realistic situation in which, for example, the cost of entry may be different (and greater) for new entrants or where delays in response to a change in market conditions can give the existing firm an opportunity to earn rents temporarily.
9. California has been pressuring both Massachusetts and New York to maintain their position on requiring a percentage of electric vehicles in the fleet early in the next decade. California is required to have some electric vehicles, and would benefit from other states adopting similar requirements due to economies of scale.
10. Smith (1994) argues against this solution for the countries in the European Union (EU) since monitoring and enforcing compliance becomes very difficult compared to monitoring and enforcing compliance with an EU-determined tax. His argument may hold for carbon emissions where one can tax the pollutant directly, but, since ozone is not directly emitted and its formation is complicated and dependent on local conditions, it may be more efficient to allow for more decentralized control over choice of ozone policies.
11. 'Zero emission vehicles' do not actually have zero emissions when the entire fuel cycle is considered. For example, the generation of electricity for running electric vehicles will result in emissions which will vary with the fuel used.
12. The assumption of competition is probably reasonable for current car markets and, in any case, no information about excess profit margins was available.
13. In fact, discussions with industry officials reveal that new car prices will not necessarily reflect the emissions control components on the car. Higher standards in one region may end up getting spread across costs of cars sold everywhere. This is not the case examined here, but it would be interesting to look at the efficiency and distributional consequences of that kind of pricing.
14. The Sierra Research analysis assumed that labour costs would decline by 5 per cent as labour became more experienced with any particular car, and that engineering, tooling and equipment costs would decrease by 50 per cent for each 5-year production cycle. It was also assumed that new vehicle dealers would only be able to realize 50 per cent of their standard price mark-up (Sierra Research Inc. 1994, p. 98).
15. These estimates are between high cost estimates from the auto industry and lower estimates from the California Air Resources Board (Automotive Consulting Group 1993; CARB 1990).

16. Vehicle populations for 1994 are taken from the Motor Vehicle Manufacturers' Association (1994).
17. The successively tighter Californian standards are currently packaged as a whole that regions can either adopt or not adopt. However, it is clear from the welfare estimates presented that packaging them may not be appropriate. Some of the early year standards appear to be much more cost-effective than those of the later years.
18. The calculation of costs and benefits here is slightly different from the dark areas depicted in Figure 6.1. First, benefits are constant for each type of vehicle in each region, instead of increasing with the number of vehicles as Figure 6.1 shows. Second, we have not included the costs or benefits of reduced car sales that would result when there are higher prices for the less-polluting cars – the areas resulting from a decline in cars from N_D to N_C.
19. Since costs exceed benefits in California in the later years, there is no side-payment to be made.
20. The '49-state car' option is not evaluated here but should be much more cost-effective for the OTR. The question, however, is the cost it imposes on other regions of the country.
21. The assumptions here about the benefits of reduced emissions are relatively high compared to the range of estimates in the literature.
22. It was clear to nearly all observers that the waiver limits in many states were absurdly low, too low to permit meaningful emission repair. In very few states were the waivers high enough to allow the replacement of a catalyst or oxygen sensor, two components that, once having failed, would have dire consequences for emissions.
23. Harrington and McConnell, 1994. This study used EPA's own estimates of the 'identification rate' and rate of 'errors of commission' of various tailpipe tests (USEPA 1992). The identification rate is the fraction of excess emissions detected by an emission test. Errors of commission are complying vehicles incorrectly found in violation.
24. EPA claims that more sophisticated tests are needed to detect vehicles that have been tampered with (Personal communication, Gene Tierney). However, EPA never tested the IM240 test against attempts to cheat, so it remains an open question as to whether any regularly-scheduled programme can detect cheating reliably.
25. Centralized programmes are presumably impervious to these perverse incentives, although they are of course vulnerable to old-fashioned bribery by motorists. Corruption has been found, for example, in New York's centralized programme.
26. California is considering a large-scale programme that would target polluting vehicles through an I&M programme and offer owners the option to sell the car in lieu of repair.

References

Alberini, A., W. Harrington and V. McConnell (1996), 'Estimating an emissions supply function from accelerated vehicle retirement programs', *Review of Economics and Statistics*, **78** (2), 251–65.

Aroesty, Jerry, Lionel Galway, Louise Parker, Milt Kamins, Pamela W. Wicinas, Gwen Farnsworth and David Rubenson (1994), 'Restructuring Smog Check: A Policy Synthesis', RAND Report No. DRU–885–CSTC, prepared for the California Senate Transportation Committee.

Automotive Consulting Group (1993), *Low Emission/Ultra Low Emission Vehicles: A Systems Cost Analysis*, Ann Arbor, Michigan, 25 January.

Beaton, Stuart P., G.A. Bishop, Yi Zhang, L.L. Ashbaugh, D.R. Lawson and D.H Stedman (1995), 'On-road vehicle emissions: regulations, costs and benefits', *Science*, **268**, 19 May, 991–3.

Bishop, Gary A. and Donald H. Stedman (1994), 'Remote sensing and vehicle emissions variability', paper presented at the Fourth Annual CRC On-Road Vehicle Workshop, March.

California Air Resources Board (CARB) (1990), *Proposed Regulations for Low Emission Vehicles and Clean Fuels: Staff Report and Technical Support Documents*, Sacramento, California, 13 August.

California I&M Review Committee (1993), 'Evaluation of the California Smog Check Program and Recommendations for Program Improvements: Fourth Report to the Legislature', Sacramento, California.

Calvert, J.B., J.B. Heywood, R.F. Sawyer and J.H. Seinfeld (1993), 'Achieving acceptable air quality: some reflections on controlling vehicle emissions', *Science*, **261**, 2 July, 37–45.

Cebula, Francis J. (1994), 'Report on the Sunoco Emissions Systems Repair Program', Sun Oil Company, Philadelphia, Pennsylvania.

Elliott, E. Donald, Bruce A. Ackerman and John C. Millian (1985), 'Toward a theory of statutory evolution: the federalization of environmental law', *Journal of Law, Economics, and Organization*, **1** (2), Fall, 313–40.

Energy and Environmental Analysis (1993), 'Draft Working Paper on Emissions-based Registration Fees', report prepared for Maricopa County, Arizona, Association of Governments (Arlington, Va.).

Federal Register (1992), 'Vehicle Inspection and Maintenance Requirements for State Implementation Plans', **57** (215), 5 November.

Hall, Jane V., Arthur M. Winer, Michael T. Kleinman, Frederick W. Lurmann, Victor Brajer and Steven D. Colome (1995), 'Valuing the health benefits of clean air', *Science*, **255**, 14 February, 812–17.

Harrington, Winston and Virginia McConnell (1994), 'Modeling in-use vehicle emissions and the effects of inspection and maintenance programs', *Journal of Air and Waste Management Assocation*, **44** (6), June, 794–99.

Harrington, Winston, Margaret A. Walls and Virginia McConnell (1995), 'Shifting gears: new directions for cars and clean air', *Issues in Science and Technology*, Winter, **XI** (2), 26–32.

Krupnick, Alan J. and Paul R. Portney (1991), 'Controlling urban air pollution: a benefit-cost assessment', *Science*, **252**, 26 April.

Krupnick, A.J., M. Walls and C. Hood (1993), 'The Distributional and Environmental Implications of an Increase in the Federal Gasoline Tax', Energy and Natural Resources Division Discussion Paper ENR93–24, Resources for the Future, Washington, DC, September.

Lawson, Douglas R., P.J. Groblicki, D.H. Stedman, G.A. Bishop and P.L. Guenther (1990), 'Emissions from in-use motor vehicles in Los Angeles: a pilot study of remote sensing and the inspection and maintenance program', *Journal of the Air and Waste Management Association*, August, **40**, 1096–1105.

Lodder, Tymon S. and Kim Bruce Livo (1994), 'Review and Analysis of the Total Clean Cars Program', report by the Colorado Air Quality Control Commission.

Lyons, Carol E. and Donald H. Stedman (1991), 'Remote Sensing Enhanced Motor Vehicle Emissions Control for Pollution Reduction in the Chicago Metropolitan Area: Siting and Issue Analysis', final report for the Illinois Department of Energy and Natural Resources, Chicago, October.

Mason, Alpheus T. (1972), *The States' Rights Debate*, 2nd ed, New York: Oxford University Press.

Motor Vehicle Manufacturers' Association of the United States, Inc. (1994), 'MVMA Motor Vehicle Facts & Figures '94", Motor Vehicle Manufacturers' Association of the United States, Inc., Public Affairs Division.

Oates, Wallace E. (1993), *Fiscal Federalism*, Brookfield, Vermont: Ashgate.

Oates, Wallace and Robert M. Schwab (1988), 'Economic competition among jurisdictions: efficiency enhancing or distortion inducing', *Journal of Public Economics*, **35** (3), April, 333–54.

Portney, Paul (1990), 'The evolution of federal regulation', in Paul Portney (ed.), *Public Policies for Environmental Protection*, Washington, DC: RFF, pp. 7–25.

Rose-Ackerman, Susan (1981), 'Does federalism matter? Political choice in a federal republic', *Journal of Political Economy*, **89** (1), February, 152–65.

Sierra Research (SRI) (1994), 'The Cost-Effectiveness of Further Regulating Mobile Source Emissions', Report No. SR94–02–04, 28 February.

Small, Kenneth A. and Camilla Kazimi (1995), 'On the costs of air pollution from motor vehicles', *Journal of Transport Economics*, January, **29**, 7–32.

Smith, Stephen (1994), 'Federal issues in environmental taxation', paper presented at the 50th Congress of the International Institute of Public Finance, Cambridge, MA, 22–25 August.

Tiebout, C.M. (1956), 'A pure theory of local government expenditures', *Journal of Political Economy*, **64**, October, 416–24.

US Environmental Protection Agency (USEPA) (1992), 'I/M costs, benefits and impacts analysis', Office of Mobile Sources, Ann Arbor, Michigan, February.

Walsh, P.A., D.R. Lawson and P. Switzer (1994), 'An analysis of US roadside survey data', presented at the Fourth Annual CRC On-Road Vehicle Workshop, March.

Appendix 6AI

Assume a country with two regions, A and B, and one manufacturer supplying a product (in this case automobiles) to consumers in both. The welfare consequences of allowing the regions to set emission standards independently of the setting of a uniform standard by the central government will be compared here. So suppose independent standards e_A and e_B, with $e_A < e_B$ (that is, e_A is more stringent). The unregulated firm has three choices:

1. Produce one vehicle for sale in both regions, capable of meeting emission standard e_A.
2. Produce two distinct vehicles for the two regions.
3. Produce one vehicle meeting emission standard e_B and exit the market in region A.

For simplicity, let it be assumed that in producing each vehicle type the firm incurs a fixed cost of F and constant marginal costs that depend on the design emission level. Thus, the cost function for producing N_A vehicles for sale in region A is:

$$C(N_A) = F + k(e_A)N_A \qquad (6A1.1)$$

Average costs are clearly declining, making the firm a natural monopoly. The price it will charge for each vehicle will be bounded above by the monopoly price, where marginal revenue equals marginal cost. However, its ability to charge at this level might be limited by the possibility of entry by a rival firm. The price is bounded below by average cost. The latter is the competitive case which is discussed in the text above. The firm will be indifferent between (1), (2) and (3) above, since it will have the same profits under any of these. Residents in the two regions are not indifferent, and the most likely outcome is two different cars in the two regions. However, as discussed in the text, the welfare-maximizing result may or may not occur without central government intervention.

If the firm can act as a monopoly, the results are somewhat different. Suppose the firm is able to charge the monopoly price in each region and let $N_A(p)$ and $N_B(p)$ be the demand curves for vehicles. Suppose that the price elasticities of the two demand curves are the same (at the same prices). To be investigated are the circumstances under which the firm will choose (1), (2) or (3) above. Now, (3) can be eliminated immediately as long as the demand curve $N_A(p)$ in region A lies above the average cost curve at any point. Suppose that is the case. The profit function for (2) is

$$\pi^2 = p_A N_A(p_A) + p_B N_B(p_B) - 2F - k(e_A)N_A - k(e_B)N_B \qquad (6A1.2)$$

If ε_A and ε_B are the demand elasticities, then the prices satisfy:

$$-\frac{1}{\varepsilon_A} = \frac{p_A - k(e_A)}{p_A} \quad \text{and} \quad -\frac{1}{\varepsilon_B} = \frac{p_B - k(e_B)}{p_B} \qquad (6A1.3)$$

For (1) there is a single market with the same price p in both regions, and the demand for vehicles is $N(p) = N_A(p) = N_B(p)$, and the price satisfies:

$$-\frac{1}{\varepsilon} = \frac{p - k(e_A)}{p} \qquad (6A1.4)$$

At any price, p, the single-market elasticity ε is a weighted average of the elasticities in the individual markets. If $\varepsilon_A = \varepsilon_B$ at every price, then both must equal the unified-market elasticity ε. In that case, comparison of (6AI.4) and (6AI.3) shows that $p = p_A$. In other words, consumers in region A are no better off than they would have been under (2). But since $p_A > p_B$, consumers in B pay higher prices for vehicles, although they do enjoy higher environmental quality than they otherwise would have.

As for the firm, its revenues will be lower, and its variable costs higher, when producing for the unified market. However, it does enjoy the possibly greater advantage of avoiding half the set-up costs. These costs may be so great that the firm will prefer to make only one type of vehicle to sell in both markets. In this simple model, for the firm to decide to produce only one car, the conditions must be as follows:

$$\Delta = N_B(p_B) [k(e_A) - k(e_B)] - [N_B(p_A) - N_B(p_B)] [p_B - k(e_a)] < F \qquad (6A1.5)$$

Now consider the possible strategic interaction of the two regional governments in this case. Suppose the standard in each region is initially at level e_B, and region A decides to make its standard more stringent. The price in region A will increase to p_A regardless of how the firm responds. But in region B the price *is* affected by the firm's decision to produce one or two cars, and as (6AI.5) suggests, that decision is the more likely the smaller the cost difference between the two standards. The only tool that the authorities in region B have to prevent the one-car outcome is to change the standard e_B. To make it more attractive for the firm to produce two separate cars, region B must reduce its emission standard. In deciding whether to take this action, the authorities in B will weigh the advantage of less expensive vehicles against the disadvantage of reduced air quality. In either case, social welfare in B is lower than it was before region A acted. This example suggests that in the case of monopoly, the existence of economies of scale can also lead to spillovers that might justify action by the federal government.

7. Deriving and selecting policy instruments to meet air quality standards in the European Union

Zeger Degraeve, Gert Jan Koopman, Cécile Denis and Leen Teunen*

Introduction

This chapter develops a methodology to select a least-cost mix of transport and other policy measures in different regions of the European Union (EU) to reach air quality standards by the year 2010. In carrying out this task two fundamental characteristics of air quality problems in Europe are addressed: their variation across regions and the interregional linkages between some forms of pollution (notably ozone). Therefore, the questions to be answered are *which* policies should be introduced *where* in order to arrive at a least-cost solution for the Union as a whole. As all policy instruments analysed in this chapter have an, albeit different, impact on the various pollutants, the solution approach has to ensure that all objectives are satisfied simultaneously.

Traditionally, in Europe, policies have focused heavily on mandating emission limits for certain technologies. This is the approach that was taken in the case of the Large Combustion Plant Directive and in setting tailpipe emission standards for vehicles. Notwithstanding certain additional restrictions introduced at the national level, the emphasis in Europe was on European-wide technology standards. As far as vehicles are concerned, this can, to a large extent, be explained by the current legal and institutional requirements of the internal market which lead to full technical harmonization at the European level.[1] Where passenger cars and heavy duty vehicles are concerned, European legislation was introduced in the seventies and the emission limits have gradually been tightened since. Significant improvements have been achieved and regulated emissions per vehicle kilometre are now generally 90 per cent lower than in 1970. However, increased vehicle mileage and poor maintenance have partly offset the impact on total emissions and air quality.

* We would like to thank Willy Gochet, Matthias Mors and Stef Proost for their support, comments and suggestions and Heinz Jansen for invaluable assistance with the data collection. The views expressed in this chapter are those of the authors and do not necessarily reflect the position of the European Commission.

Moreover, the regional variation in air quality problems is very significant because of climate and other factors. In fact, whereas various air quality standards are practically always met in certain regions, other areas suffer major problems all year round. Both in Europe and in the US this situation has triggered an interest in more targeted instruments that can be better geared towards specific regional/local problems. This approach would suggest that coordination across policy levels (European, national, regional) is required to devise a least-cost mix of policy measures, that are, partly, regionally differentiated. As problems are highly variable across regions, it would be excessively costly to require identical policy instruments to be introduced across the whole of the EU.

Following two decades of tightening emission standards, the marginal costs of such abatement measures have increased. The search for a more cost-effective selection of instruments has, therefore, intensified. There are calls for broadening the tool kit. As a result there is currently much interest in measures that target the worst polluters rather than uniquely focusing on new technologies. Economic instruments have a potentially important role to play in this respect. The same holds for inspection and maintenance and nontransport measures. Clearly, an approach that explicitly recognizes the spatial dimension of air quality problems and the variety of possible instruments will have major implications for environmental policy-making in the EU.

In recognition of the need for a wider selection of possible instruments, the most recent EU Directive (94/12/EC) mandating tailpipe emission standards for cars in the EU for the period 1996 to 1997 requires, in Article 4, a review of a variety of instruments – among which are measures aiming at the internalization of environmental costs and measures to stimulate public transport – to be undertaken with explicit consideration of their cost-effectiveness, prior to making new proposals for tailpipe standards for the year 2000. The European Commission has carried out this analysis in collaboration with the car and oil industries, in the context of the so-called Auto/Oil Programme.

This chapter draws upon data from the Auto/Oil Programme and aims at developing a cost-effective mix of instruments to meet air quality standards. Although Directive 94/12/EC does not explicitly require the regional dimension to be taken into account, this chapter attempts to provide some preliminary insights into this field.

The outline of this chapter is as follows. The next section describes the nature and dimensions of the problem more precisely. It sets out the regions analysed, the air quality standards used, the relation between emissions and pollution employed in the analysis, as well as the effectiveness and costs of the various policy instruments. The second section presents the conceptual framework that was developed to analyse the matter and the third section sets out the formal model. As the dimensions of the model are too large to solve through standard algorithms, a specific solution technique had to be developed. This is explained in the fourth section. The description of the data is given in the fifth section. In the sixth section, we report the baseline results and provide a comparison of our minimum cost proposals with alternatives sometimes advocated in the public debate. Finally, we round up with conclusions and present an overview of unresolved matters that should be further examined.

The definition of the problem

Both in the US and in the EU the basic approach to air quality problems consists of requiring the attainment of uniform air quality standards. Obviously, the first step is the definition of these standards. In the EU, air quality standards are based on World Health Organization guidelines and are set at uniform levels across the EU for concentrations of pollutants at different places during different time intervals.[2] These levels are generally thresholds above which health risks become serious or significant damage to vegetation and agriculture occurs. It is important to emphasize that this policy aims at protecting (the weakest) individuals equally across the EU and, therefore, differs from a cost–benefit analysis (CBA) approach which would require balancing the costs of air quality improvements with the associated benefits. A CBA approach would not lead to uniform limit concentrations, but rather to a variation of 'optimal' concentrations across regions.

The analysis in this chapter is based on underlying air quality objectives for ozone (O_3), and urban NO_x concentrations. According to available forecasts, CO and HC levels will decrease with current policies such that air quality standards concerning these pollutants will be reached by 2010. This study does not take account of particulate matter (where insufficient data are available) and CO_2 emissions (for which emission reduction objectives based on air quality standards cannot be derived). The methodology developed can, however, easily be extended to these (and other) pollutants. As NO_x and HC are ozone precursors, reductions in these concentrations will affect air quality through two channels. The distinction between local pollution and regional pollution (ozone) is made in the following way: for the local pollution problem, urban emissions are the ones that matter, while for regional pollution total (urban and non-urban) emissions of precursors are the focus. Each measure is therefore characterized by reductions in urban NO_x, regional NO_x and regional HC emissions.

It has to be borne in mind, however, that whereas air quality is expressed in terms of concentrations, policies can only affect emissions. This implies that relations between emissions and concentrations will have to be incorporated in the analysis. With the exception of ozone, these relations are linear, for example, a 1 per cent reduction in NO_x emissions lowers NO_x concentrations by 1 per cent. For ozone, these relations are highly nonlinear, but they can be approximated by linear functions over certain ranges.

Moreover, ozone, in contrast to the other pollutants, is transported over significant distances. This unique feature of ozone will have to be taken into account explicitly in the analysis.

Based on these relations, expected economic growth as well as already scheduled measures in a variety of sectors, a forecast has been made by the Commission of 'baseline' emissions and air quality levels for the year 2010 in seven representative European cities/regions. A comparison of those levels with the air quality standards gives a set of reductions in local emissions (NO_x, HC, CO). These emission reductions are based on mandating full compliance of all grid squares – into which individual regions can be broken down – with 8-hour maxima of the World Health Organization guidelines. It has to be pointed out that more than 50 per cent of the grid squares already satisfy the required air quality levels.[3]

The approach taken for ozone is, however, different. The ozone reduction objectives represent percentage reductions from forecast ozone AOT90 (Accumulative exposure Over a Threshold) figures. AOT90 is defined as the sum of ozone concentrations exceeding 90 ppb (parts per billion) during the months May, June and July and is computed as follows:

$$AOT90 = \int \max([O_3] - 90.0)dt$$

The AOT90 values are calculated for the base-case year 2010 with the EMEP MSC–W model of the Swedish Environmental Research Institute (Simpson 1991, update September 1995). The target imposed results from keeping excess ozone levels less than 5 ppb, which will require very significant reductions in ozone levels from forecast 2010 levels (which are already some 60 per cent lower than 1990 levels). As a result, the ozone reduction objective here aims at substantial reductions in *peak* ozone concentrations measured during the periods where they are most prevalent. It is justified to look at the ozone problem in this manner because manmade emissions (from transport and nontransport sources) are the main cause of peak ozone concentrations during the summer months. Peak ozone concentrations occur on top of average ozone concentration levels which consist mainly of ozone occurring naturally in the environment. As an extension of the analysis, the potential of emission regulatory instruments for traffic and industry on average annual ozone concentration levels has also been investigated. It was observed that throughout the EU about a 3 per cent reduction in average annual ozone concentrations could be achieved at best. However, even these reductions would not suffice to reach some of the stringent ozone standards that have recently been advocated in the literature (Nilsson 1995). It can be strongly suggested, then, that the ozone objectives used contribute significantly to solving ozone problems, to the extent that these are caused by human activities.[4]

The percentage reductions in urban emissions as well as in ozone concentrations that are required to bring down air pollution to acceptable levels by the year 2010 are reported in Table 7.1. As can be seen, the seven regions are substantially different in terms of the severity of air quality problems. The specific regions were selected because they are fairly representative for the distribution of air quality problems across Europe.

The analysis presented in this chapter takes as its input the costs and effectiveness (in terms of emissions reduction), as established by other researchers working in the context of the Auto/Oil Programme, of a large number of policy instruments in the areas of vehicle technology, fuel quality, inspection and maintenance and a large number of measures aimed at behavioural change. It has to be pointed out, however, that these instruments are largely economic instruments which, in addition to changing transport behaviour, could also affect technology choices. In the remainder of this chapter, this category is labelled 'nontechnical' measures. The data are mainly derived from two reports, Touche Ross (1995) and the European Commission (1995). In all cases estimates of incremental costs by the year 2010 have been used.

Table 7.1 Required emissions and ozone concentration reductions in seven European regions

Pollutant	Regions						
	Athens *Greece*	*Cologne* *Germany*	*The Hague* *Netherlands*	*London* *UK*	*Lyons* *France*	*Madrid* *Spain*	*Milan* *Italy*
Urban NO_x (%)	55	25	5	40	40	50	50
Ozone % (AOT90)	60	90	90	90	90	0	80

The analysis contains one aggregate category of measures that can be introduced outside the transport sector, denoted by 'nontransport' measures. The incorporation of this category of measures in the analysis allows an efficient emission reduction objective to be allocated to transport. Clearly, the aggregate nature of these measures implies that in case policy proposals have to be drawn up for the nontransport sector, more work on precise instruments will have to be undertaken. The section on 'Description of the data' below, discusses how the cost and effectiveness of the nontransport measures used in this chapter have been estimated.

In this analysis, most measures considered can be introduced autonomously at the level of the individual regions[5] in which the various cities are located. The major exception to this rule consists of vehicle technology standards which, given the present legal and institutional framework, can only be introduced at the same intensity throughout the EU as a whole and are subsequently called 'global' measures. The analysis therefore also addresses the question as to which measures should be taken at the European level and at member state level, respectively. In all computations presented in this chapter, the least-cost policy mix is derived by minimizing the total unweighted costs of measures introduced across all seven regions.

The air quality objectives and the costs of policy measures are taken to be representative of the countries in which the regions are situated. This means, for example, that the total costs of a fuel measure introduced in the Athens region consists of the per vehicle cost (annual mileage times cost per litre) multiplied by the size of the entire Greek vehicle fleet. Implicitly, therefore, the analysis covers the following countries: Greece, Germany, the Netherlands, the United Kingdom, France, Spain and Italy. Clearly, this procedure assumes a significant degree of averaging within countries. A lack of more disaggregated data prevents a more detailed analysis. Several consequences arise from this assumption. First, although there is no guarantee that the air quality objectives are reached everywhere in a particular country, it nevertheless seems reasonable to assume that large parts of the country satisfy the standard as the objectives have been formulated for cities, where, generally speaking, air quality problems are relatively severe. Second, to the extent that local measures can only be introduced in those parts of a country where they are really necessary, their 'true' costs are likely to be overestimated. Third, not all member states of the Union are covered, which implies that the least-cost mix found in this analysis need not necessarily coincide with a least-cost package of measures for the Union as a whole. Also, as far as ozone abatement is concerned, some deviation from the least-cost solution might occur due to the fact that cheap abatement options for ozone precursors in countries that are not covered by the analysis are ignored. However, as stated above, the distribution of cities/regions is found to be representative for the EU as a whole. Moreover, the countries covered represent more than 80 per cent of the EU's population and GDP. Therefore, it seems reasonable to conclude that, although the analysis is not complete, it can provide pointers for efficient policies to meet air quality standards in the Union as a whole.

The conceptual framework

Throughout this chapter, a measure is defined as a single instrument capable of reducing emissions. A measure will typically belong to only one of five different categories that are distinguished in the model. The first four categories are transport-related measures. A fifth category includes measures targeted at emissions originating from nontransport sources such as power plants and industrial combustion. The four transport-related categories are: (1) *technical* measures, that is, improvements in vehicle engine technology (for example, pre-heat catalytic converters), imposed by means of *standards*;[6] (2) *mandatory fuel standards* requiring the introduction of clean fuels; (3) *nontechnical* measures aimed at changing transport choices (for example, economic instruments such as tax incentives or traffic management tools such as parking and circulation restrictions); and (4) *inspection and maintenance*-related measures.

It is important to underline at the outset that the so called nontechnical measures can have an important impact on technologies chosen by consumers. For example, fiscal instruments differentiating between vehicles and fuels with different environmental characteristics can direct consumer demand towards cleaner cars and fuels. Therefore, both standards and economic instruments, as two different policy measures, can lead to technology change, albeit in different ways (that is, by making change compulsory or by triggering it through incentives, respectively).

In addition, a measure is classified according to its geographical scope. *Global* measures, which in this analysis are restricted to technical vehicle measures (category 1), must be introduced simultaneously throughout the European Union. Measures from the remaining four categories are assumed to be *local*. Local measures can be tailored to a specific regional situation and hence can be introduced at various intensities throughout the EU.

Sets of measures are defined within each of the five categories and consist of a grouping in various combinations of individual measures belonging to the particular category. However, different technologies are available for gasoline and diesel vehicles. Consequently, different sets of measures were constructed for those two engine types. As a result, the category 'technical' vehicle measures is subdivided into two subcategories, for gasoline engine and for diesel engine vehicles, respectively. The sets of measures constructed for fuels comprise different gasoline–diesel packages, implying that a subdivision of the fuel category is unnecessary. For the nontechnical category, four different subcategories were given for the effectiveness and cost of sets of measures related to various levels of (1) subsidies to public transportation; (2) road pricing to discourage traffic during peak hours; (3) scrapping schemes for old vehicles; and (4) circulation taxes based on the amount of pollutants emitted per kilometre. No subcategories were considered for inspection and maintenance and for the nontransport-related sets of measures. For more details on the data, see the later section, below.

Table 7.2 gives an illustrative example. Within the five categories and the resulting nine subcategories in the columns of Table 7.2, letters (A, B, C, and so on) represent sets of measures (possibly consisting of only one measure). The numbers denote combinations of sets of measures, zero indicating the empty set, implying that no measure from this subcategory is selected. Global measures are indicated in bold. Each set of measures is characterized by its cost and by its emission reduction potential (that is, its effectiveness) expressed in terms of the percentage reduction in economy-wide emissions forecast in 2010 if no additional policy action is taken.

The problem is then how to combine the sets of measures across the subcategories, taking exactly one set from each subcategory, into a *bundle* that would achieve emission standards at the least cost. For example, Table 7.2 shows that a bundle could comprise set 2 from the gasoline and set 3 from the diesel subcategory of technical measures, set 1 from the fuel measures, sets 0 from both public transportation and road pricing, set 2 from the scrapping schemes and set 0 from the circulation tax subcategories of nontechnical measures, set 1 from inspection and

Table 7.2 Sets of measures

Technical Measures		Fuel Measures	Nontechnical Measures				Inspection and Maintenance	Non transport Measures
Gasoline	Diesel		Public Transport	Road Pricing	Scrapping Schemes	Circulation Tax		
0∅	0∅	0∅	0∅	0∅	0∅	0∅	0∅	0∅
1 {A}	1 {D}	1 {G}	1 {J}	1 {L}	1 {N}	1 {Q}	1 {S}	1 {U}
2 {B}	2{E}	2 {H}	2 {K}	2{M}	2{O}	2{R}	2{T}	2 {V}
3 {C}	3{F}	3 {I}	...	...	3 {P}	...	3 {S,T}	3 {W}
4 {A,B}	4{E,F}	...			...		...	4 {V,W}
5 {A,B,C}	...							...

maintenance and finally, set 2 from the nontransport category. This gives in terms of the notation of Table 7.2, {2 {B}, 3 {F}, 1 {G}, 0 Ø, 0 Ø, 2 {O}, 0 Ø, 1 {S}, 2 {V}}. Observe also that sets of measures within subcategories are not disjoint. However, in a bundle, care must be taken to ensure that each individual measure can only appear once. The use of the discrete sets of measures is not restrictive for the modelling purposes: the same instrument, such as a reduction in public transport fares but applied at a different intensity (for example, 10 per cent and 40 per cent rebate), is considered to be a different type of measure.

Clearly, interaction effects among the various sets of measures belonging to the four different transport categories have to be eliminated. This requires the effectiveness of bundles of measures to be partly endogenous. When two sets of measures from different transport categories (for example, fuel, and inspection and maintenance) are applied simultaneously, the impact on emissions reduction is not always the sum of the reductions of the individual sets. In some cases there are synergy effects implying that the simultaneous introduction of two sets leads to an abatement of emissions that is larger than the sum of the emission reduction potential of the individual measures. In particular, this will be the case when one set of measures induces the use of the other set of measures, or when both sets of measures are complementary, Generally, however, the joint impact will be lower than the sum of the two emissions reductions. This is because a second set of measures can only be applied to the emissions level remaining after the first set has had its effect. Unless otherwise given, it is assumed that this type of interaction effect prevails.

The example in Table 7.3 illustrates the net effect on the abatement of some pollutant for several sets of measures applied simultaneously. In the first and second line of Table 7.3, we arbitrarily start with the introduction of a gasoline and diesel set of measures which, in the example, have individual emission reduction effects of 9 per cent and 21 per cent, respectively. There is no interaction between the sets of measures from those two subcategories and the net effect of 30 per cent is simply obtained by adding the effects of the two sets separately. Subsequently, a fuel set of measures, line three of Table 7.3, is introduced with an individual emissions reduction effect of 25 per cent. Clearly, in the case where we could simply add the effects of the sets of measures, the additive effect would be 55 per cent (= 30 per cent + 25 per cent). However, the net effect after accounting for interaction is only 47.5 per cent, considering that the effectiveness of the fuel set can be applied only to the emissions level which remains after the selected sets of gasoline and diesel measures have had their effect. This reasoning can be continued for the introduction of, for example, scrapping, road pricing and inspection and maintenance sets

Table 7.3 Illustration of the net effect on emissions reduction

Set of Measures	Reduction of some pollutant (%)		
	Individual effect (%)	*Additive effect (%)*	*Net effect*
Gasoline	9	9	9%
Diesel	21	30	30%
Fuel	25	55	47.5% = $100*[1-(1-0.09-0.21(1-0.25)]$
Scrapping schemes	15	70	55.375% = $100*[1-(1-0.09-0.21)(1-0.25)(1-0.15)]$
Road Pricing	20	90	64.3% = $100*[1-(1-0.09-0.21)(1-0.25)(1-0.15)(1-0.2)]$
Inspection and maintenance	5	95	66.085% = $100*[1-(1-0.09-0.21)(1-0.25)(1-0.15)(1-0.2)(1-0.05)]$

of measures. Observe the significant difference between the additive reduction effect of 95 per cent and the reduction effect of 66.085 per cent when interaction effects are taken into account. Clearly, this difference is not to be neglected. Moreover, the resulting net reduction effect is independent of the order of introduction of the different sets of measures.

Obviously, as far as emissions reduction is concerned, there are no interaction effects between the transport- and the nontransport-related measures.

Lastly, an important spatial effect is also considered. The formation of ozone (O_3), a compound with a strong oxidizing potential which is formed by complex chemical reactions between HC, NO_x and oxygen in the presence of sunlight, entails a transboundary impact which is of particular importance to Europe. The ozone precursors HC and NO_x are transported over long distances from the emission source and eventually contribute to ozone formation in another country (see, for example, Mayeres et al. 1993 and Stedman and Williams 1991). Consequently, the abatement of the ozone precursors in one region is observed to have an impact on the ozone level in other regions. Over certain ranges of ozone abatement, these effects can be approximated by linear relations, linking emissions reduction in region *i* to changes in ozone levels in region *j*. This, in turn, can be summarized in so-called blame matrices. As our ozone reduction objective is stated in terms of AOT90 figures (see section on 'the definition of the problem', above), the entries of the two blame matrices (one for (regional) HC and one for (regional) NO$_x$) give the percentage reduction in AOT90 in a particular region due to a 1 per cent reduction of the corresponding precursor in another region. The blame matrices were derived by the Swedish Environmental Research Institute (Simpson 1991, update September 1995). For the other pollutants, such a spatial interdependency is not observed in practice, and hence they are called local pollutants.

The formal model

Before stating the formal model, the notation used will be defined. Capital letters in bold are used for set names whose elements are sets already.

set definitions :
TG : set of (sets of) technical gasoline engine measures
TD : set of (sets of) technical diesel engine measures
T : set consisting of the cross-product of technical gasoline and diesel engine measures, $\mathbf{T} = \mathbf{TG} \times \mathbf{TD}$
F : set of (sets of) fuel measures
NU : set of (sets of) nontechnical public transport measures
NR : set of (sets of) nontechnical road pricing measures
NS : set of (sets of) nontechnical scrappage incentives
NC : set of (sets of) nontechnical circulation tax measures
N : set consisting of the cross-product of nontechnical public transport, road pricing, fuel tax and circulation tax measures, $\mathbf{N} = \mathbf{NU} \times \mathbf{NR} \times \mathbf{NS} \times \mathbf{NC}$
M : set of (sets of) inspection and maintenance
BT : set of all transport-related sets of measures, $\mathbf{BT} = \mathbf{T} \cup \mathbf{F} \cup \mathbf{N} \cup \mathbf{M}$
BN : set of all nontransport-related sets of measures
G : set of global measures
L : set of local measures
C : set of regions
P : set of pollutants

parameter definitions
d_{lj} : required abatement of pollutant l in region j as a percentage of emissions level in 2010, $\forall\, l \in P,\, \forall\, j \in C$
c_{Rj} : cost of introducing set of measures R in region j, $\forall\, R \in \mathbf{BT} \cup \mathbf{BN},\, \forall j \in C$
e_{Rjl} : effectiveness of set of measures R for abatement of pollutant l

in region j, $\forall R \in \mathbf{BT} \cup \mathbf{BN}$, $\forall l \in P$, $\forall j \in C$

$e_{R1R2R3R4R5R6R7R8jl}$
: net effectiveness of the particular combination of sets of measures, for the abatement of pollutant l in region j,

$\forall l \in P$, $\forall j \in C$, $= 100[1-(1-e_{R1jl}-e_{R2jl})(1-e_{R3jL})(1-e_{R4jl})(1-e_{R5jl})(1-e_{R6jl})$
$(1-e_{R7jl})(1-e_{R8jl})]$, $\forall R1 \in \mathbf{TG}$, $\forall R2 \in \mathbf{TD}$, $\forall R3 \in \mathbf{F}$, $\forall R4 \in \mathbf{NU}$,
$\forall R5 \in \mathbf{NR}$, $\forall R6 \in \mathbf{NS}$, $\forall R7 \in \mathbf{NC}$, $\forall R8 \in \mathbf{M}$

a_{ijl} : entries of the blame matrix, impact of reducing the ozone precursor l in region i on the reduction of ozone in region j, $\forall i,j \in C$, $l = HC, NO_x$

variable definition
x_{Rj} = 1, if set of measures R will be introduced in region j, 0, otherwise, $\forall R \in \mathbf{BT} \cup \mathbf{BN}$, $\forall j \in C$

As the input data are based on sets of measures, the decision variable x_{Rj} is also based on sets of measures. Using the notation defined, the formal model is then as follows.

i. Minimize total cost of introducing sets of measures

$$\min \sum_{R \in \mathbf{BT} \cup \mathbf{BN}} \sum_{j \in C} c_{Rj} x_{Rj} \tag{7.1}$$

subject to

ii. Achieve the required emissions abatement

$$\sum_{\substack{R1 \in \mathbf{TG}, R2 \in \mathbf{TD}, R3 \in \mathbf{F}, R4 \in \mathbf{NU}, \\ R5 \in \mathbf{NR}, R6 \in \mathbf{NS}, R7 \in \mathbf{NC}, R8 \in \mathbf{M}}} e_{R1R2R3R4R5R6R7R8jl} x_{R1j} x_{R2j} x_{R3j} x_{R4j} x_{R5j} x_{R6j} x_{R7j} x_{R8j}$$

$$+ \sum_{R9 \in \mathbf{BN}} e_{R91} x_{R9j} \geq d_{lj} \quad \forall l \in P \setminus \{O_3\}, \forall j \in C \tag{7.2}$$

iii. Achieve the required ozone abatement

$$\sum_{l=HC,NO_x} \sum_{i \in C} a_{ijl} \left(\sum_{\substack{R1 \in \mathbf{TG}, R2 \in \mathbf{TD}, R3 \in \mathbf{F}, R4 \in \mathbf{NU}, \\ R5 \in \mathbf{NR}, R6 \in \mathbf{NS}, R7 \in \mathbf{NC}, R8 \in \mathbf{M}}} \right.$$

$$e_{R1R2R3R4R5R6R7R8il} x_{R1i} x_{R2i} x_{R3i} x_{R4i} x_{R5i} x_{R6i} x_{R7i} x_{R8i}$$

$$\left. + \sum e_{R9il} x_{R9i} \right) \geq d_{O_3 j} \quad \forall j \in C \tag{7.3}$$

iv. Choose only one set of measures from each subcategory

$$\sum_{R \epsilon TG} x_{Rj} = 1, \quad \sum_{R \epsilon TD} x_{Rj} = 1 \quad \forall j \epsilon C$$

$$\sum_{R \epsilon F} x_{Rj} = 1$$

$$\sum_{R \epsilon NU} x_{Rj} = 1, \quad \sum_{R \epsilon NR} x = 1, \quad \sum_{R \epsilon NS} x_{Rj} = 1, \quad \sum_{R \epsilon NC} x = 1$$

$$\sum_{R \epsilon M} x_{Rj} = 1$$

$$\sum_{R \epsilon BM} x_{Rj} = 1 \tag{7.4}$$

v. Global measures can only be introduced throughout the EU

$$\sum_{R \epsilon BT | k \epsilon R} x_{Rj} = \sum_{R \epsilon BT | k \epsilon R} x_{Rj+1} \quad \forall k \epsilon G, \forall j \epsilon C \tag{7.5}$$

vi. Define the variables 0/1

$$x_{Rj} \epsilon \{0,1\} \quad \forall R \epsilon BT \cup BN, \forall j \epsilon C \tag{7.6}$$

In the objective function (7.1), the sum of the costs of all sets of measures that are selected in all regions is minimized. As discussed before, the interaction effects are negligible and the additive functional form is quite acceptable. However, the model could easily be extended to cope with interaction among costs if such interaction would be observed. Constraints (7.2) make sure that the required emissions reductions are achieved for all pollutants except ozone. Constraints (7.3) model the same requirement for ozone. Here, the regional interdependencies are considered explicitly through the blame matrix modelling the chemical relations between ozone precursors and ozone. As discussed above, one and only one set of measures (including the zero set) must be selected from each one of the nine subcategories considered. Constraints (7.4) model this requirement. Clearly, it has to be ensured that global measures are introduced throughout the EU. Constraints (7.5) impose this by requiring that for each global measure, the sum of all the variables modelling the sets of measures containing that global measure, should be equal for two consecutive regions in the set C. Finally, constraints (7.6) enforce the proper integrality conditions.

Model (7.1) – (7.6) is a nonlinear integer programming problem for which no efficient solution methods have been developed for realistic problem sizes. Given the dimensions of the sets involved (see section on 'Description of the data', below), the model is of a very large size and therefore unsolvable as such. However, a special decomposition technique will allow us to build a customary solution algorithm. This solution's approach is introduced in the next section.

The solution approach[7]
Because of the specific nature of the model (7.1)–(7.6) as an integer nonlinear program and its formidable dimensions, we are forced to develop a customized solution approach which is described in this section. Our solution algorithm is an implementation of the Dantzig–Wolfe decomposition principle, also called column generation (see, for example, Dantzig and Wolfe 1960).

Description of the decomposition technique
The task of model (7.1)–(7.6) essentially consists of constructing, for each region, the single cheapest bundle across the nine subcategories, which achieves the emission abatement objectives. This entails taking into account regional interdependencies for ozone and ensuring that, in the case where some region introduces global measures, those global measures are also introduced in all other regions (included in the selected bundles for the regions) or they are not introduced at all in the final solution. The structure of the problem allows us to separate the task of the model into two different but interdependent problems. The key criterion for the separation decision, the decomposition principle, is the interaction among the regions for emissions reduction.

Interaction among the regions exists for ozone abatement and for the introduction of global measures. However, regions can decide on their own which bundle best achieves (as cheaply as possible) the required reduction in urban NO_x emissions. We call this second task the 'regional selection' problem. The first task will basically be a coordination mechanism among the individual regional bundle proposals considering the ozone interdependencies and the introduction of global measures. Clearly, the regions will not be fully coordinated immediately by their first bundle choices. Consequently, the algorithm proceeds iteratively with the regions making bundle selections which are subsequently considered by the coordination mechanism. The coordination problem, called the master program, feeds coordination information back to the regional selection problems which use this information to generate new bundle proposals. The iterative procedure stops when the regions have generated enough bundle proposals to become coordinated with respect to the ozone abatement objectives and the introduction of global measures. At each iteration, the coordination information reflects the fact that ultimately, the regions have to choose only one bundle from those selected thus far while achieving the ozone abatement objectives, and that for some of the regions, global measures have been included in the bundle proposals. Specifically, in linear programming terms, the coordination information consists of the dual prices of the master problem solved as a linear program.

Before formally stating the coordination problem, the following additional notation is defined:

set definition
Q_j : set of bundle selection proposals at some iteration of the algorithm for region j, $\forall\, j \in C$

parameter definition
f_{rj} : cost of bundle r for region j, that is, the sum of the costs of all the sets of measures comprised in the bundle, $\forall\, j \in C, \forall\, r \in Q_j$

eb_{rjl}: net effectiveness of the sets measures in bundle r for the abatement of pollutant l in region j, $l = HC, NO_x$, $\forall\, j \in C, \forall\, r \in Q_j$

variable definition
z_{rj} = 1, if region j selects bundle r from the bundle proposals generated thus far, 0, otherwise, $\forall\, j \in C, \forall\, r \in Q_j$.

It is important to realize that the bundles appearing in the master program have already been generated by the regions individually to satisfy the local emission abatement objectives, so that only ozone constraints are included at this stage. How this is done is explained later. The master problem is then as follows :

i. Minimize the total cost of the bundles chosen for each region:

$$\min \sum_{\substack{j \in c \ r \in Q_j}} \sum f_{rj} z_{rj} \tag{7.7}$$

subject to

ii. Choose only one bundle from all the proposals thus far for each region: dual price

$$\sum_{r \in Q_j} z_{rj} = 1 \qquad \forall j \in C \qquad\qquad \pi_{j0} \tag{7.8}$$

iii. Achieve the ozone abatement in each region: dual price

$$\sum_{1=HC,NO_x} \sum_{i \in C} \sum_{r \in Q_i} (a_{iji} eb_{ril}) z_{ri} \geq d_{O3j} \qquad \forall j \in C \quad \mu_j \qquad (7.9)$$

iv. Global measures can only be introduced throughout the EU: dual price

$$\sum_{r \in Q_j, k \in r} \Sigma Z_{rj} = \sum_{r \in Q_{j+1}, k \in r} \Sigma z_{rj+1} \quad \forall k \in G, \forall j \varepsilon C \qquad v_{j,j+1,k} \qquad (7.10)$$

v. Define the variables nonnegative:

$$Z_{rj} \geq 0 \quad \forall j \in C, \forall r \in Q_j \qquad (7.11)$$

In the objective function (7.7), we minimize the sum of the costs of the bundles selected for each region noting that this cost is just the sum of the component sets of measures. Constraints (7.8) ensure that for each region, only one bundle proposal will be chosen from the ones generated thus far. The required ozone abatement is enforced by conditions (7.9) taking into account the regional interactions through the blame matrices. Constraints (7.10) model the requirement that for some region, a bundle proposal containing a global measure can only be chosen if the other regions choose bundles that also contain that global measure. In order to obtain the dual price information to be provided to the regional bundle selection problems, the master program must be solved as a linear program. Therefore, we need to add the proper nonnegativity conditions (7.11).

Given the dual price information $(\pi_{j0}, \mu_j, v_{i,j+1,k,s}, \forall j \in C, \forall k \in G)$ of the coordination program (7.7) – (7.11), the regional bundle selection problems, also called the subproblems, need to construct a bundle from the different sets of measures across the nine subcategories. At each iteration, this bundle is currently the most attractive one given the coordination information and at the same time it satisfies the objective for urban NO_x levels. The bundle construction problem is a difficult nonlinear integer programming problem given the interactions among the efficiencies of the sets of measures. We circumvent this problem by explicitly enumerating, during the pricing operation, all the possible bundles that can feasibly be constructed for each region. Consequently, at each iteration of the algorithm, for each region, it suffices to incorporate the coordination information into each bundle and select the most attractive one. Clearly, during the bundle construction phase, we can immediately take into account the nonlinearities which exist among the efficiencies of the sets of transportation related measures.

Specifically, the iterative coordination algorithm proceeds as follows. The dual price information μ_j, $\forall j \in C$ reflects how well the ozone abatement has already been achieved for each region with the bundles generated so far. Particularly, μ_j will be high if the ozone reduction is not yet easily achieved and low for the opposite situation. Dual prices $v_{j,j+1,k}$, $\forall j \in C$, $\forall k \in G$ have a similar interpretation, but apply to global measures. Basically, the $v_{j,j+1,k}$ will be high if either region j or $j+1$ has already selected global measures while the other region has not yet done so, and be low for the opposite situation. To create new attractive bundles for each region, the dual prices lead to a modification of the bundle's costs. In linear programming terms, the reduced cost of bundle r is then computed as follows:

$$f_{rj} - \pi_{j0} - \sum_{l=HC,NO_x} \sum_{i \in C} (a_{jil,} \, eb_{rjl}) \mu_j + \sum_{k \in G} v_{j-1,jk} - \sum_{k \in G} v_{j,j+1,k} \qquad \forall j \in C$$

This cost modification causes different bundles to become more or less attractive during the iterations of the coordination algorithm reflecting the situation of the master program as described above. At each iteration, the most attractive bundle for each region is, in linear programming terms, the one with the most negative reduced cost. This bundle will be added to the list of bundles generated Q_j, $\forall j \in C$ and added to the master program in the form of a new z_{rj} variable. If the new bundles have been added to the master, it is solved again as a linear program to obtain new dual prices and a new iteration can start. The procedure stops when for each region, we cannot find a bundle with a negative reduced cost. Traditionally, at that point, the master problem is solved as an integer program in order to find the single best bundle for each region. For more details on the column generation process, we refer the reader to any advanced text on decomposition of linear programs, for example, Lasdon (1970).

The decomposition algorithm is more suitable than model (7.1)–(7.6) with the bundles listed explicitly because it allows us to implicitly consider all the bundles while explicitly adding only a small subset of them to the master program. The approach therefore ensures that the determination of solutions is feasible with reasonable computational resources.

We have programmed our algorithm in FORTRAN 77 using the NDP486 Compiler V4.3.0 and linked with the LINDO optimization library version 5.1 from Schrage (1992). All experiments were run on an IBM compatible 486, 66 Mhz PC. Typical computation times range from 24 up to 36 hours.

Achieving 'good' solutions using column generation
Although we are confronted with a discrete optimization problem, because of its dimensionality we have to resort to column generation, which is a

continuous (linear programming)-based solution technique. This technique relaxes only the integrality conditions on the variables maintaining all other constraints. Consequently, the column generation master program is a relaxation of the discrete optimization problem and its optimal solution, found at the moment when no new columns (= bundles) price out, provides an unattainable lower bound on the total cost of the optimal discrete solution. Computational experience indicates that only an extremely small number of columns need to be generated to achieve the master's LP optimum. Traditionally, at that point, an integer program is solved searching for the optimal discrete solution among the columns generated. In so far as we have only a small number of the potentially millions of possible columns, the resulting discrete solution may be arbitrarily inaccurate.

To tackle this problem, we follow an idea suggested by Degraeve (1992) for a column generation approach to solving the general integer cutting-stock problem. Degraeve suggests adding a fixed number of potentially 'good' columns initially before starting the column generation phase, thereby achieving excellent quality integer solutions. From an academic standpoint, column generation remains interesting for finding the lower bound total cost which can subsequently be used to judge the quality of the discrete solution's total cost found afterwards. The quality of the discrete solution, called the gap, is given by the percentage deviation of its total cost from the lower bound total cost. Specifically for this problem, the potentially 'good' initial columns for each region consist of a fixed number of cheapest bundles of sets of measures that achieve the required reduction in urban NO_x emissions.

Table 7.4 compares the total costs and corresponding gaps for the optimal discrete solution without and with the 'good' initial columns. The first column in Table 7.4 lists the unattainable lower bound on the total costs of the emissions' abatement in the seven regions. Obviously, this bound is identical for both models.

Table 7.4 Impact of adding 'good' initial columns on solution quality

Unattainable total cost lower bound (MECU)	*Without 'good' initial columns*		*With 'good' initial columns*	
	Total cost (MECU)	*Gap (%)*	*Total cost (MECU)*	*Gap (%)*
9956.75	*12756.64*	*21.95*	*10060.84*	*1.03*

Observe in Table 7.4 that with 'good' initial columns, we find an integer solution which costs about 104.09 million ECU more than the unattainable lower bound on the total costs. Although we cannot scientifically prove that we have indeed found the optimal integer solution, we can certainly claim that for this practically relevant problem of formidable dimensions, our algorithms were able to find the best possible solution.

Description of the data
In this section we describe the different measures for each of the five categories (nine subcategories) and discuss some cost and effectiveness aspects. Figure 7.1 presents the organization of the transport-related measures: four subcategories of technical (regulatory) measures, and four subcategories of nontechnical measures (which can, however, include technical measures). The remaining category, nontransport, which covers the reduction of emissions from stationary sources is not included in Figure 7.1.

Technical measures: vehicle standards
Input data for the technical vehicle measures is derived from Touche Ross (1995) which specifies sets of measures to meet particular emission reduction scenarios presented in Tables 7.5a and 7.5b. These sets consist of combinations of various technologies which have been determined by Touche Ross (1995) as 'engineering packages'.

Table 7.5a Sets of technical measures and impact on emissions for gasoline engines

	Passenger cars and light duty vehicles (LDV)	
Scenario 1	A: NO_x–20%, CO–20%, HC–20%	Cars
	D: NO_x–20%, CO–20%, HC–20%	Light duty vehicles
Scenario 2	B: NO_x–40%, CO–30%, HC–40%	Cars
	E: NO_x–40%, CO–30%, HC–40%	Light duty vehicles
Scenario 3	C: NO_x–65%, CO–45%, HC–65%	Cars
	F: NO_x–65%, CO–45%, HC–65%	Light duty vehicles

Table 7.5b Sets of technical measures and impact on emissions for diesel engines

	Passenger cars, light duty vehicles, heavy duty vehicles and buses	
Scenario 1	A: NO_x–20%, CO–25%, HC–10%, PM–20%	Cars
	D: NO_x–20%, CO–25%, HC–10%, PM–20%	Light duty vehicles
	G: NO_x–15%, PM–15%	Heavy duty vehicles and buses
Scenario 2	B: NO_x–35%, CO–40%, HC–20%, PM–35%	Cars
	E: NO_x–35%, CO–40%, HC–20%, PM–35%	Light duty vehicles
	H: NO_x–30%, PM–30%	Heavy duty vehicles and buses
Scenario 3	C: NO_x–50%, CO–50%, HC–30%, PM–50%	Cars
	F: NO_x–50%, CO–50%, HC–30%, PM–50%	Light duty vehicles
	I: NO_x–50%, PM–50%	Heavy duty vehicles and buses

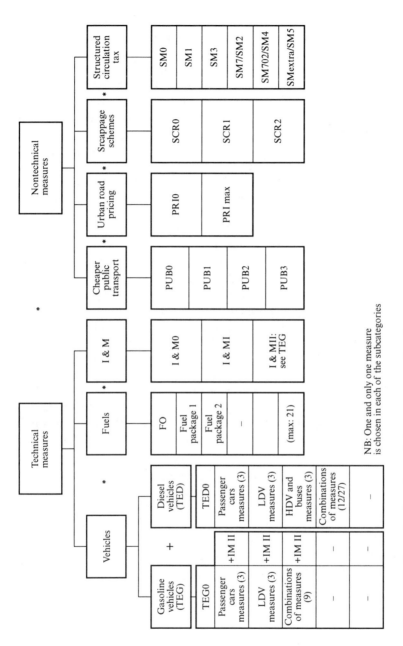

Figure 7.1 Organization chart of the transport-related measures

Combining the sets of measures for each of the emission scenarios listed in Table 7.1 allows the data for the model to be constructed. We need to mention here that data for gasoline vehicles include enhanced durability standards. The effects of these enhanced durability standards were not distinguished, in the available data, from the effects of inspection and maintenance. Technical standards for gasoline vehicles therefore also implicitly assume improved inspection and maintenance.[8] As a result, we consider 16 possible sets of measures for gasoline vehicles (the empty set, the three intensities for passenger cars, the three intensities for LDV, and the nine combinations) and 22 different sets of measures for diesel vehicles (the empty set, the three intensities for passenger cars, the three intensities for LDV, the three intensities for HDV and buses, and twelve selected combinations). This leads to 352 possible sets of measures for this first category. All measures are being considered as global. The empty set refers to the situation in which no technologies are being introduced. A list of the combinations is presented in Table 7.6 (letters refer to measures as defined in Table 7.5).

The total (percentage) reductions in CO, HC, NO_x (and particulate matter) emissions per kilometre travelled presented above (based on Touche Ross 1995) have been translated into percentage reductions in economy-wide emissions. This adjustment is detailed in Denis (1996) and leads to the 'effectiveness' parameters (denoted e_{Rjl} in the previous section) needed to run the model. Given the different shares of the various emission sources in the different regions analysed in the model, the emission reduction 'effectiveness' parameters vary across the regions.

The same study also specifies costs for each set of measures in ECU per vehicle. Based on the simulation results with the EUCARS model,

Table 7.6 List of technical standards for vehicle emissions.

TEG 1	∅
TEG 2–4	{A,G}, {B,G}, {C,G}
TEG 5–7	{D,H}, {E,H}, {F,H}
TEG 8–16	{A,G,D,H}, {A,G,E,H}, {A,G,F,H}, {B,G,D,H}, {B,G,E,H}, {B,G,F,H} {C,G,D,H}, {C,G,E,H}, {C,G,F,H}
TED 1	∅
TED 2–4	{A},{B},{C}
TED 5–7	{D},{E},{F}
TED 8–10	{G},{H},{I}
TED 11–22	{A,D,G}, {B,E,H}, {C,F,I}, {A,D,H}, {B,E,G}, {B,E,I}, {C,F,H}, {A,D,I}, {C,F,G}, {A,E,H}, {B,F,I}, {A,F,I}

which allow for the determination of additional welfare costs (Koopman and Denis 1995), we obtain total cost figures in ECU per set of measures and per region (see Denis 1996).

Technical measures: fuel standards
The study of Touche Ross (1995) also presents 24 scenarios for different combinations of gasoline and diesel fuels. The composition and the emission effects (per litre of fuel used) of the fuel options are listed in Tables 7.7a and 7.7b.

We assume that all fuels can be introduced locally. We do not have subcategories here (as is the case for vehicle measures), because the Touche Ross (1995) data already include the relative proportions of the two different engine types in use by the year 2010. More fundamentally, gasoline and diesel fuels are produced in a joint process and one cannot assess independently the changes in the two fuels. Furthermore, not all combinations between gasoline and diesel fuels from Tables 7.7a and 7.7b are possible or give useful results. As a consequence, we consider the 18 sets of measures in the fuel category listed in Table 7.8.

The effectiveness (as a percentage reduction) and the total incremental cost (in net present value and in ECU) of each set of measures for each of the pollutants are also provided by the Touche Ross (1995) study. To obtain the relevant figures for the effectiveness of measures expressed in

Table 7.7a Composition of gasoline fuel options

	Base	I	II	III	IV
Emission reductions					
(% of PC emissions):					
NO_x reduction	0	6.28	2.89	−2.75	−6.36
HC reduction	0	8.75	13.43	14.16	18.62
CO reduction	0	9.24	13.89	13.38	17.16
Fuel characteristics					
Benzene (vol.%)	2.3	2.1	1.8	1.0	0.7
Aromatics (vol.%)	40	37	36	30	25
Olefins (vol.%)	11	9	10	9	8
Ether (% O_2)	0.6	< 1.0	< 1.7	~1.6	~2.0
Distillation E 100 (%)	53	55	56	62	65
Distillation E 150 (%)	84	85	88	89	92
Sulphur (wt ppm)	300	30	30	100	100
RVP (summer) (kPa)	68	58	58	58	58

Table 7.7b Composition of diesel fuel options

	Base	I	II	III	IV
Emission reductions (% of PC and LDV emissions)					
NO$_x$ reduction	0	0.53	0.54	0.99	1.46
HC reduction	0	10.68	15.92	19.75	32.00
CO reduction	0	10.60	15.99	20.28	31.84
PM reduction	0	9.95	15.44	21.26	22.64
Emission reductions (% of HDV and buses emissions)					
NO$_x$ reduction	0	2.15	3.32	4.56	5.47
HC reduction	0	2.20	3.97	4.83	3.53
CO reduction	0	0.39	0.24	0.27	3.48
PM reduction	0	3.22	5.02	7.56	8.49
Fuel characteristics					
Cetane number	51	53	54	55	58
Density (kg/m^3)	843	835	831	828	825
Polyaromatics (vol.%)	9	6	4.5	2.2	1
T 95 (°C)	355	~350	~345	~340	~340
Sulphur (wt ppm)	450	300	200	50	30

Table 7.8 Fuel combinations for gasoline and diesel cars

Identifier	*Gasoline fuels*	*Diesel fuels*
F0	Gas base	Diesel base
F1	Gas I	Diesel base
F3	Gas III	Diesel base
F4	Gas IV	Diesel base
F5	Gas base	Diesel I
F6	Gas I	Diesel I
F7	Gas II	Diesel I
F8	Gas IV	Diesel I
F9	Gas base	Diesel II
F10	Gas I	Diesel II
F11	Gas II	Diesel II
F12	Gas III	Diesel II
F13	Gas IV	Diesel II
F14	Gas base	Diesel III
F18	Gas IV	Diesel III

economy-wide percentage emissions reductions, similar adjustments had to be made as in the case of the vehicle technology measures. These are detailed in Denis (1996).

The cost per litre of gasoline and diesel is provided by the Touche Ross (1995) study. Region dependent cost figures are calculated based on the total amount of litres consumed in the EU, weighted by the relative number of cars in a particular region.

Technical measures: inspection and maintenance
The data on inspection and maintenance measures are taken from Touche Ross (1995). This study gives the three scenarios shown in Table 7.9. Note that they only concern gasoline vehicles in this analysis. This subcategory consists of three sets of measures. Each measure can be locally introduced. As mentioned before, I&M scenario 2 is treated with the technical measures for gasoline vehicles. We therefore have only two options left in this subcategory: either no changes to the existing situation or I&M scenario 1. Moreover, as I&M scenario 2 includes I&M scenario 1, we have to make sure that in the program technical standards for gasoline vehicles (which include I&M scenario 2) are not chosen together with I&M scenario 1. This exclusion condition reduces the total number of bundles.

Similar adjustments on effectiveness and costs had to be made as in the case of the vehicle technology measures and fuel measures.

The nontechnical measures
The nontechnical measures include local measures, but also economic and fiscal incentives which change behaviour but also lead to technical

Table 7.9 Inspection and maintenance scenarios

Scenario	Measures
0	Keeping the existing control procedures (application of Directive 92/55/EC, with no further enhancements)
1	Introduction of a short transient test cycle (1a) or remote road side sensing of vehicle emissions (1b)
2	Along with the improved testing procedure (scenario 1), introduction of on-board diagnostics (OBD II) on all new vehicles sold, together with vehicle design to 160 000 km durability, supplemented by a programme to monitor and enforce the conformity of vehicles in circulation (CVC) with these higher standards

changes. Input data for the nontechnical measures are based on a report of the European Commission (1995). We refer the reader interested in the specific details of the measures to this study. Particularly, the effects of the measures listed in Table 7.10 are considered in this study. Note that the EUCARS model used in this study focuses on passenger cars and uses data at an EU–12 level of aggregation.

Combinations of all of these measures would lead to an extremely large number of sets (the total number of possible combinations of sets increases exponentially when adding additional sets). We therefore restrict our analysis to four effective (cost/effectiveness ratio) measures leading to the four nontechnical subcategories. These measures are detailed in Table 7.11. The analysis of the effects of other combinations is left for future research.

Combining the sets of measures for each of the local measures listed in Table 7.11 allows us to construct the data for the model. As a result, we consider four possible sets of measures for public transport, labelled PUB (the empty set, and the three intensities), two possible sets for road pricing, PRI (the empty set, and the maximum intensity, which is the

Table 7.10 Nontechnical measures

Type	Measure
Cheaper public transport	Public transport subsidy (percentage reduction in fares)
Traffic management	Traffic restrictions (percentage reduction in urban traffic) associated with improvements in public transport
Urban road pricing	Percentage increase of existing price per km
Scrappage (2001-2005)	Various scrappage subsidies based on car age
Fuel tax	Percentage increase in price of fuel
Structured fuel tax	Percentage increase in price of reference fuel (tax rate is based on NO_x emission factor)
Structured purchase tax	Purchase tax proportional to emissions (tax rate is based on NO_x emission factor)
Structured purchase tax with target	Purchase tax based on emissions above target (tax rate is based on NO_x emission factor)
Structured annual circulation tax 1	Tax proportional to absolute emissions (tax rate is based on NO_x emission factor and mileage)
Structured annual circulation tax 2	Tax proportional to emissions per km (tax rate is based on NO_x emission factor)

Table 7.11 Nontechnical sets of measures

Subcategory	Code	Specifications
Cheaper public transport	PUB1	10% fares reduction
	PUB2	25% fares reduction
	PUB3	40% fares reduction
Road pricing	PRI1	+5% of existing price per km
	(PRI2)	+15% of existing price per km
	(PRI3)	+25% of existing price per km
	(PRI4)	+35% of existing price per km
	PRI5	+50% of existing price per km
Scrapping schemes	SCR1	Scrapping subsidy equal to 2000 ECU per car older than 10 years (1996–2000)
	SCR2	Subsidy equal to 23% of the price of a new car, provided it replaces an old car (2008–2009)
Structured annual circulation tax	SM1	0.005 ECU/g emitted NO_x
	SM2	0.015 ECU/g emitted NO_x
	SM4	0.025 ECU/g emitted NO_x
	SM5	0.035 ECU/g emitted NO_x
	SM3	0.05 ECU/g emitted NO_x
	SM6	0.025 ECU/g emitted NO_x and replacing the existing circulation tax
	SM7	0.025 ECU/g emitted NO_x and replacing 50% of the fuel excises
	SM702	0.035 ECU/g emitted NO_x and replacing 50% of the fuel excises
	SMextra	Linear extrapolation of SM7, SM702 results

Notes: Estimations of the costs and effects of scrappage schemes based on previous Greek experience. Data given in Touche Ross (1995).

cheapest because of positive effects on congestion), and three possible sets of measures for scrapping schemes, SCR (the empty set, and the two different schemes). For the fiscal instrument, structured annual circulation tax, we have two possible sets of measures: either with fiscal reform, or without. In either case, we have six possibilities in total: the empty set, SM1, SM3, in addition to three other possibilities, either SM7, SM702 and SMextra if revenue recycling is applied, or SM2, SM4, SM5 if not. This leads to a total of 144 possible sets of measures which can be introduced locally.

The effectiveness and the total cost (in ECU) of each measure for the whole European Union are region dependent and are given by the EUCARS framework (European Commission 1995). Again we take into account the relative part of emissions for which the passenger cars sector was responsible in each region. Urban road-pricing data were extended to all vehicles (not only passenger cars) on the basis of urban mileage. The costs are weighted by the relative number of inhabitants in a certain region against the total in the EU.

The nontransport category

For the nontransport sector, we rely on national cost curves established for the total economy. Possible reductions of NO_x and SO_x were found in Klaassen (1992) and in the data base used by the RAINS model (Alcamo et al. 1990). Reductions in HC emissions were taken from an AEA study (1995). Because of the lack of general information on cross-effects, we took the conservative assumption that 100 per cent of costs are to be allocated to the reduction of the main pollutant, with the hypothesis that no change occurs for other pollutants.[9] One general and major difference with the costing methodology applied to mobile sources is that welfare costs were not estimated here, because of the lack of relevant data.

It has to be acknowledged that base data refer to countrywide emissions in the framework of regional pollution problems (ozone or acidification). We do not have specific abatement costs for the urban nontransport sector, which means that the urban/countrywide distinction does not exist as such in the stationary data. The difficulty was overcome by using existing information on urban shares of mobile and stationary sources: data for reduction in urban NO_x from nontransport sources are therefore made up from the national cost curves and the urban shares of transport in 2010. The main source of pollution in cities is, of course, transportation anyway.

The eleven nontransport measures can be introduced locally in our model. The emissions reductions are weighted by the part of the nontransport sector for each pollutant over the total emitted amounts. Below we describe how the cost/effectiveness data were derived for NO_x and HC emissions.

1. *Reduction in NO_x emissions.* As the basis for our data, we use national cost curves established for the year 2000 which are also used in the RAINS model (Alcamo et al. 1990). The scenario incorporates the legislation changes expected up to 2000. The first step is to eliminate

all the points on the cost curve that pertain to changes in the transport sector in order to keep only measures that would reduce emissions from nontransport sources (for example, cleaner technologies for power plants).Ten points are then chosen on each national curve. The same source was used by the Auto-Oil Programme to establish emission attenuation profiles up to 2010 for nontransport sources. Reasonable consistency can therefore be assumed for the impact.

2. *Reduction in HC emissions* The study AEA (1995) builds national cost curves for the reduction in HC from UK 1990 data. Total HC emissions exclude biogenic emissions. The cost curves were cleared of the transport measures and the already agreed measures, such as Stage I measures in refuelling stations. Biogenic emissions were added to the total of emissions from stationary sources to obtain reduction in percentage of nontransport emissions. Ten points were chosen on each curve, as for the NO_x cost curves.

3. *Aggregated (HC and NO_x) reduction from stationary sources* A simple additive rule was taken: cost of measure X is the sum of the costs of step X for the NO_x curve, and step X for the HC curve; emission reductions are unchanged. This is a conservative assumption.

Number of possible bundles
It has to be stressed that, although the number of sets of measures in each subcategory is limited, the resulting total number of bundles is very large. However, because of the nature of the so-called nontechnical measures and the specific problem mentioned for I&M scenario 2, the total number of bundles for each city is not simply the product of the number of sets of measures in each subcategory.

The EUCARS model used to evaluate the consequences of the nontechnical measures analyses the reactions of rational economic agents to changes in prices and travel conditions (taxation, car and fuel prices, congestion, and so on) and quantifies the resulting impact on emissions and consumer welfare. To the extent that nontechnical measures give consumers an incentive to buy cleaner cars and/or fuels, in addition to reducing mobility, measures from a variety of categories are selected.

This is particularly the case for the structured circulation tax based on car emissions. Imposing this tax induces rational consumers to select a set of measures from the inspection and maintenance subcategory which reduces emissions at costs that are lower than the tax. In addition, the structured circulation tax also induces consumers to select particular sets of measures from the gasoline and diesel subcategory of technical measures. The EUCARS results for the effectiveness and cost of the structured circulation tax thus implicitly comprise measures from other categories. Clearly, technical change can either be mandated through standards or induced by economic instruments, but, in order to avoid double counting, only one of these policy instruments can be selected.

The implication of this for the bundle composition process is that when a set of measures from the structured circulation tax subcategory is chosen, the model must be prohibited from choosing sets of measures from the inspection and maintenance and technical categories because they are already implied by the structured circulation tax. Clearly, the same applies to structured circulation taxes when technical standards are selected. Hence, certain combinations of sets of measures across subcategories are excluded.[10] The same applies to inspection and maintenance measures and technical measures for gasoline vehicles, to avoid double counting, as explained before.

The resulting total number of bundles for each region is 1 122 000. This means that the full-blown discrete optimization program for the seven regions contains 7 854 000 variables. The column generation procedure for the model without 'good' initial columns has explicitly generated exactly 665 of them at the master's linear programming optimum.

Discussion of the results

The modelling approach presented above has been used to evaluate different policy scenarios, each of which ensures that air quality standards are met throughout the seven regions included in the analysis. The detailed results of these scenarios are presented in Table 7.12. The rows of Table 7.12 contain seven sections, one for each region. Each section indicates both the cost and the composition of the selected bundle, the percentage reductions in emissions of urban NO_x, and regional HC and NO_x, as well as the contribution made by the various regions towards meeting the seven ozone objectives.

The base case (labelled SPEU1) generates a package of measures that implies annual costs of some 10 BECU. Several features of this base case are noteworthy. First, European-wide standards for passenger cars are not selected, but technical change is triggered through a vehicle tax reform including the introduction of a structured circulation tax on emissions. Tax rates and, therefore, the improvements in vehicle technology differ significantly across the regions: the strongest improvements are selected in The Hague and Madrid, intermediate tax levels are introduced in Athens and Cologne, while London and Lyons opt for more modest improvements. In all cases the tax reform consists of recycling a large part of the revenues from the new circulation tax back to car owners through lower fuel excises. The underlying data (European Commission 1995)

Table 7.12 Computational results

	SPEU1 To	SPEU1 From	SPEU1A To	SPEU1A From	SPEU2 To	SPEU2 From	SPEU2A To	SPEU2A From	BAT To	BAT From
ATHENS Cost	507.59		196.34		485.23		209.48		1204.40	
Bundle composition										
Technical gas	TEG6		TEG6		TEG4		TEG4		TEG15*	
Technical diesel	TEG9		TED9		TED8		TED8		TED1*	
Fuel	FUL0		FUL0		FUL4		FUL4		FUL9*	
Public transport	PUB1		PUB0		PUB1		PUB0		PUB3	
Road pricing	PRI1		PRI1		PRI1		PRI1		PRI1	
Scrapping scheme	SCR2		SCR2		SCR2		SCR0		SCR0	
Structured circulation tax	extraSM		extraSM		extraSM		extraSM		SM0	
Inspection and maintenance	IAM0		IAM0		IAM0		IAM0		IAM4*	
Nontransport	IND8		IND8		IND8		IND8		IND10	
Emissions reduction										
NO_{xurb} ≥ 55.0%	55.41		55.16		55.08		34.64		51.05	
HC ≥ 40.00%	45.03		44.82		47.55		49.14		47.09	
NO_x ≥ 0.00%	64.33		64.31		64.00		58.41		69.85	
O_3 Athens	76.17	76.17	75.79	75.79	80.88	80.88	84.46	84.46	79.37	79.37
Cologne	0.00	0.00	0.00	0.00	0.00	0.00	0.00	0.00	0.00	0.00
The Hague	0.00	0.00	0.00	0.00	0.00	0.00	0.00	0.00	0.00	0.00
London	0.00	0.00	0.00	0.00	0.00	0.00	0.00	0.00	0.00	0.00
Lyons	0.00	0.00	0.00	0.00	0.00	0.00	0.00	0.00	0.00	0.00
Madrid	0.00	0.00	0.00	0.00	0.00	0.00	0.00	0.00	0.00	0.00
Milan	0.00	0.00	0.00	0.00	0.00	0.00	0.00	0.00	0.00	0.00
O_3 ≥ 60.00%		76.17		84.02		80.88		84.46		79.37
COLOGNE Cost	4398.73		2108.21		4398.75		1715.69		5532.69	
Bundle composition										
Technical gas	TEG6		TEG6		TEG6		TEG6		TEG15*	
Technical diesel	TED9		TED9		TED8		TED9		TED1*	
Fuel	FUL4		FUL4		FUL4		FUL4		FUL9*	
Public transport	PUB1		PUB0		PUB1		PUB0		PUB1	
Road pricing	PRI1		PRI1		PRI1		PRI1		PRI1	
Scrapping scheme	SCR0		SCR0		SCR0		SCR0		SCR0	
Structured circulation tax	extraSM		extraSM		extraSM		extraSM		SM0	
Inspection and maintenance	IAM0		IAM0		IAM0		IAM0		IAM4*	
Nontransport	IND8		IND8		IND8		IND8		IND8	
Emissions reduction										
NO_{xurb} ≥ 25.00%	68.40		68.02		68.34		66.84		60.64	
HC ≥ 0.00%	62.13		61.95		62.08		61.91		57.71	
NO_x ≥ 0.00%	59.61		59.48		59.62		56.79		59.65	
O_3 Athens	0.00	0.00	0.00	0.00	0.00	0.00	0.00	0.00	0.00	0.00
Cologne	112.06	112.06	111.79	111.79	112.04	112.05	108.31	108.31	109.58	109.58
The Hague	45.66	11.89	45.54	10.67	45.64	11.89	44.49	11.87	44.06	11.45
London	15.59	0.54	15.54	0.59	1.57	0.52	15.85	0.52	13.97	0.59
Lyons	133.15	16.01	132.81	17.29	133.10	16.01	129.92	17.29	128.21	18.24
Madrid	0.00	0.00	0.00	0.00	0.00	0.00	0.00	0.00	0.00	0.00
Milan	18.484	0.22	18.43	0.21	18.45	0.22	18.07	0.21	17.73	0.22
O_3 ≥ 90.00%		140.72		140.55		140.68		138.20		140.08

* Denotes an imposed measure since the model's task is to supplement those measures to form bundles

Table 7.12 Computational Results (Continued)

		SPEU1		SPEU1A		SPEU2		SPEU2A		BAT	
THE HAGUE	Cost	1414.49		303.79		1414.48		982.82		1542.45	
	Bundle composition										
	Technical gas	TEG6		TEG6		TEG6		TEG6		TEG15*	
	Technical diesel	TED9		TED9		TED9		TED9		TED1*	
	Fuel	FUL8		FUL5		FUL8		FUL8		FUL9*	
	Public transport	PUB1		PUB0		PUB1		PUB0		PUB1	
	Road pricing	PRI2		PRI1		PRI1		PRI1		PRI1	
	Scrapping scheme	SCR0		SCR0		SCR0		SCR0		SCR0	
	Structured circulation tax	extraSM		extraSM		extraSM		extraSM		SM0	
	Inspection and maintenance	IAM0		IAM0		IAM0		IAM0		IAM4*	
	Nontransport	IND10		IND6		IND10		IND10		IND10	
	Emissions reduction										
	NO_{xurb} ≥ 5.00	61.83		58.40		61.79		64.57		66.81	
	HC ≥ 0.00%	77.39		70.03		77.43		77.26		71.93	
	NO_x ≥ 0.00%	63.09		55.58		63.06		62.98		65.72	
		To	From	To	From	To	From	To	From	To	From
	O_3 Athens	0.00	0.00	0.00	0.00	0.00	0.00	0.00	0.00	0.00	0.00
	Cologne	11.89	45.66	10.67	45.54	11.89	45.64	11.87	44.49	11.45	44.06
	The Hague	19.52	19.52	17.41	17.41	19.52	19.52	19.49	19.49	19.35	19.35
	London	4.00	10.92	3.71	12.08	4.01	10.63	4.00	10.64	3.31	11.86
	Lyons	14.19	14.21	12.73	15.38	14.20	14.21	14.17	15.38	13.71	16.16
	Madrid	0.00	0.00	0.00	0.00	0.00	0.00	0.00	0.00	0.00	0.00
	Milan	0.22	0.00	0.20	0.00	0.22	0.00	0.22	0.00	0.21	0.00
	O_3 ≥ 90.00%		90.31		90.40		90.00		90.01		91.43
LONDON	Cost	519.09		-425.50		277.02		-994.88		2523.00	
	Bundle composition										
	Technical gas	TEG6		TEG6		TEG4		TEG5		TEG15*	
	Technical diesel	TED9		TED9		TED6		TED7		TED1*	
	Fuel	FUL0		FUL0		FUL0		FUL0		FUL9*	
	Public transport	PUB1		PUB0		PUB1		PUB0		PUB1	
	Road pricing	PRI1		PRI1		PRI1		PRI1		PRI1	
	Scrapping scheme	SCR0		SCR0		SCR0		SCR2		SCR0	
	Structured circulation tax	SM7		extraSM		SM7		SM7		SM0	
	Inspection and maintenance	IAM0		IAM0		IAM0		IAM0		IAM4*	
	Nontransport	IND5		IND5		IND5		IND5		IND5	
	Emissions reduction										
	NO_{xurb} ≥ 40.00%	48.31		57.92		43.48		44.20		62.59	
	HC ≥ 0.00%	37.55		41.85		37.34		37.22		39.38	
	NO_x ≥ 0.00%	42.70		46.13		38.77		39.56		51.21	
		To	From	To	From	To	From	To	From	To	From
	O_3 Athens	0.00	0.00	0.00	0.00	0.00	0.00	0.00	0.00	0.00	0.00
	Cologne	0.54	15.59	0.59	15.54	0.52	15.57	0.52	15.85	0.59	13.97
	The Hague	10.92	4.00	12.08	3.71	10.63	4.01	10.65	4.00	11.86	3.30
	London	73.04	73.04	81.26	81.26	72.28	72.28	72.13	72.13	77.20	77.20
	Lyons	5.86	1.90	6.49	2.08	5.70	1.90	5.72	2.08	6.37	2.14
	Madrid	0.00	0.00	0.00	0.00	0.00	0.00	0.00	0.00	0.00	0.00
	Milan	0.00	0.00	0.00	0.00	0.00	0.00	0.00	0.00	0.00	0.00
	O_3 ≥ 90.00%		94.52		102.59		93.76		94.05		96.62

* Denotes an imposed measure since the model's task is to supplement those measures to form bundles

Table 7.12 Computational Results (Continued)

		SPEU1		SPEU1A		SPEU2		SPEU2A		BAT	
LYONS	Cost	780.75		-154.95		780.77		-154.95		2383.38	
	Bundle composition										
	Technical gas	TEG6		TEG6		TEG6		TEG6		TEG15*	
	Technical diesel	TED9		TED9		TED9		TED9		TED1*	
	Fuel	FUL4		FUL4		FUL4		FUL4		FUL9*	
	Public transport	PUB1		PUB0		PUB1		PUB0		PUB1	
	Road pricing	PRI1		PRI1		PRI1		PRI1		PRI1	
	Scrapping scheme	SCR0		SCR0		SCR0		SCR0		SCR0	
	Structured circulation tax	SM3		extraSM		SM7		extraSM		SM0	
	Inspection and maintenance	IAM0		IAM0		IAM0		IAM0		IAM4*	
	Nontransport	IND6		IND6		IND6		IND6		IND6	
	Emissions reduction										
	NO_{xurb} ≥ 40.00%	50.33		56.05		50.30		56.07		60.50	
	HC ≥ 5.00%	43.26		49.12		43.24		49.08		47.28	
	NO_x ≥ 0.00%	45.63		47.97		45.63		47.99		53.03	
		To	From	To	From	To	From	To	From	To	From
	O_3 Athens	0.00	0.00	0.00	0.00	0.00	0.00	0.00	0.00	0.00	0.00
	Cologne	16.02	133.15	17.29	132.81	16.01	133.10	17.29	129.92	18.24	128.21
	The Hague	14.21	14.19	15.39	12.73	14.21	14.20	15.39	14.17	16.16	13.71
	London	1.90	5.86	2.07	6.49	1.90	5.71	2.07	5.72	2.14	6.37
	Lyons	42.97	42.97	45.72	45.73	42.96	42.96	45.72	45.74	49.48	49.48
	Madrid	37.84	0.00	40.57	0.00	37.83	0.00	40.57	0.00	43.34	0.00
	Milan	24.69	1.88	26.64	1.74	24.68	1.81	26.64	1.74	28.13	1.80
	O_3 ≥ 90.00%		198.06		199.49		197.78		197.28		199.57
MADRID	Cost	1087.06		-74.75		1818.01		-146.51		1497.82	
	Bundle composition										
	Technical gas	TEG6		TEG6		TEG6		TEG6		TEG15*	
	Technical diesel	TED9		TED9		TED6		TED6		TED1*	
	Fuel	FUL1		FUL0		FUL4		FUL5		FUL9*	
	Public transport	PUB1		PUB0		PUB1		PUB0		PUB1	
	Road pricing	PRI1		PRI1		PRI1		PRI1		PRI1	
	Scrapping scheme	SCR0		SCR2		SCR0		SCR0		SCR0	
	Structured circulation tax	extraSM		extraSM		extraSM		extraSM		SM0	
	Inspection and maintenance	IAM0		IAM0		IAM0		IAM0		IAM4*	
	Nontransport	IND7		IND7		IND7		IND7		IND7	
	Emissions reduction										
	NO_{xurb} ≥ 50.00%	50.03		51.47		50.01		50.14		50.78	
	HC ≥ 30.00%	47.22		45.63		48.68		49.06		39.81	
	NO_x ≥ 0.00%	52.22		53.40		49.30		49.55		53.06	
		To	From	To	From	To	From	To	From	To	From
	O_3 Athens	0.00	0.00	0.00	0.00	0.00	0.00	0.00	0.00	0.00	0.00
	Cologne	0.00	0.00	0.00	0.00	0.00	0.00	0.00	0.00	0.00	0.00
	The Hague	0.00	0.00	0.00	0.00	0.00	0.00	0.00	0.00	0.00	0.00
	London	0.00	0.00	0.00	0.00	0.00	0.00	0.00	0.00	0.00	0.00
	Lyons	0.00	37.84	0.00	40.57	0.00	37.83	0.00	40.57	0.00	43.33
	Madrid	67.77	67.77	68.49	68.48	65.25	65.25	65.63	65.63	66.34	66.34
	Milan	0.21	00.00	0.20	00.00	0.20	0.00	0.20	0.00	0.19	0.00
	O_3 ≥ 0.00%		105.61		109.05		103.09		106.20		109.67

* Denotes an imposed measure since the model's task is to supplement those measures to form bundles

Table 7.12 Computational Results (Continued)

		SPEU1		SPEU1A		SPEU2		SPEU2A		BAT	
MILAN	Cost	1353.13		1112.34		1324.66		-240.03		2664.22	
	Bundle composition										
	Technical gas	TEG6		TEG6		TEG6		TEG6		TEG15*	
	Technical diesel	TED9		TED9		TED9		TED9		TED1*	
	Fuel	FUL5		FUL0		FUL4		FUL0		FUL9*	
	Public transport	PUB1		PUB0		PUB1		PUB0		PUB1	
	Road pricing	PRI1		PRI1		PRI1		PRI1		PRI1	
	Structured fuel tax	SCR0		SCR0		SCR2		SCR0		SCR0	
	Structured circulation tax	SM7		extraSM		SM702		extraSM		SM0	
	Inspection and maintenance	IAM0		IAM0		IAM0		IAM0		IAM4*	
	Nontransport	IND7		IND6		IND6		IND6		IND6	
	Emissions reduction										
	NO_{xurb} ≥ 50.00%	50.10		55.00		50.04		50.08		50.35	
	HC ≥ 30.00%	54.82		61.30		52.58		49.51		51.48	
	NO_x ≥ 0.00%	48.72		50.72		46.96		46.55		48.32	
		To	From	To	From	To	From	To	From	To	From
	O_3 Athens	0.00	0.00	0.00	0.00	0.00	0.00	0.00	0.00	0.00	0.00
	Cologne	0.22	18.47	0.24	17.99	0.22	18.47	0.21	18.07	0.22	17.73
	The Hague	0.00	0.22	0.00	0.19	0.00	0.22	0.00	0.22	0.00	0.21
	London	0.00	0.00	0.00	0.00	0.00	0.00	0.00	0.00	0.00	0.00
	Lyons	1.88	24.69	2.06	26.98	1.81	24.69	1.74	26.65	1.80	28.14
	Madrid	0.00	0.20	0.00	0.21	0.00	0.20	0.00	0.20	0.00	0.19
	Milan	342.53	342.53	368.19	368.19	329.45	329.45	319.04	319.41	331.79	331.79
	O_3 ≥ 80.00%		386.13		413.56		373.03		412.64		378.05
Total cost lower bound (MECU)		9956.75		1587.85		9566.21		1314.20		16876.45	
Total cost (MECU)		10060.84		1713.11		9600.03		1371.63		17347.96	
GAP (%)		1.03		7.31		0.35		4.19		2.72	

* Denotes an imposed measure since the model's task is to supplement those measures to form bundles

Table 7.12 Computational Results (Continued)

		Z1		Z1A		Z2		Z2A	
ATHENS	Cost	1371.84		1101.17		739.17		411.84	
	Bundle composition								
	Technical gas	TEG6		TEG5		TEG6		TEG6	
	Technical diesel	TEG9		TED9		TED9		TED9	
	Fuel	FUL0		FUL0		FUL6		FUL8	
	Public transport	PUB2		PUB2		PUB1		PUB0	
	Road pricing	PRI1		PRI1		PRI1		PRI1	
	Scrapping scheme	SCR2		SCR2		SCR2		SCR2	
	Structured circulation tax	SM2		SM3		SM3		SM3	
	Inspection and maintenance	IAM0		IAM0		IAM0		IAM0	
	Nontransport	IND10		IND10		IND8		IND8	
	Emissions reduction								
	NO_{xurb} $\geq 55.0\%$	55.41		55.07		55.03		55.22	
	HC $\geq 40.00\%$	45.96		45.89		45.93		45.61	
	NO_x $\geq 0.00\%$	70.55		70.46		65.04		65.28	
		To	From	To	From	To	From	To	From
	O_3 Athens	77.19	77.19	77.07	77.07	77.77	77.77	77.14	77.14
	Cologne	0.00	0.00	0.00	0.00	0.00	0.00	0.00	0.00
	The Hague	0.00	0.00	0.00	0.00	0.00	0.00	0.00	0.00
	London	0.00	0.00	0.00	0.00	0.00	0.00	0.00	0.00
	Lyons	0.00	0.00	0.00	0.00	0.00	0.00	0.00	0.00
	Madrid	0.00	0.00	0.00	0.00	0.00	0.00	0.00	0.00
	Milan	0.00	0.00	0.00	0.00	0.00	0.00	0.00	0.00
	O_3 $\geq 60.00\%$		77.19		77.07		77.77		77.14
COLOGNE	Cost	4207.20		2699.60		3814.66		2714.92	
	Bundle composition								
	Technical gas	TEG6		TEG5		TEG6		TEG6	
	Technical diesel	TED9		TED9		TED8		TED9	
	Fuel	FUL4		FUL5		FUL5		FUL5	
	Public transport	PUB1		PUB0		PUB1		PUB0	
	Road pricing	PRI1		PRI1		PRI1		PRI1	
	Scrapping scheme	SCR0		SCR0		SCR0		SCR0	
	Structured circulation tax	SM3		SM5		SM2		SM5	
	Inspection and maintenance	IAM0		IAM0		IAM0		IAM0	
	Nontransport	IND8		IND8		IND8		IND8	
	Emissions reduction								
	NO_{xurb} $\geq 25.00\%$	54.27		59.02		52.75		59.22	
	HC $\geq 0.00\%$	57.47		59.02		57.46		59.03	
	NO_x $\geq 0.00\%$	55.07		57.89		52.22		58.04	
		To	From	To	From	To	From	To	From
	O_3 Athens	0.00	0.00	0.00	0.00	0.00	0.00	0.00	0.00
	Cologne	103.56	103.56	108.08	108.08	99.90	99.90	108.27	108.27
	The Hague	11.55	42.20	43.86	11.67	41.10	11.44	43.92	11.70
	London	0.72	14.43	14.66	0.71	14.76	0.72	14.64	0.70
	Lyons	15.84	123.09	127.83	13.64	120.06	16.64	128.00	13.85
	Madrid	0.00	0.00	0.00	0.00	0.00	0.00	0.00	0.00
	Milan	0.21	17.08	17.72	0.22	16.70	0.21	17.74	0.21
	O_3 $\geq 90.00\%$		131.88		134.32		128.90		134.73

* Denotes an imposed measure since the model's task is to supplement those measures to form bundles

Table 7.12 Computational Results (Continued)

		Z1		Z1A		Z2		Z2A	
THE HAGUE	Cost	1575.91		1182.05		1557.50		1189.08	
	Bundle composition								
	Technical gas	TEG6		TEG5		TEG15		TEG6	
	Technical diesel	TED9		TED9		TED12		TED9	
	Fuel	FUL8		FUL9		FUL8		FUL9	
	Public transport	PUB1		PUB0		PUB2		PUB0	
	Road pricing	PRI1		PRI1		PRI1		PRI1	
	Scrapping scheme	SCR0		SCR0		SCR0		SCR0	
	Structured circulation tax	SM5		SM3		SM0		SM3	
	Inspection and maintenance	IAM0		IAM0		IAM0		IAM0	
	Nontransport	IND10		IND10		IND10		IND10	
	Emissions reduction								
	NO_{xurb} ≥ 5.00	57.89		58.57		66.94		59.20	
	HC $\geq 0.00\%$	74.69		75.46		71.91		75.58	
	NO_x $\geq 0.00\%$	62.26		62.96		65.69		63.21	
		To	From	To	From	To	From	To	From
	O_3 Athens	0.00	0.00	0.00	0.00	0.00	0.00	0.00	0.00
	Cologne	11.55	42.20	11.67	43.86	11.44	41.10	11.70	43.92
	The Hague	19.07	19.07	19.28	19.28	19.34	19.34	19.33	19.33
	London	14.87	3.78	3.82	14.76	3.31	14.97	3.82	14.53
	Lyons	14.09	13.80	13.94	12.12	13.70	14.71	13.98	12.30
	Madrid	0.00	0.00	0.00	0.00	0.00	0.00	0.00	0.00
	Milan	0.00	0.22	0.22	0.00	0.21	0.00	0.22	0.00
	$O_3 \geq 90.00\%$		90.23		90.02		90.12		90.09
LONDON	Cost	2233.24		923.94		2200.54		726.74	
	Bundle composition								
	Technical gas	TEG6		TEG5		TEG4		TEG4	
	Technical diesel	TED9		TED9		TED7		TED7	
	Fuel	FUL0		FUL0		FUL10		FUL0	
	Public transport	PUB1		PUB0		PUB1		PUB0	
	Road pricing	PRI1		PRI1		PRI1		PRI1	
	Scrapping scheme	SCR0		SCR0		SCR0		SCR0	
	Structured circulation tax	SM1		SM1		SM1		SM1	
	Inspection and maintenance	IAM0		IAM0		IAM0		IAM0	
	Nontransport	IND8		IND8		IND8		IND8	
	Emissions reduction								
	NO_{xurb} $\geq 40.00\%$	50.15		48.93		46.53		44.96	
	HC $\geq 0.00\%$	52.89		52.55		54.18		52.44	
	NO_x $\geq 0.00\%$	51.88		51.33		49.00		48.09	
		To	From	To	From	To	From	To	From
	O_3 Athens	0.00	0.00	0.00	0.00	0.00	0.00	0.00	0.00
	Cologne	14.43	0.72	0.71	14.66	0.72	14.76	0.70	14.64
	The Hague	3.78	14.87	14.76	3.82	14.97	3.31	14.53	3.82
	London	102.09	102.09	101.41	101.41	104.17	104.17	100.90	100.90
	Lyons	1.90	7.98	7.92	1.63	8.03	1.93	7.80	1.65
	Madrid	0.00	0.00	0.00	0.00	0.00	0.00	0.00	0.00
	Milan	0.00	0.00	0.00	0.00	0.00	0.00	0.00	0.00
	$O_3 \geq 90.00\%$		122.20		121.51		124.17		121.01

* Denotes an imposed measure since the model's task is to supplement those measures to form bundles

Table 7.12 Computational Results (Continued)

		Z1		Z1A		Z2		Z2A	
LYONS	Cost	1183.77		-686.80		1337.882		-656.51	
	Bundle composition								
	Technical gas	TEG6		TEG5		TEG9		TEG5	
	Technical diesel	TED9		TED9		TED12		TED9	
	Fuel	FUL5		FUL1		FUL5		FUL5	
	Public transport	PUB1		PUB0		PUB1		PUB0	
	Road pricing	PRI1		PRI1		PRI1		PRI1	
	Scrapping scheme	SCR0		SCR0		SCR0		SCR2	
	Structured circulation tax	SM1		SM1		SM0		SM1	
	Inspection and maintenance	IAM0		IAM0		IAM0		IAM0	
	Nontransport	IND7		IND6		IND6		IND6	
	Emissions reduction								
	NO_{xurb} $\geq 40.00\%$	48.41		42.65		55.57		44.23	
	HC $\geq 5.00\%$	44.85		37.99		41.38		38.21	
	NO_x $\geq 0.00\%$	44.03		38.25		49.26		39.04	
		To	From	To	From	To	From	To	From
	O_3 Athens	0.00	0.00	0.00	0.00	0.00	0.00	0.00	0.00
	Cologne	15.84	123.10	13.64	127.83	16.64	120.06	13.85	128.00
	The Hague	13.80	14.09	12.12	13.94	14.71	13.70	12.30	13.98
	London	7.98	1.90	1.63	7.92	1.93	8.03	1.65	7.80
	Lyons	41.94	41.94	36.28	36.28	45.57	45.57	36.94	36.94
	Madrid	0.00	37.19	32.10	0.00	39.71	0.00	32.64	0.00
	Milan	1.73	24.41	21.03	1.75	25.66	1.72	21.35	1.71
	$O_3 \geq 90.00\%$		188.53		187.73		189.09		188.43
MADRID	Cost	2081.73		740.81		1098.96		517.91	
	Bundle composition								
	Technical gas	TEG6		TEG5		TEG12		TEG12	
	Technical diesel	TED9		TED9		TED12		TED12	
	Fuel	FUL0		FUL0		FUL5		FUL6	
	Public transport	PUB1		PUB0		PUB1		PUB0	
	Road pricing	PRI1		PRI1		PRI1		PRI1	
	Scrapping scheme	SCR2		SCR2		SCR2		SCR2	
	Structured circulation tax	SM5		SM5		SM0		SM0	
	Inspection and maintenance	IAM0		IAM0		IAM0		IAM0	
	Nontransport	IND9		IND9		IND7		IND7	
	Emissions reduction								
	NO_{xurb} $\geq 50.00\%$	50.97		50.43		50.16		50.29	
	HC $\geq 30.00\%$	47.41		46.98		34.43		34.89	
	NO_x $\geq 0.00\%$	60.17		59.98		52.88		53.12	
		To	From	To	From	To	From	To	From
	O_3 Athens	0.00	0.00	0.00	0.00	0.00	0.00	0.00	0.00
	Cologne	0.00	0.00	0.00	0.00	0.00	0.00	0.00	0.00
	The Hague	0.00	0.00	0.00	0.00	0.00	0.00	0.00	0.00
	London	0.00	0.00	0.00	0.00	0.00	0.00	0.00	0.00
	Lyons	0.00	37.19	0.00	32.10	0.00	39.71	0.00	32.64
	Madrid	75.92	75.92	75.60	75.60	64.49	64.49	64.88	64.88
	Milan	0.00	0.22	0.22	0.00	0.18	0.00	0.18	0.0
	$O_3 \geq 0.00\%$		113.11		107.69		104.20		97.51

* Denotes an imposed measure since the model's task is to supplement those measures to form bundles

Table 7.12 Computational Results (Continued)

		Z1		Z1A		Z2		Z2A	
MILAN	Cost	1549.98		271.89		1538.65		266.82	
	Bundle composition								
	Technical gas	TEG6		TED5		TEG4		TEG4	
	Technical diesel	TED9		TED9		TED9		TED9	
	Fuel	FUL0		FUL0		FUL0		FUL0	
	Public transport	PUB1		PUB0		PUB1		PUB0	
	Road pricing	PRI1		PRI1		PRI1		PRI1	
	Structured fuel tax	SCR0		SCR2		SCR0		SCR0	
	Structured circulation tax	SM1		SM1		SM1		SM1	
	Inspection and maintenance	IAM0		IAM0		IAM0		IAM0	
	Nontransport	IND8		IND8		IND8		IND8	
	Emissions reduction								
	NO_{xurb} ≥ 50.00%	51.10		51.93		50.57		50.08	
	HC ≥ 30.00%	47.93		48.71		47.53		49.51	
	NO_x ≥ 0.00%	48.31		49.10		48.11		46.55	
		To	From	To	From	To	From	To	From
	O_3 Athens	0.00	0.00	0.00	0.00	0.00	0.00	0.00	0.00
	Cologne	0.21	17.08	0.22	17.72	0.21	17.74	0.21	18.07
	The Hague	0.22	0.00	0.00	0.22	0.00	0.22	0.00	0.22
	London	0.00	0.00	0.00	0.00	0.00	0.00	0.00	0.00
	Lyons	24.41	1.72	1.75	21.03	1.71	21.35	1.74	26.65
	Madrid	0.22	0.00	0.00	0.22	0.00	0.18	0.00	0.20
	Milan	322.03	322.03	327.29	327.29	320.15	320.15	319.04	319.41
	O_3 ≥ 80.00%		363.96		366.47		359.64		412.64
Total Cost Lower Bound (MECU)		14114.50		6114.28		12158.47		5079.80	
Total Cost (MECU)		14203.68		6232.67		12287.36		5170.81	
GAP (%)		0.63		1.90		1.05		1.76	

* Denotes an imposed measure since the model's task is to supplement those measures to form bundles

show that this is a highly cost-effective option that induces technical change at lower cost than can be achieved through the imposition of vehicle standards. This is because it entails a certain degree of switching from improvements in fuel efficiency (triggered by the fuel tax) to reducing noxious pollutants: the cost savings achieved by the former significantly bring down the overall cost of the package.

The data set does not contain economic instruments to trigger technical improvements for buses and light and heavy duty vehicles. In the computations, these can, therefore, only be introduced through technical standards. Moreover, in the base case it has been assumed that these standards have to be applied on a European-wide scale. For light and heavy duty vehicles as well as for buses the highest available standards are selected, in combination with a stringent inspection and maintenance regime (I&MII) for gasoline-powered vehicles.[11]

Nontransport measures also play an important role in reaching air quality standards. The intensity at which these are applied also varies significantly across the EU.

The reduction in emissions brought about by nontransport measures and fiscally induced improvements in new cars accounts for the lion's share of emission reduction. However, it has to be pointed out that the share differs across the various regions, reflecting differences both in contributions from various sources as well as in intensities at which the policy instruments are applied.

In addition, all regions apply a road-pricing scheme which has a significant impact on emissions (5–7 per cent), but comes at a negative cost. The simulation results with the EUCARS model that were used to generate the input data for this instrument suggest that it is a 'no-regrets' option because it reduces congestion and in the process also curbs emissions.

There is a significant degree of variation in the introduction of clean fuels. Only Lyons and Cologne select the same fuel type; the other cities adopt more tailor-made solutions. This clearly shows that the introduction of one 'Euro-fuel' quality would be an economically inefficient solution.

Finally, all cities introduce improved public transportation links. Although this option does not lead to strong reductions in emissions, it is low cost because it reduces congestion. Athens also selects the introduction of a scrapping scheme which makes an important contribution to reducing emissions from the existing car fleet. The relatively very high age of cars in Athens makes this an attractive option.

In a subsequent analysis (labelled SPEU1A), it was assumed that the marginal costs of public funds are 1.3 (instead of 1). The implicit hypothesis used for this analysis is thus that any government revenues generated by an air quality policy are used to cut distortionary taxes elsewhere in the economy. As a result, air quality policy instruments that are revenue raising become more attractive. This scenario has dramatically lower costs (1.7 BECU) than the base case. Interestingly, the selection of policy instruments does not change very much. The main change consists in an increased reliance on fiscal instruments for limiting car emissions, since any revenues from tax restructuring within the transport system can now be put to good use elsewhere in the economy. Also, subsidies to public transportation become less attractive and are no longer selected. Given the greater reduction in emissions from cars, the intensities at which measures are selected to reduce emissions from stationary sources are generally reduced.

The conclusion is that the policy mix is fairly stable, but becomes less costly since its revenues are assumed to be put to good use.

In a third analysis (labelled SPEU2), it was tested whether technical vehicle standards would become a more attractive option if they could be varied across the Union, that is, mandated at the level of the individual regions in contrast to being global. However, it was found that, even under this condition, standards for passenger cars are less attractive than economic instruments that induce technical change. Also, some variation is now introduced in the mix of standards for LDVs, HGVs and buses (where no economic instruments are available in the data set). Still, on the whole, the results presented in Table 7.12 show that the least-cost policy mix is fairly close to the base case. Accordingly, costs are lower (9.7 BECU), but the difference is fairly small (about 3 per cent). Assuming that the marginal costs of public funds equal 1.3 (analysis labelled SPEU2A) again brings down the overall costs of the package and induces a shift towards revenue-raising instruments. Total compliance costs are now just under 1.4 BECU (compared to 1.7 BECU in the case where no regional flexibility can be introduced).

These computational results suggest that using transport tax revenues to cut taxes elsewhere in the economy and allowing regional variation in emission standards (where these are applied) can bring down the costs of meeting air quality standards very significantly: the numerical experiments reported above suggest a sevenfold cost difference.

The above experiments have been repeated for a case where tax restructuring in the transport sector, an instrument that is selected in all regions in the base case (SPEU), albeit at different intensities, is assumed to be no longer available. This instrument is particularly cost-effective as it implies that revenues from a circulation tax on emissions are used to cut fuel excises: the induced technical costs of cleaner vehicles are partly offset by cost savings from less fuel efficient vehicles.[12] However, as a result, there is an increase in CO_2 emissions of up to 10 per cent (see European Commission 1995). As other instruments, by and large, have a neutral or slightly negative effect on CO_2 emissions and these emissions contribute to global warming (and, therefore, impose a cost on society), policy scenarios which contain this instrument are not fully comparable with scenarios not relying on this measure.

The results of this scenario (labelled Z1), however, indicate that technical standards for passenger cars are still not selected. Cities that had selected tax restructuring measures in the base case (SPEU1) replace it by purely revenue-raising circulation taxes on emissions. However, as these measures are costlier than tax restructuring, they are introduced at significantly lower tax rates as a result of which the reduction in emissions from cars is much lower than in the base case. As a result, the contribution from new technology in passenger cars to the required emission reductions is also smaller than in the base case. This is compensated by larger reductions from stationary sources. The total cost of the package (13.3 BECU) rises by some 30 per cent compared to the base case.

Computations without tax restructuring measures have been replicated for all the other experiments reported above. The results of these computations are presented in Table 7.12 (the experiments are denoted by Zx, where x refers to the name of the analysis). Broadly speaking, the pattern of policy measures does not change significantly in these computations compared to the relevant analysis with tax restructuring measures. However, costs are much higher and the percentage difference in costs between the two cases is especially large for the most 'flexible' case (with marginal costs of public funds of 1.3 and full flexibility in standards); the cost difference here amounts to nearly a factor of 4.

Finally, a scenario was run in which a traditional best available technology (BAT) approach to vehicle and fuel standards was tested. The strictest possible vehicle standards were mandated and a fuel specification was imposed that makes the largest technically possible contribution to bringing down NO_x emissions in Athens (the urban NO_x objective in Athens proved to be the binding constraint in this analysis – see below). Also, the most rigorous inspection and maintenance scheme available was made mandatory. All these measures were imposed at a European-wide level and it was left to the model to complement emission reductions, where necessary, by selecting additional instruments for the seven regions. However, in keeping with the regulatory nature of the BAT approach, the model was prohibited from selecting emissions-based circulation taxes.

The results of this scenario indicate that under these conditions the urban NO_x objective in Athens cannot be met. The maximum achievable reduction is 51 per cent. This clearly indicates that relying on a pure BAT approach could have environmental drawbacks because in certain regions changes in transport patterns are needed to bring about the required reductions in emissions. The scenario was re-run with the lower emission constraint for Athens. Total costs are approximately 17.3 BECU. The 70 per cent increase in costs compared to the base case results from the higher costs of vehicle and fuel technologies.

It was also evaluated whether the results are sensitive to changes in cost estimates. In particular, it was analysed to what extent the results would change if vehicle tax restructuring measures were 25 per cent costlier than in the base case. This sensitivity run (not reported) aims at developing some understanding for potential economies of scale in vehicle manufacturing. However, it was found that also in this case no 'global measures' are selected and that the pattern of instruments is very similar to the base case (results not reported).

It is worth underlining that reductions from stationary sources play an important role in all regions and scenarios. While the data collected for stationary sources are largely illustrative and the results have, therefore, to be interpreted with great care, this nevertheless suggests that undue reliance on transport options is unwarranted. More detailed work is necessary to assess the precise implications of this point.

Finally, the ozone constraint has an important impact on the results. As can be clearly seen from Table 7.12, The Hague and Lyons depend heavily on London and Cologne for reaching ozone constraints. Clearly, an important conclusion to be drawn from this is that, in defining emission reduction objectives for the local pollutants NO_x and HC, ozone has to be taken into account, preferably through the type of cost-effectiveness analysis presented in this chapter. A consecutive approach which first aims at reaching local air quality objectives and subsequently tags on ozone considerations is likely to be unnecessarily costly.

Conclusions and directions for future research

The analysis presented in this chapter suggests that a rebalancing of the air quality policy mix could result in substantial cost-savings if greater use were made of economic instruments. Although the results of this study are not comprehensive and more work is needed on improving the underlying data and the geographical coverage, cost differences of up to a factor 10 between a centralized standard-based approach and a decentralized approach relying on economic instruments such as those found in this study, suggest that serious thought should be given to ways of broadening the existing policy mix. However, in this respect, we would like to mention the critique of Oates et al. (1989) on the cost-effectiveness methodology used in this chapter. In the current version of the bundle selection programme, a zero value is attached for all air pollution reductions beyond the air pollution constraints. A centralized standard-based approach generally results in 'overcontrol' beyond the air pollution constraints. If there is no value to this overcontrol, the BAT-type of solution was shown to be more expensive than the decentralized approach relying on economic instruments. If, however, reduced concentrations below the level of the standards bring with them further improvements in health or the environment, the centralized standard-based approach will produce greater benefits than the decentralized or incentive-based approach. In further research, we will investigate how the additional benefits associated with the BAT-type solution can be offset against the cost advantages enjoyed by their incentive-based counterparts. Also, given the strong variation in air quality levels across the EU and the interregional nature of ozone formation, the introduction of greater regional detail could have an important impact on the numerical results of this analysis. Therefore, although the methodology developed in this chapter can be extended to incorporate these issues, it is clear that the results need to be interpreted with care.

In all computational results with the model, technical change in vehicle technology plays an important role in meeting air quality standards.

Triggering these changes through economic instruments is, however, attractive since this allows the strong geographical variation of air quality problems found in the EU to be accommodated. In addition, it must be pointed out that the present analysis does not exhaustively address all the issues that have to be considered. For example, further research into the importance of certainty for planning investment decisions in vehicle industries as well as economies of scale is needed. We believe that there is no contradiction in our approach of making technical standards on cars 'global' measures while the same technical improvements can be introduced locally when selected as a result of local tax incentives. However, globally enforcing technical standards could result in lower costs for the technology compared to a local introduction because of potential benefits of economies of scale in manufacturing. This has not been taken into account in this analysis as data related to economies of scale in manufacturing were not available at the time of writing this chapter. Future research should examine this issue.

Clean fuels also play an important role in the cost-effective scenarios analysed in this chapter. However, different clean fuels are generally selected for different regions. Therefore, if clean fuels are not required for reasons of complementarity with vehicle technologies (for example, unleaded petrol needed for cars with catalytic converters), ambitious European-wide fuel standards covering a large number of parameters would seem hard to defend on grounds of cost-effectiveness.

Road pricing seems to play an important role in cost-effective policy mixes to curb air pollution. It is always selected in the scenarios presented in this chapter, albeit at varying intensities. This results from the fact that road pricing brings in significant benefits through reduced congestion. In fact, the contribution to emission reduction is a secondary effect and the reductions in emissions from this tool are a 'by-product' that is, however, not to be overlooked. Tighter inspection and maintenance schemes can bring benefits, but are not found to be among the most cost-effective options.

Emission reductions from nontransport sources are of major importance in all scenarios studied in this chapter. Significant differences across the various regions hint at the importance of differentiating the intensity at which this instrument is applied. More information on the costs of nontransport measures is needed to arrive at a careful allocation of global emission reduction requirements to this sector.

The analysis presented in this chapter can be extended in various ways. For example, other air emissions, such as CO_2 and particulates, can be integrated in this framework. Sufficient data were not available at the time of writing. However, given the interdependencies existing between policies aimed at reducing these emissions and those analysed in this chapter, this extension could be of particular importance. Moreover, an increase in the number of regions analysed could also be envisaged, as well as a further differentiation within certain regions. This could modify the results, because of ozone-linkages and the significant degree of differentiation found within countries such as Germany. Finally, air quality problems usually occur during certain periods of the year. Therefore, it would, *a priori*, seem attractive to evaluate the potential of instruments that can vary in time. Cost-estimates would have to be made and reflection would have to be given to how this temporal dimension could be integrated into the model.

Finally, in this research we have focused on the identification of the cost-effective solution for the European Union as a whole. This is a necessary step. However, because of the interregional nature of ozone formation, policies result that, although being cost-effective globally, might not be the most attractive for local governments in terms of cost. Future research should address issues regarding how local governments can implement policies that are not necessarily in their own interest.

Notes

1. Of course, in the US two sets of emissions standards exist: the Californian standards and the federal standards. States are free to choose between adopting either system, but no other is allowed. The system is much disliked by the US car industry which claims that it implies high costs since two different sets of vehicles have to be produced and marketed, preventing the full exploitation of economies of scale.
2. For example, ozone concentrations can be evaluated according to different criteria: 1–hour maxima, 1–hour values for the 99th percentile, 8–hour maxima and 8–hour values for the 99th percentile. This illustrates that ozone values vary over time and across regions and that these characteristics have to be taken into account when drawing up guidelines. Moreover, in view of the uncertainty surrounding the health effects, there are upper and lower bounds for each criterion.
3. Air Quality Studies for the Auto-Oil Programme, European Commission, 1996. The 'Baseline' emissions and air quality levels incorporate the impact of the already agreed upon legislative proposals.
4. While the emission reduction objective for urban NO_x was directly derived from the work carried out in the context of the Auto/Oil Programme, the ozone target has been developed by the authors.
5. Data implicitly refer to the introduction of most measures at the national level, but for some measures the distinction is made between the urban zone and the entire country.
6. These measures also include enhanced durability standards, as will be explained later.
7. This section can be skipped without loss by a reader not interested in the technical details of the algorithm.
8. Improved inspection and maintenance (I&M) can be applied to gasoline cars and light duty vehicles, with two different intensities, the second one implying changes in new cars sold (enhanced durability specification, recall procedures, conformity of vehicles in circulation (CVC), on-board diagnostic (OBD)). This makes interactions with the technical vehicle packages difficult to handle, both for costs and emissions. It was therefore decided to combine the second intensity of I&M with the technical instruments

related to gasoline vehicles. Actually, because of the effectiveness of I&M, all technical standards for gasoline vehicles include this second I&M package.

9. According to Klaassen in a personal communication, most technologies used to reduce NO_x emissions are pollutant specific, and secondary benefits for reduction of VOC should be negligible for measures outside the transport sector.

10. Clearly, combinations of fiscal incentives and (multiple) standards can also be envisaged. Such packages could, for example, comprise minimum standards and fiscal incentives that lead to further reductions in emissions. Such packages can, in principle, be evaluated in the current framework. This issue is left for further research.

11. The standards for light duty diesel-powered vehicles are not tightened because, in the data set, they only occur in combination with standards for passenger cars (the latter are not selected because technical change is triggered through economic incentives and the exclusivity conditions imply that when either one is chosen the other cannot be adopted at the same time).

12. This is because, in the EUCARS model, fuel efficiency on new vehicles is produced up to the point where the technical costs are no longer outweighed by the (discounted) value of future fuel savings. A cut in fuel excises reduces the latter variable and therefore gives an incentive to produce less fuel efficient vehicles (which are also cheaper).

References

(AEA) Technology Consultancy Services (1995), 'HC Emissions in Europe: An Assessment of the Potential for Abatement and an Estimate of the Associated Costs', Report to the EC, DGXI.

Alcamo, J., L. Hordijk, and R. Shaw (1990), *The RAINS Model of Acidification: Science and Strategies in Europe*, Dordrecht/Boston/London: IIASA/Kluwer Academic Publishers.

Amann, M. and G. Klaassen (1995), 'Cost-effective strategies for reducing nitrogen deposition in Europe', *Journal of Environmental Management*, **43**, 289–311.

Dantzig, G.B. and P. Wolfe (1960), 'Decomposition principle for linear programs', *Operations Research*, **8**, 101–11.

Degraeve, Z. (1992), 'Scheduling Joint Product Operations with Proposal Generation Methods', PhD Dissertation, University of Chicago, Graduate School of Business, Chicago, Illinois.

Degraeve, Z., G.J. Koopman, C. Denis, and L. Teunen (1996), 'A Spatial Cost-Effectiveness Study of Transport Policy Measures Aimed at Achieving Air Quality Standards in the European Union', Research Report no. 9619, Department of Applied Economic Sciences, Katholieke Universiteit Leuven, Belgium.

Denis, C. (1996), 'Data Sources for the Optimization Model', in Z. Degraeve, G.J. Koopman, C. Denis and L. Teunen, 'Deriving and Selecting Policy Instruments to Meet Air Quality Standards in the European Union', European Commission, Technical Report, DGII.

European Commission (1995), 'A Welfare Cost Assessment of Various Measures to Reduce Pollutant Emissions from Passenger Road Vehicles for the Year 2010', Final Report, DG II, DOC II/576/95–EN.

European Commission (1996), 'Air Quality Studies for the Auto-Oil Programme', Report of Subgroup 2, DGXI, Doc XI/433/96, Brussels, Belgium.

Klaassen, G. (1992), 'Marginal and Average Costs of Reducing Nitrogen Oxides and Sulfur Dioxide Emissions in Europe', European Federation for Transport and Environment, T&E Report 93/2, Copenhagen.

Koopman, G.J. and C. Denis (1995), 'EUCARS: A Partial Equilibrium European Car Emissions Simulations Model, Version 2', European Commission, Technical Report, DGII.

Lasdon, L.S. (1970), *Optimization Theory for Large Systems*, New York: Macmillan.

Mayeres, I., S. Proost and D. Miltz (1993), 'The Geneva Hydrocarbon Protocol: economic insights from a Belgian perspective', *Environmental and Resource Economics*, **3**, 107–27.

Nilsson, M. (1995), 'To Clear the Air over Europe', European Federation for Transport and Environment, T&E Report 95/8, Brussels.

Oates, W.E., P.R. Portney and A.M. McGartland (1989), 'The net benefits of incentive-based regulation: a case study of environmental standard setting', *American Economic Review*, **79** (5), 431–53.

Schrage, L. (1992), *LINDO: An Optimization Modeling System*, Danvers, MA: Boyd & Fraser.

Simpson, D. (1991), 'Long Period Modeling of Photochemical Oxidants in Europe', EMEP, Cooperative Programme for Monitoring and Evaluation of the Long Range Transmission of Air Pollutants in Europe, Swedish Environmental Research Institute, EMEP MSC–W Report 2/91, Update September 1995.

Stedman, J.R. and M.L. Williams (1991), 'A trajectory model of the relationship between ozone and precursor emissions', Warren Spring Laboratory, Working Paper No. W91027.

Touche Ross (1995), 'A Cost-effectiveness Study of Various Measures Likely to Reduce Pollutant Emissions for Road Vehicles for the Year 2010, Final Report', Edinburgh, UK.

8. Central versus local regulation of gasoline-related automobile emissions: the contrasting cases of lead, CO and precursors

Jane V. Hall

Introduction

Emissions from transport are significant contributors to ambient air pollutants that threaten ecosystems, including human health, on a large scale. The scope of vehicular emissions is large. Multiple primary and secondary pollutants result from poorly controlled emissions. As vehicle use grows and industrial sources of pollution simultaneously become better controlled, reduction of vehicular emissions becomes more urgent.

One significant issue is whether vehicular emissions should be regulated at the central (federal) or local level. For the case of stationary (largely industrial) pollution sources the primary reason to regulate centrally is to manage transboundary pollutants or their precursors. A secondary reason, with somewhat weaker economic support (Jaffe et al. 1995), is to reduce the incentive for regions to compete via less stringent regulations. In the absence of these two considerations, local jurisdictions could determine the optimal means of regulation. For vehicles, however, mobility is a complication. That is, vehicles do not remain in any one jurisdiction, but must refuel when needed, regardless of location.

Even with this factor, some choices might be made locally, in so far as they affect aspects of fuel composition that directly reduce hydrocarbon or carbon monoxide emissions from the vehicle's fuel or exhaust system. A primary exhaust control technology – the catalytic converter – is, however, fouled by the use of leaded gasoline. Consequently, even if catalytic converters were necessary only to meet 'local' air quality objectives, unleaded gasoline must be available anywhere that vehicles with this technology are likely to refuel. Essentially, unleaded gasoline is a perfect complement to the catalytic converter in the reduction of hydrocarbon, carbon monoxide and nitrogen oxide emissions.

This chapter first provides a brief background on why vehicle-related regulation is necessary; the nature of relevant pollutants; the environmental objectives of emissions regulation; and the role of transport emissions in air quality management. It then describes the role of fuel composition in emissions reductions and contrasts the cases of lead and hydrocarbon control. Finally, the factors that determine whether local or central control is more appropriate are discussed and a framework is suggested to assist in making such determinations.

Background
Automobile emissions are regulated because that is the only means to approximate an efficient reduction in the environmental impacts they cause. Further, those impacts are potentially severe, cumulative and persistent.

The theoretical basis for regulation
In general, competitive markets achieve (or adequately approximate) the objective of efficiency. For many environmental goods, including improvements in air quality, an efficient outcome will not be reached by markets alone. First, no market exists in which cleaner air can be privately purchased as a discrete good. Second, polluting emissions are a classic externality. Third, even with clearly assigned property rights the transaction costs of reaching an efficient solution among interested parties would preclude such a result.[1]

Furthermore, efficiency is not the sole factor in social welfare. Equity considerations may also justify regulation (Stokey and Zeckhauser 1978). Finally, markets may optimize locally, but scale effects could still require central action (Daly 1991) if effects aggregated across regions are large. Thus, there are three possible objectives of regulation: increasing efficiency in allocation, increasing equity in distribution, and accounting for scale effects.

All of these are factors in seeking to optimize the 'community welfare function' (Munda et al. 1994). Clearly, it is then also necessary to define the boundaries of the community. For environmental effects, the boundaries must encompass both the sources and receivers of pollutants.

Fuel and combustion by-products and transformation products
Vehicles directly emit a wide array of compounds. Lead (Pb), carbon monoxide (CO) and sulphur dioxide (SO_2) are harmful in the form in which they are emitted and are therefore called primary pollutants. Hydrocarbons (HC) and nitrogen oxides (NO_x) contribute to the formation of other compounds that are harmful, which are called secondary pollutants. (Sulphur oxides also contribute to secondary pollutants.) Figure 8.1 illustrates the association between emitted compounds and primary and secondary pollutants.

The distinction between primary and secondary pollutants is an important factor in assessing the appropriate level of government intervention because the impacts of primary pollutants are more likely to be limited in geographic area and because some emissions generate joint

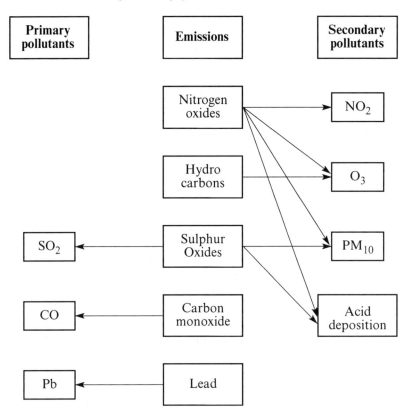

Figure 8.1 Emissions and resulting primary and secondary pollutants.

products. Carbon monoxide, for example, tends to concentrate locally, and does not contribute to formation of any secondary pollutants. Nitrogen oxides, in contrast, contribute to NO_2 locally, ozone locally and downwind, fine particulate matter (PM_{10}) locally and downwind, and acid deposition at great distances.

Another important factor is whether targeted pollutants can be reduced by fuel reformulation or only with emissions controls on the vehicle, or whether a carefully coordinated combination of these two approaches is required.

Effective regulatory options – those that meet environmental objectives at least cost – are constrained by these factors: the complex patterns of transformation of emissions into multiple compounds at various distances, and the technical approaches that can effectively address both the scope and the scale of pollutants.

Environmental objectives

Taken broadly, the ecosystem impacted by vehicular emissions extends from the human lung to large areas of forest and limnetic systems. The movement of pollutants within a large air mass defines the scale of this ecosystem. The scale therefore differs by pollutant. The number of pollutants originating at a source defines the scope.

At the local level, health is the dominant issue; downwind, acid deposition and ozone impacts on forest and limnetic systems are of concern. With the limited exceptions of CO and lead, vehicular emissions have the potential to contribute to pollution across all scales of the ecosystem.

Breathing elevated fine particulates is associated with increased risk of death, respiratory illness and reduced worker productivity (Dockery and Pope 1994). Four thousand people died during one five-day period during the infamous London pollution episode of 1952 (Cochran and Peilke 1992). Sulphur dioxide is also associated with increased respiratory illness and lost work days. Sulphur, along with nitrogen oxides, contributes to acid deposition, which is calculated to cause the loss of more than $30 billion each year in European forest ecosystem output (Brown 1993). Emissions of sulphur and nitrogen oxides are also precursors of PM_{10} components.

Carbon monoxide reduces the blood's capacity to carry oxygen, a particular risk to those with cardiovascular conditions. Lead affects learning ability in children through its action on the central nervous system and increases the risk of hypertension in adults.

Ozone's (O_3) most serious effect may be reduced lung capacity after long-term exposure and there is some evidence of an association with premature death (Lippman 1989, 1993). It also causes eye irritation, coughs, sore throats and headaches, as well as damaging forests and reducing crop yields. The health benefits of reducing ozone and PM_{10} to US air quality standards are estimated at about ten billion dollars annually for the Los Angeles region (Hall et al. 1992).

The growing role of transport

Transport emissions are a large and growing source of total emissions in Europe. The Organization for Economic Cooperation and Development (OECD) has reported that transport contributes 60 per cent of total nitrogen oxides (NO_x), 78 per cent of carbon monoxide (CO) and 50 per cent of hydrocarbons (HC) (OECD 1991a).

Another indicator of emissions potential is the increasing proportion of commercial energy used in transport (WRI 1992). As Table 8.1 shows, the per cent has risen throughout Europe, generally to about 25 to 30 per cent in most countries. At the same time, kilometres driven have risen rapidly throughout Europe. The percentage increase from 1970 to 1989 ranges from under 60 per cent in Belgium to nearly 300 per cent in Greece, as shown in Table 8.2 (OECD 1991b).

The dominant fuel in meeting the growing demand for mobility is gasoline.[2] A number of advantages over other potential fuels suggest that gasoline will continue to be dominant for the foreseeable future. These include energy density, existing infrastructure, existing engine technology and relative cost (Calvert et al. 1993). This means that reducing transport emissions will require cleaner engines, cleaner fuels, or a combination of engine/fuel strategies.

Table 8.1 Percentage of total commercial energy used in transport

Country	1979	1989
Austria	23	27
Belgium	16	23
Denmark	23	32
France	22	29
Germany	19	26
Italy	23	28
Netherlands	15	20
United Kingdom	25	30

Source: World Resources Institute (1992).

Table 8.2 Change in European road traffic

Country	Percentage change in vehicle–kilometres, 1970–1989	Billions of vehicle kilometres, 1989
Austria	147	54
Belgium	57	52
France	99	414
Germany	82	427
Greece	293	36
Italy	103	297
Netherlands	85	89
Spain	185	100
Sweden	73	61
Turkey	283	23
United Kingdom	99	357

Source: OECD (1991b).

The contribution of transport emissions is important because: it is growing relative to total pollution; transport demand is rising, especially in the southern regions of Europe; control may be more cost-effective than further regulation of other sources; transport is highly dependent on liquid fossil fuels; and even in cases where local effects are the primary concern, local jurisdictions have limited control over emissions from vehicles moving through the area.

The case of regulating gasoline

Gasoline must meet a wide array of vehicle performance objectives. Three of the most important characteristics are octane rating, vapour pressure and distillation range. Octane number is the anti-knock rating of the fuel and is a key factor in how well the engine will perform. Vapour pressure must be high enough for a cold engine to start and low enough to avoid vapour lock at high temperatures or altitudes. The distillation range affects performance and mileage.

Over time, gasoline has been modified to meet changing engine requirements (especially higher compression ratios). Engine technology has also changed, accommodating fuel changes that are environmentally beneficial. Valve seat materials, for example, have been substituted such that they do not require leaded gasoline to protect them from rapid wear. Vapour pressure and other fuel characteristics have also been regulated to reduce vehicular emissions. Whether such changes require extensive capital investment in refining technology or can be achieved more simply depends on which elements of the fuel must be modified and how extensively.

When gasoline composition is regulated to reduce air pollution, it is to reduce the total mass of emissions. However, in the case of hydrocarbons, it may also be to reduce the reactivity of emissions. There are six characteristics of gasoline that are important in the reduction of either mass or reactivity. These are: olefin content, oxygenates, sulphur, vapour pressure, aromatic content and distillation characteristics (see Appendix 8AI for definitions of these terms). Of these, reductions of the first four clearly reduce emissions of CO, HC or NO_x, either directly or by improving the efficiency of the vehicle's control system (Calvert et al. 1993).

The ways in which emissions reductions result vary with each component. When sulphur is reduced, efficiency of the catalytic converter increases. Reductions in vapour pressure reduce hydrocarbon emissions that evaporate from the vehicle's fuel system, even when not in operation. Light olefins tend to be more reactive, a factor in ozone formation; reducing them reduces the ozone-forming potential of HC emissions. Adding oxygenates (such as methyl tertiary butyl ether, MTBE) reduces CO and increases octane.

Changing any single component of gasoline to meet environmental objectives, however, requires one or more compensating changes to maintain those characteristics that are important for vehicle performance. Optimization across these sets of variables is complex, and requires that the dual functioning of the fuel and engine be taken into account.

The approach chosen will depend on the scope of pollutants to be reduced, the relative environmental scale of their effects, and the technological alternatives available in the refining and blending of fuels. Each of these factors plays a role in the relative gains and losses society will experience as a result of fuel reformulation.

Lead and the catalytic converter
Lead is a common gasoline additive in areas where catalytic converter technology is not required on vehicles. It is a low cost means of boosting octane because relatively little is needed and its use avoids investment in expensive refinery equipment and more intensive use of crude feedstocks. For (generally older) vehicles it also protects valve seats from wear.

In the United States, however, lead has gradually been phased out of gasoline, beginning in the mid-1970s. California banned it outright as a fuel additive in 1992. Many other regions around the world are now in various stages of lead reduction.

The reasons for restricting use of this inexpensive additive are threefold. First, lead emissions produce elevated lead levels in ambient air. At relatively low concentrations severe adverse health effects result. Second, lead damages some components of the engine and exhaust system. Finally, catalytic converters are 'poisoned' – disabled and rendered ineffective – by small amounts of lead. Catalysts on vehicles mis-fuelled with leaded gasoline have HC idle emissions nine times, and CO emissions three times, the level allowed in California in 1990 (CARB 1990a, 1990b). As little as three tanks of leaded fuel can render the catalyst useless (Hall et al. 1995).

Catalytic converter technology in current use is capable of substantially reducing exhaust emissions of HC, CO and NO_x. It is the most effective and most cost-effective (lowest cost per ton) means of reducing exhaust emissions to an equivalent level now available. Consequently, regulations that require exhaust emissions at the level adopted in 1992 by the Commission of the European Communities effectively mandate catalytic converters on gasoline-powered passenger vehicles. The 1992 standards are close to the US federal 1980 standards, and the standards proposed for 1994 and to be implemented in 1996, for HC and NO_x combined, approximate the Californian 1980 standards (Small and Kazimi 1995).

The central decision to apply these exhaust standards throughout the European Union (EU) introduces the necessity of preventing mis-fuelling with leaded gasoline to ensure the effectiveness of the catalytic converter over the life of the vehicle. At a minimum, this implies two additional federal regulations. First, unleaded fuel must be available throughout the EU. Second, filler inlet restrictors (to prevent fuelling from the larger nozzles on pumps dispensing leaded fuel) are necessary on cars equipped with catalytic converters, and must be inspected to ensure that they have not been removed.

Unleaded fuel and the catalytic converter are perfect complements in producing reduced exhaust emissions. Consequently, adoption of catalytic converter technology to meet vehicular emissions standards introduces the further necessity of federal regulation requiring widespread availability and use of unleaded gasoline. The fact that lead is in and of itself harmful to human health increases the net benefits of these regulations.

Reformulated gasoline

Reformulated gasoline (RFG) is 'gasoline with modified chemical and physical properties' intended to reduce the mass and air quality impact of vehicular emissions (Calvert et al. 1993). Current and proposed RFG requirements in the US are aimed at both reducing emissions from the existing fleet and enhancing the effectiveness of new emissions controls on automobiles.

The potential scope of ambient pollution reduction from RFG is wide, including reductions in O_3, NO_2, CO, PM_{10} and acid deposition. Some of these pollutants are primarily of local concern and others have impacts far downwind from their emissions sources. Changes in fuel composition necessary to achieve pollution reductions can be generalized into those that can be undertaken solely to meet local objectives and those that are necessary to meet environmental objectives at distant receptors.

Carbon Monoxide Carbon monoxide is a pollutant that may be controlled locally. It is a primary pollutant, contributes to no secondary pollutant(s), and tends to concentrate in places where there is heavy vehicular traffic. Consequently, where catalytic converters do not reduce CO adequately to meet health standards, further control is possible by adding oxygenates to gasoline. This requirement can be limited to only those areas with elevated CO and can be seasonal. Further, the addition of oxygenates boosts octane and is accomplished by blending, rather than by more complex refining processes.

Ozone, PM_{10} and Acid Deposition Moving beyond CO, the picture becomes much more complicated. Ozone is a secondary pollutant, requiring HC and NO_x for its formation in the atmosphere. The relative contribution of HC and NO_x to ozone formation varies, however, with location and the mix of emissions in the regional air mass. Therefore, in regions that are 'NO_x-limited', reducing NO_x emissions will be more effective in controlling O_3 than would HC reductions. This is because in a relatively HC-rich atmosphere, NO_x emissions significantly increase ozone production. The reverse is true for regions that are HC-limited. Suburban and rural areas downwind of cities tend to be NO_x-limited because there are fewer industrial sources and less traffic (Finlayson-Pitts and Pitts 1993).

Ozone reduction, however, is not the only reason to control NO_x emissions. Nitrogen oxides are also precursors to PM_{10}, acid deposition and an array of other compounds. Consequently, even in areas that are HC-limited for ozone formation, NO_x reductions may be necessary to prevent downwind effects outside the local jurisdiction.

Apart from CO control, it is apparent that local control might not be adequate to meet environmental objectives. Where reducing local ambient ozone is the sole objective of HC control, or where such control simultaneously reduces downwind ozone effects to a level acceptable in the downwind area(s), local regulation of fuels to reduce the ozone-forming potential would be adequate. Where more hydrocarbon reduction is necessary to protect downwind areas, or where NO_x control is necessary to reduce PM_{10} or acid deposition, local ozone-related regulations will not necessarily achieve overall air quality goals. This is because local jurisdictions will be disinclined to incur costs to reduce effects falling beyond their boundaries. Unless the degree of control necessary to meet local objectives coincides with that needed to reduce downwind effects, local control is likely to be inadequate.

Gasoline reformulation Ozone, NO_2, PM_{10} and acid deposition are all reduced by NO_x reductions that can be gained from improved catalytic converter efficiency and reduced engine wear resulting from sulphur limits, and from reducing the aromatic content of gasoline (CARB 1994a). Nitrogen oxide exhaust emissions are predicted to fall an additional 11 per cent as a result of implementation of the California Air Resources Board (CARB 1994b) proposed Phase II RFG standards which limit sulphur content to 40 ppmw and aromatics to 25 per cent of volume. These restrictions go further than the federal limits set by the Environmental Protection Agency (EPA) under the 1990 Clean Air Act Amendments and will require investment in sophisticated refining equipment.

Many of the requirements of RFG are directed at reducing HC mass and reactivity. Vehicles emit HCs in two ways: evaporative losses from the fuel system and incompletely combusted HC from the exhaust.

Evaporative losses can be a significant portion of a vehicle's total HC emissions. Evaporative HC emissions result from three processes. Diurnal HC emissions result from variations in daily temperature that cause fuel in the vehicle's tank to expand, even when the engine is not running. Higher ambient temperatures mean higher emissions rates. Running losses are the result of higher temperatures while the vehicle is operating. Hot soak emissions come from the carburettor after the engine has been turned off, but not yet cooled. The primary method to reduce evaporative emissions is to restrict vapour pressure by various means. (This will also reduce HC emissions during re-fuelling and from fuel storage and transport.) Vapour pressure is generally measured by Reid Vapor Pressure (RVP) expressed as psi (pounds per square inch).

The simplest way to reduce vapour pressure is to reduce the amount of butane added to gasoline. Butane is blended into gasoline because it is an excellent octane booster (and therefore a logical substitute for lead), and is inexpensive. It is also very volatile. This is an advantage in ensuring high enough vapour pressure for engine performance, but increases emissions simultaneously. Reducing butane content means that something else must be substituted to maintain octane levels necessary for acceptable engine performance. There are three basic ways to do this: use more expensive blending agents (oxygenates), refine more crude oil and produce less gasoline per barrel, or use more sophisticated refining methods (fluid catalytic cracking, alkylation and isomerization) that are more capital intensive.

The choice then is to reduce RVP by blending alternative octane-boosting feedstocks or by investment in refining capacity. Reducing gasoline reactivity also reduces ozone-forming potential, even if mass emissions are not significantly reduced. The HC that are emitted then have less capability to mediate the transformation of NO_x into ozone. Reducing light olefin content is the primary means to achieve this (Calvert et al. 1993; CARB 1994a).

Effective regulation

Reducing ambient CO, ozone and other secondary pollutants with catalytic converter technology requires the simultaneous availability of unleaded gasoline and enforcement of fill pipe restrictor requirements. The noble metal component of the catalyst is so sensitive to the disabling effect of lead that even occasional mis-fuelling will render the catalyst ineffective. The catalytic converter is the 'first line' means to achieve exhaust standards. Decisions to deploy this technology (or to impose exhaust standards that can be met no other way) must be federal, and are effectively decisions to require the sale of unleaded fuel and to undertake other measures to prevent mis-fuelling. A phase-out of lead in gasoline may eventually be required to protect health and further reduce mis-fuelling.

Reductions of CO, HC and NO_x emissions (beyond those accomplished by the catalyst) to meet local air quality objectives can be achieved with reformulation of gasoline. Replacing butane with oxygenates, for example, reduces CO and the ozone-forming potential of HC simultaneously. Where downwind effects are at issue, more sophisticated reformulation involving refinery reconfiguration and processing changes are necessary to improve catalyst efficiency, reduce NO_x and further reduce reactivity.

The appropriate level of government to undertake any action therefore depends on whether control beyond the catalyst is necessary only to meet local objectives or also to meet objectives outside the jurisdiction(s) where vehicle emissions occur.

Issues of scale and scope

The regulating jurisdiction must have the ability to set and achieve environmental objectives. The boundaries will then be determined by the scope and scale of fuel-related vehicular emissions. Scope refers to the size of the set of pollutants that result from emissions. Scale refers to the geographic reach of pollution and the aggregate impacts (costs and benefits) of reducing those pollutants. Scope and scale together determine whether federal action is necessary and whether it is worthwhile.

Ecological factors

From an ecosystem perspective, regulatory jurisdiction must reach to the boundary of adverse effects resulting from vehicular emissions. The dominant ecological factors in determining the boundary are the complexity of atmospheric chemistry and mobility of large air masses. Hydrocarbon and NO_x emissions from vehicles are involved in numerous complex atmospheric interactions. The products of these pollutants vary fundamentally with local conditions, notably meteorology and the ratio of pollutants present in the atmospheres near the point of emission and downwind. The ultimate effects of these emissions also depend on the aggregate level of pollution and the existence of sensitive receptors.

For the case of controlling HC to reduce ozone, the effectiveness of reducing HC emissions to achieve the goal depends upon whether the atmosphere is already rich in HC. If so, and especially if biogenic HC are an important constituent, NO_x control will also be necessary to reduce ozone (Finlayson-Pitts and Pitts 1993). The scope of regulation must then reach to both pollutants.

If downwind areas are susceptible to acid deposition, or PM_{10} is elevated locally or downwind, NO_x control will be necessary in any event. This means that fuel regulation must extend beyond those characteristics affecting HC and also introduces the possibility that NO_x exhaust standards must be set at absolute levels, not as a function of HC (Hall and Hall 1997).[3]

Economic considerations
Environmentally, jurisdiction should be defined by the boundary of effects on the largest defined element of the ecosystem (Zerbe 1974). For air pollution, this will be the downwind reach of acid-generating emissions. From an economic perspective, jurisdiction should be large enough to encompass the benefits and the costs of abatement (Baumol and Oates 1988). Otherwise, the transaction costs of agreement may be so large as to preclude effective regulation, even if compensation is possible. In theoretical terms, this means that jurisdiction can vary by the scope and scale of what is emitted, as long as the regulating authority accounts for all costs and benefits of abatement.

In practice, the regulation of HC and NO_x is technically complex. The generation of ozone is represented by a non-convex production function and both HC and NO_x produce joint products. There is no unique robust least-cost HC abatement strategy for ozone because of the non-convexities in the atmospheric production of ozone (Repetto 1987). This is not a significant policy issue, however, where NO_x also generates other pollutants with adverse effects because the level of NO_x abatement will be determined by other factors, constraining the set of HC reductions that will reduce local ozone.

Further confounding economic considerations is the joint product problem. Logically, before any regulation is undertaken we want to know the approximate economic benefits that will result from abatement. This means estimating the reduction in the frequency of adverse effects that are associated with a quantity of emissions and placing a value on avoiding those effects. The marginal benefit of reducing HC- or NO_x-related ozone, however, depends on the level of other 'inputs'. Necessary emissions reductions will also reduce other pollutants, and those pollutants have multiple effects. Damage related to a pollutant generated by multiple precursors cannot be allocated back to individual units of emissions when one or more precursors have joint products (Hall et al. 1992; Hall and Hall 1993). One consequence is that the use of standard economic tools – net benefit estimation and cost-effectiveness comparisons – cannot lead to unambiguous conclusions about the appropriate scope or scale of regulation (Hall and Hall 1997).

Implications

Regulation of air pollution is a complex task. Determining the appropriate jurisdictional level to regulate any aspect of it will be a function of
both the scope and scale of emissions and resulting pollutants, and the
reach of their adverse effects. For cases, such as the catalytic converter,
where exhaust control technology and some fuel specifications are
complementary factors in emissions reductions, fuel must be regulated at
the governmental level that can ensure that supplies of that fuel are available (and used) wherever vehicles equipped with that technology re-fuel.

When reformulation of gasoline is also necessary to reduce HC mass
or reactivity, CO or NO_x, the level of jurisdiction will be determined by
the boundary of the affected ecosystem. Thus, if local ozone is the issue,
restricting vapour pressure of local fuel during seasons when ozone is
elevated may be an adequate strategy. This can be accomplished relatively
simply by blending different feedstocks into the fuel or by more complex
refining, depending on which is less costly.

If, however, extensive reduction in HC reactivity is necessary or NO_x
reduction from greater catalyst efficiency is an objective, the necessary
capital investment in refinery retro-fitting will be large and federal action
may be necessary.

Standard economic tools, notably cost–benefit assessment, will not be
adequate to answer either the question of how much to regulate or which
approach to adopt. Consequently, it may be useful to undertake an
alternative assessment and then determine what level of government
jurisdiction must be involved to achieve the preferred outcome.

Multicriteria evaluation

One emerging means of assessing alternatives when, for one or more
reasons, quantitative measures such as cost–benefit analysis are not
likely to yield useful results is multicriteria evaluation. It proceeds from
the concept that community welfare is a multidimensional variable
encompassing private and social economic impacts, environmental and
energy impacts, and the physical environment (infrastructure). The
underlying principle is that there is no way to optimize for all criteria or
quantify all variables, so a formal basis for compromise is needed
(Munda et al. 1994).

The first step is to define the problem. In the case discussed in this
chapter that means defining the scope and scale of fuel-related emissions
and pollution impacts from vehicles. Second, alternative solutions need
to be generated. Some of those have been discussed here, focusing on
fuel specifications. A broader set would include land use, transit alternatives, alternative fuels, more sophisticated catalyst systems, and engine

modifications, among others. Third, criteria to evaluate the alternatives are selected.[4] These criteria will relate to efficiency, equity and scale. Finally, the preference system of decision-makers is considered.

This exercise is then conducted in a systematic framework that can help to identify the source of jurisdictional conflicts and make 'the trade-offs in a complex situation more transparent to decision-makers' (Munda et al. 1994). Whether action will ultimately be taken locally or centrally will then logically depend on which level can implement the effective level of regulation necessary to carry out the alternative that best meets the chosen criteria.

Multicriteria evaluation in context

The US recently undertook an extensive effort to evaluate regulation of pollution, including that from vehicles, in an atmospherically complex regional context wherein the federal government was seeking advice from state governments, tribes, industry and other groups. Specifically, in the 1990 amendments to the federal Clean Air Act, Congress recognized that visibility in the western parks and monuments had been reduced by pollution originating at great distances from the receptor sites, and that cooperation among all of the western states and tribes would be necessary to prevent future degradation and to begin to reverse the visibility losses that had already occurred. The Grand Canyon Visibility Transport Commission (GCVTC), including nine governors and four Tribal Leaders, was established to recommend actions to the federal government. A significant part of the Commission's work was to develop a better understanding of the physical relationships between visibility and pollution sources throughout the west, and to assess the impacts of potential regulatory alternatives on the economy of the region (and on identifiable subgroups) and on equity, the environment, and other social values. In effect, the starting-point was to carry out the first two steps of a multicriteria analysis.

The Commission initiated a series of studies, the general objective of which was to construct an integrated assessment system to support easy comparison of visibility and social impacts among competing emissions-reducing policies (Mathai 1995). The results of this assessment were intended to also support a secondary assessment, which would evaluate in detail how a set of Commission-specified criteria would be affected by alternative regulatory approaches to visibility improvement (GCVTC 1994). These criteria addressed non-air quality environmental changes, demographic changes, equity, social impacts and similar consequences that would be expected as a result of significant changes in the economic activities of one or more major sectors in the eleven state region, and represent the third step in multicriteria analysis. The foundation for economic impact estimation was a regional economic model.

The direct and indirect impacts on economic activity are one of the more easily quantified consequences of regulation. However, myriad other changes can result from regulations and these will generate social gains and losses not easily captured by economic models. One objective of the Commission was to evaluate social impacts on a much broader basis, incorporating factors that cannot be readily distilled into one common denominator in either regional economic modelling or cost–benefit analysis.

The Commission issued its recommendations in June 1996. These differed in some quite significant ways from the alternatives that were initially identified. For example, a number of transport-related measures to reduce emissions are included, including a 49-state (or federal) low emission vehicle. While this could represent higher costs than some other alternatives, it avoided unacceptable distributional consequences in rural and tribal areas near the parks. This alternative also would generate benefits not directly related to the Commission's mandate. The Commission also recommended adoption of policies to encourage renewable energy and conservation as a means to reduce the power generation contribution to visibility reduction, although these measures were explicitly left out of the initial set of alternatives. These quite significant changes in the policy options ultimately recommended to the federal government emerged from a process that incorporated quantitative and qualitative information and provided for extensive re-evaluation and re-assessment of alternatives relative to the established criteria while the process went forward. In the end, a mix of federal, regional and local policies was recommended to effectively achieve the common goal of improved visibility in national parks. Multiple criteria were accommodated effectively in a circumstance in which agreement could not have been reached on the use of any single criterion as a basis for choosing among alternatives. There was a large role for the general framework of cost–benefit analysis and extensive discussion of economic impacts, but the overall framework for choice was inclusive of factors not readily accommodated by the use of cost–benefit analysis alone (Puri and Hall 1996).

Conclusions

The European Union is moving towards harmonizing technical standards for vehicles and fuels. Restriction of lead content is consistent with this approach and is required both to protect the catalytic converter necessary for meeting new exhaust standards and to protect public health. Further, reductions in leaded fuel will tend towards levelling the playing field for refineries in northern and southern Europe.

Reduced hydrocarbon and nitrogen oxide emissions may be necessary to reduce ozone locally, or to reduce local and downwind fine particulate matter, downwind ozone and acid deposition. Regulation of fuel characteristics other than lead may be appropriately carried out at either the federal or local level. This depends on the degree to which emissions reductions are needed to meet both local and downwind environmental objectives, and whether refinery processing must be changed significantly, or requirements can be met by blending. The socially optimal solution will therefore depend on atmospheric conditions, and other technical factors, along with community objectives. Analyses to support decision-making may need to extend to techniques beyond the benefit–cost framework, such as multicriteria evaluation.

Notes

1. Limited trading markets in air emissions exist, but have as their objectives lowering the cost of reducing emissions rather than achieving an efficient level of environmental pollution.
2. Diesel is also important, but presents different technical issues.
3. NO_x and HC interact to generate ozone. To some degree, controls can emphasize reduction of one relative to the other, depending on cost and other considerations. Where NO_x also contributes to elevated levels of pollutants other than ozone, the degree of NO_x control will not be as flexible.
4. Selecting the criteria after the alternatives are identified may prevent some options from being pre-selected out of the action set.

References

Baumol, W.J. and W.E. Oates (1988), *The Theory of Environmental Policy*, 2nd edn, Cambridge, UK: Cambridge University Press.

Brown, L.R.(1993), 'A new era unfolds', in *State of the World*, New York: W.W. Norton, pp. 3–21.

California Air Resources Board (CARB) (1990a), *Reformulated Gasoline: Proposed Phase 1 Specifications, Technical Support Document*, 13 August, Sacramento, CA.

California Air Resources Board (CARB) (1990b), *Reformulated Gasoline: Proposed Phase 1 Specifications, Staff Report*, 13 August, Sacramento, CA.

California Air Resources Board (CARB) (1994a), *Proposed Amendments to the California Phase 2 Reformulated Gasoline Regulations, Including Amendments Providing for the Use of a Predictive Model*, Staff Report, 22 April, Sacramento, CA.

California Air Resources Board (CARB) (1994b), *RFG Newsletter*, Sacramento, CA.

Calvert, J.G., J.B Heywood, R.F. Sawyer and J.H. Seinfeld (1993), 'Achieving acceptable air quality: some reflections on controlling vehicle emissions', *Science*, **261** (5117), 37–44.

Cochran, L.S. and R.A. Peilke (1992), 'Selecting international receptor-based air quality standards', *Journal of the Air and Waste Management Association*, **42**, 1657–72.

Daly, H. (1991), 'Elements of environmental macroeconomics', in Robert Costanza (ed.), *Ecological Economics: The Science and Management of Sustainability*, New York: Columbia University Press.

Dockery, D.W. and C.A. Pope III (1994), 'Acute respiratory effects of particulate air pollution', *Annual Review of Public Health*, **15**, 107–32.

Finlayson-Pitts, B.J. and J.N. Pitts Jr (1993), 'Atmospheric chemistry of tropospheric ozone formation: scientific and regulatory implications', *Journal of the Air and Waste Management Association*, **43**, 1050–100.

Grand Canyon Visibility Transport Commission (GCVTC) (1994), *Outline of Criteria for Evaluation of Emission Management Options*, Denver, CO: Western Governors' Association.

Hall, D. and J.V Hall (1997), 'Estimating the benefits of emissions reductions in complex atmospheres', *International Journal of Global Energy*, **9** (5), June 1997.

Hall, J., J. Aplet, S. Levy, G. Meade, and A. Puri (1995), *The Automobile, Air Pollution Regulation and the Economy of Southern California 1965–1990*, Fullerton, CA: Institute for Economic and Environmental Studies, California State University.

Hall, J. and D. Hall (1993), 'Damage functions: applications and limitations', Working Paper, Institute for Economic and Environmental Studies, Fullerton, CA: California State University.

Hall, J., A.M. Winer, M. Kleinman, F. Lurmann, S.D. Colome, and V. Brajer (1992), 'Valuing the health benefits of clean air', *Science*, **255**, 812–17.

Jaffe, A.B., S.R. Peterson, P.R. Portney, and R.N. Stavins (1995), 'Environmental regulation and the competitiveness of U.S. manufacturing: what does the evidence tell us?', *Journal of Economic Literature*, **33** (1), 132–63.

Lippman, M. (1989), 'Health effects of ozone – a critical review', *Journal of the Air Pollution Control Association*, **39**, 672–95.

Lippman, M. (1993), 'Environmental toxicology and exposure limits for ambient air', *Applied Occupational Environmental Hygiene*, **12**, 847–58.

Mathai, C.V. (1995), 'The Grand Canyon Visibility Transport Commission and Visibility Protection in Class I Areas', *Environmental Manager*, **1**, 29–31.

Munda, G., P. Nijkamp and P. Rietveld (1994), 'Qualitative multicriteria evaluation for environmental management', *Ecological Economics*, **10** (2), 97–112.

Organization for Economic Cooperation and Development (1991a), *The State of the Environment*, Paris OECD.

Organization for Economic Cooperation and Development (1991b), *Environmental Indicators: A Preliminary Set*, Paris, OECD.

Penwell Publishing Co. (1990), *International Petroleum Encyclopedia*, Tulsa, OK: Penwell.

Puri, A. and J. Hall (1996), 'Assessing the social impacts of Grand Canyon Visibility Regulations', Working Paper, Institute for Economic and Environmental Studies, Fullerton, CA: California State University.

Repetto, R. (1987), 'The policy implications of non-convex environmental damages: a smog control case study', *Journal of Environmental Economics and Management*, **14** (1), 13–29.

Small, K. and C. Kazimi (1995), 'On the costs of air pollution from motor vehicles', *Journal of Transport Economics and Policy*, **24** (1), 1–17.

Stokey, E. and R. Zeckhauser (1978), *A Primer for Policy Analysis*, New York: W.W. Norton & Co., Inc.

World Resources Institute (WRI) (1992), *World Resources 1992–1993: A Guide to the Global Environment*, New York: Oxford University Press.

Zerbe, R.O. (1974), 'Optimal environmental jurisdictions', *Ecology Law Quarterly*, **4** (2), 193–245.

Appendix 8AI- Glossary of terms

Aromatics: A class of chemicals with a closed ring of six carbon atoms. Benzene is an important example.

Distillation characteristics: For example, T90. The temperature at which 90 per cent of mass will evaporate by distillation.

Fluid catalytic cracking: Breaking large molecules into smaller ones at high temperature and pressure in the presence of silica and alumina. An important refining technology.

Olefins: A class of unsaturated hydrocarbons that tend to be chemically reactive because of an unstable double bond between two carbon atoms.

Oxygenates: Compounds added to gasoline to boost octane and reduce carbon monoxide emissions. Two of the most common are ethanol and MTBE (methyl tertiary butyl ether).

Reactivity: A measure used to indicate a compound's ability to mediate the formation of ozone in the atmosphere.

Reformulated gasoline (RFG): Gasoline with chemical or physical properties modified to reduce the mass and air quality impact of vehicular emissions.

Vapour pressure: A measure of volatility and a characteristic important to reducing the mass of hydrocarbon emissions.

9. Regional and federal interests in transport and environment policy-making: the case of Belgium[1]

Bruno De Borger, Sara Ochelen, Stef Proost and Didier Swysen*

Introduction

It is well known that policy measures designed to correct for transport externalities need to take into account a number of specific characteristics of transport services. First, the demand for transport services and the impact of the associated externalities are by nature geographically differentiated. For example, travellers typically face more congestion problems and accident risks in urban regions than in rural areas; moreover, in any region these problems are more severe during peak hours than in the off-peak period. Second, some of the environmental problems linked to transportation activities have local as well as global impacts. Whereas the effect of noise, smell and particulates is very limited in space, other air pollutants have a regional, continental (acid rain and ozone) or even global impact (climate change).

Under some simplifying assumptions, the textbook prescription is to internalize the different external costs using appropriate pricing instruments. However, in the case of transportation this raises two issues, both of which call for a coordinated approach by different levels of government. First, irrespective of the government level selected, the number of instruments is limited because of administrative feasibility. For example, it may be difficult to enforce location-specific car emission regulations or fuel prices. As a consequence, there is typically no perfect match between the incidence of the various externalities and the available policy instruments. Second, some of the available instruments also fulfil important revenue functions. This may create unwanted fiscal externalities between regions if partial responsibility is left to regional governments (see, for example, Wildasin 1988).

* The authors thank Feinzaig Eliecer, Gert-Jan Koopman and Knud Munk for useful comments on the first draft of this text.

This chapter explores some of the coordination problems in the design of policies to correct for the external effects generated by transport services. The approach taken is as follows. In a first step the policy preferences of two regions in a federation are carefully examined. The first region is a small urban area (say, Brussels); the second region is the surrounding area which is less densely populated and much larger (say, the rest of Belgium). These areas differ in two respects. First they face different environmental and transport problems. Second, because of the constitution, they have different policy instruments at their disposal. Both regions have preferred policy combinations for fuel taxes, car regulations, tolls and public transport. Their preferred mix of policy instruments differs because they face different environmental and transport problems, and because they can exploit different fiscal externalities.

Of course, the two regionally preferred instrument combinations will typically differ from the optimal combination at the federal level for two reasons. First, the federal instrument mix will contain uniform values over the two regions for those instruments that cannot be regionally differentiated (for example, fuel taxes and car regulations), and differentiated values for those policy instruments that need not be uniform (for example, public transport prices and road tolls). Second, the federal government will internalize some of the environmental externalities as well as some of the fiscal externalities. Therefore, in a second step uniform values are imposed for those instruments that are assumed not to be differentiable across regions, and the resulting 'federal' optima are compared with the 'regional' optima. Although providing a full solution to the problem of optimal transport policy in a federal system is outside the scope of this chapter, the above comparison provides some important insights with regard to the costs of uniformity of policy instruments and the dangers of fiscal externalities. It can be considered a modest first step towards the design of optimal environmental and transport policies in a federal system.

The structure of the chapter is as follows. In the first section, the approach used is discussed. The assumed objectives of the two regional governments as well as those of the federal government are explained; the assumptions related to the geographic impact of the various transport externalities are reviewed; and the policy instruments available to the different governments are presented. The second section provides information on the model used to study optimal transport policies. Specifically, two different versions of the TRENEN model[1] are used, namely a model developed to study policies in the urban region and a model designed for transport in the peripheral non-urban region. The models are static partial equilibrium models of the transport market that generate optimal mixes of policy instruments for given objectives. The next three sections describe the two regionally preferred policy options and the federal solution, respectively. Conclusions are then presented in the final section.

The approach used

The approach taken in this chapter consists of two steps. First the problem of determining an optimal transport and environment policy is considered as seen from the perspective of the governments of the two regions, that is, the urban and the peripheral region. To be examined are the driving forces behind the regional governments' respective preferences for the different instruments available to them. In a second step, the solutions are compared with the 'federal' solution, the details of which are explained below. This approach can be seen as the first step towards the analysis of the more realistic, but also much more complicated, regulatory problem in which the federal government can set optimal federal instruments, taking into account the behaviour of the regional governments.

It is assumed that the urban region is surrounded by the peripheral region, both regions form a federation and this federation is in turn surrounded by other countries. The residents of the urban region live and work in their own region. In the urban area there is no freight transport, but there is intensive commuting by residents of the peripheral region to the urban region. The residents of the peripheral region make trips in their own region but also to the urban region (work, shopping, and so on). In other words, three types of individuals are distinguished: urban residents, peripheral residents who commute to the urban region and peripheral residents who do not commute. In the peripheral region freight transport is important. We distinguish between domestic freight (linked to local production or export and import) and transit freight. For passenger transport and freight transport all the transport modes (road, rail and inland waterways) except air transport are taken into account.

Table 9.1 is instrumental in describing this approach. The table contains three columns that describe three regulatory problems: the problem faced by an urban government, the problem faced by the government of the peripheral region and, finally, the problem as perceived by the federal government. In each case the corresponding objective function to be maximized, the externalities taken into account, and the set of relevant policy instruments are presented.

The *government of the urban region* is concerned with the welfare of its residents and, to a smaller extent, with the welfare of the commuters. The total welfare of the urban region consists of three components. The first

Table 9.1 Problem structure

	Urban region	Peripheral region	Federation
	Transport flows represented		
Objective function	Only passengers residents and commuters	Passengers (only residents), domestic freight and transit freights	Urban and peripheral passenger transport, domestic and transit freight
Consumer surplus	CS of residents and lower weight for CS of non-residents CS is a function of all passenger transport prices and of congestion	CS of residents CS is a function of all passenger transport prices, of congestion and of the price of a composite good which is a function of freight transport prices and congestion Zero weight transit transport CS	All passengers same weight, zero weight for transit CS
Tax revenue	Net public transport deficit and road pricing revenues taxes receipts	Public transport deficit and net road pricing, car and fuel receipts	Public transport deficit, road pricing and car and fuel tax receipts
External costs			
Accidents	Yes	Yes	Yes
Local air pollution	Yes	Yes	Yes
Regional air pollution	Only local impact	Yes	Yes
Global air pollution	No	To a small extent	To a larger extent
Road wear	No (no freight)	Yes	Yes
Noise	Yes	No	Yes
Instruments			
Emission standards	No	No	No
Public transport pricing	Urban public transport	Interregional public transport	All public transport
Fuel taxes	No (fuel tax given)	Yes	Yes
Road pricing	Yes	Yes	Yes

element is the welfare of residents and nonresidents commuting to the city. Their (indirect) utility depends, among other things, on the generalized price of passenger transport, which includes all monetary expenses as well as the relevant time costs.[2] A second component of the objective function is tax revenue. For the urban region this consists of the urban public transport deficit and the revenue from local road pricing. In order to capture a local marginal cost of public funds greater than one, tax revenues can be attributed a higher weight than consumer surplus (see, for example, Laffont and Tirole 1993).[3] The final element in the welfare function of the urban region is the external costs that affect its population. They include the external noise cost, the external accident costs and the local air pollution costs. A rational urban government cannot be expected to take air pollution with nonlocal impacts into account if it is not forced to do so by the federal government.

The set of instruments that can be used by the urban region to control transport and environmental problems is limited by the present institutional structure and by its location. It is assumed that it can decide only upon urban public transport pricing and on a local form of road pricing. Even if the local authorities were able to levy their own fuel taxes or issue their own car regulations, the degree of freedom would be very limited because of competition with the peripheral region.

The *government of the peripheral region* is assumed to have an objective function with the same structure as the urban government. However, there are three important differences. First, the peripheral region takes a slightly different set of external effects into account, which now includes road wear (due to freight transport) and regional air pollution. As illustrated in Table 9.1, a larger share of the externalities is internalized by the peripheral government. Second, the introduction of freight transport, which includes both domestic and transit transport, implies that the tax revenues on road and inland waterway transport and the surplus or deficit on rail freight transport need to be taken into account as well. Third, it is assumed that the peripheral region has a more elaborate set of instruments at its disposal than does the urban region. In addition to public transport prices and a system of road pricing, the regional government is authorized to levy fuel taxes. No price discrimination is allowed between domestic and transit freight flows. Note that the latter bring external congestion and external air pollution costs to the region without bringing any benefit except when the transit flows can be taxed.

Finally, the *federal government* is assumed to take into account the welfare of the three types of consumers, the total tax revenue, the losses of all public transport firms and all externalities.

Methodology

In this section, the TRENEN methodology used in the application considered in this chapter is described briefly. To avoid confusion, it is instructive to start with a brief review of the most important limitations of this approach. First, TRENEN assumes that the localization of households and firms is exogenously given. Second, the model is static and provides a representation of an equilibrium situation with a fully adapted stock of transport means. This implies that automobile ownership is not treated explicitly as an independent variable. Although car ownership is endogenous, a reduced-form model of modal choice is used, applicable to a time frame long enough for car ownership to adjust to changes in other variables. After a policy change, the model calculates the new equilibrium outcome, but dynamic adjustments are not described explicitly. Third, the model is not spatially disaggregated. In other words, transport is represented by one link per mode. Finally, although this is desirable from a policy viewpoint, the current version of the simulation model does not yet capture the distributional implications of transport and environmental policies: one representative consumer is assumed.

Within TRENEN, two separate models were developed. The first one was designed to study transport problems associated with an urban environment; the second model focuses on analysing interregional traffic. The models are very similar in structure but differ in the congestion function used, in the external effects taken into account, and in their treatment of freight transport. The latter is not included in the urban model, but plays a crucial role in the interregional model.

The overall model structure is represented in Figure 9.1. In the remainder of this section some additional details are provided. Since the structure of the demand and supply sides of the transport market are almost completely analogous for the urban and the interregional models, the two versions are not considered separately.

The TRENEN models simulate a regulated transport market equilibrium for a given city or region. One regulated equilibrium corresponds to the best equilibrium the regulator can obtain using a given set of instruments. Mathematically, the problem is formulated as the maximization of a weighted sum of consumers' welfare, producers' surplus, tax revenue and environmental damage under a given set of market equilibrium constraints and with regulations on the characteristics of cars and different types of taxes as instruments. The overall model structure is given in Figure 9.1. The demand and supply side is briefly described.

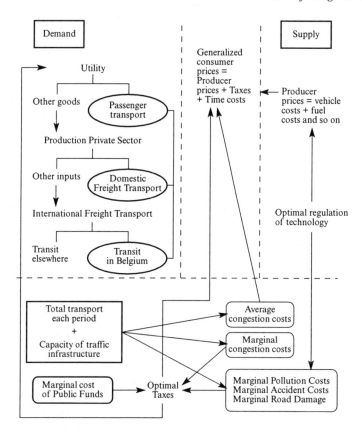

Figure 9.1 Complete model structure

Structure of the demand side

The demand for passenger transport is sufficiently disaggregated such that it captures all relevant demand categories. To structure transport demand decisions with a large number of alternatives, CES nested-utility functions were used (see Keller 1976). Calibration of this function is based on estimates of substitution elasticities at the different levels, combined with observations on prices and quantities at the lowest level of the tree structure.

Note that this approach allows the peak and off-peak periods of the day to be distinguished, includes all relevant modes (the private car (including carpooling), bus and rail), and takes account of different types of cars (for example, sub compact, compact, mid-size and full-size), as well as various fuel types (gasoline and diesel). At the highest level, total utility depends on two aggregate goods, namely transport and other goods. At the second level, the transport subutility component contains transport demands during two periods of the day (peak and off-peak) as arguments. At the third level, peak transport demand includes 'private' and 'public' peak demand. At the fourth level, public transport can be either by bus or rail. At even lower levels in the tree structure, private transport (that is, car) can occur either with 'carpooling' or 'driving solo'. Carpooling is considered as a particular mode in order to allow different prices (per car km) according to the car's occupancy rate. Through this construction, average occupancy rates are endogenous. Furthermore, two car sizes are being considered, namely big and small. Finally, there are two possible fuels, gasoline and diesel. In order to introduce congestion into the model, it is assumed that demands depend on generalized prices, defined as the sum of monetary and time expenditures.

The demand for freight transport, which is included only in the interregional version of the model, was modelled as a derived demand for inputs by a private production sector producing an aggregate private consumption good. The latter directly enters the utility function of the representative consumer at the highest level. Consumer demand for this good generates production by the private sector, in which freight transport is one among several inputs. The demand for freight transport is then assumed to be the result of cost-minimizing behaviour by producers, conditional upon the output level of the final good to be produced.

Again, a tree structure is used to represent producers' decisions with a large number of transport alternatives. It is developed in less detail than in the case of passenger transport, as the number of relevant alternatives is much smaller. For example, the peak versus off-peak decision is probably only relevant for road transportation; almost all road freight transport uses diesel, and so on. Therefore, simply the three relevant modes (road, rail and inland waterways) are distinguished, and a further distinction for road transport according to the period of the day is made. No further refinements have been considered. At all levels in the tree structure, cost functions were assumed to be of the CES type. In other words, for these levels price and quantity indices are constructed along the same lines as for passenger transport. Finally, note that generalized prices are being used here as well. This allows two factors to be taken into account: (i) that relative speeds play a role in modal choice, and (ii) that an increase in congestion level leads to time losses, yielding higher production costs.

This approach provides for a direct link between freight transport prices and consumer welfare, such that all welfare effects of both passenger and freight transport can ultimately be channelled through consumers' indirect utilities. Moreover, a constant returns to scale production function for the production sector and marginal cost pricing was assumed, implying a direct and simple relation between private goods prices and freight transport prices. Intuitively, the process by which freight transport prices affect consumers operates as follows. A rise in freight prices affects average production costs, and, under these assumptions, the private good's market price. As the price of this good increases, the indirect utility of consumers is affected. Indirect utility is introduced in the objective function to be optimized.

Structure of the supply side
The supply of the various transport modes is introduced in the model in a very simple way, namely via cost functions for the different modes and alternatives. For freight transport and public passenger transport, resource costs include expenditures on labour, energy, materials, rolling stock, and so on. For private passenger transport (that is, cars) resource costs consist of depreciation expenditures, insurance, energy, parking costs, maintenance, and so on. In the simulation exercises reported below, constant average costs per passenger-km (pass-km) and per ton-km are initially used, and this for each mode.

Note that the choice of emission technology is also captured as part of the supply component. Consider, for example, emission technologies for cars. It could be assumed that producers adjust the supply of cars passively to the quantities demanded; selling will occur at marginal cost if perfect competition is assumed. However, the supply of emission technology cannot be determined purely by consumers. Given the public good nature of cleaner technologies, this would result in underprovision of emission-reducing technologies. Therefore, an alternative approach was chosen: the emission technology used in the supply of cars is directly regulated by the government (for example, all gasoline cars need to be equipped with a catalytic converter). The choice of emission technology is optimized jointly with the taxes and public transport prices. In principle, the same logic can be followed for trucks and inland waterways. In the case of rail transport of both freight and passengers, externality-reducing technologies are decided upon as a consequence of socially optimal policies; they are then implemented by the public railroad company. Note, however, that in the simulation exercises reported below, choice between different technologies was not considered explicitly.

Structure of the external costs
The models take account of the most important externalities associated with transport services, including congestion, road surface depreciation, noise, accident risks (that is, safety) and various emissions. The latter include transport's contribution to the greenhouse effect (CO_2-equivalent),

to the ozone problem (VOC, NO_x), to acid rain (SO_2, NO_x), and to local air quality (CO, particulates).

Congestion was introduced in the model by specifying all demand functions for both passenger and freight transport in terms of generalized prices, which include monetary expenditures as well as the monetary value of travel time. The generalized prices assume that the speed of road traffic is endogenously determined according to a speed–flow relationship. This gives the traffic's speed as a function of the number of passenger car units (PCU)[4] per hour for each period considered. The functional form of Kirwan et al. (1995) was used in both the urban and interregional models. Calibration was achieved by combining observable information on current flowing and average speeds with an assumption on speed of freely floating traffic. The monetary value of travel time per kilometre is simply the value of time per hour multiplied by the inverse of the speed in kilometres per hour. Consequently, generalized prices can be written as equal to money price plus (1/speed) times the value of time.

In Table 9.2 a summary of monetary values used for all externalities other than congestion is provided. (See the appendix for the computation and sources of the valuation.)

Air pollution is caused by various vehicles' emissions. Six pollutants are considered: CO_2, NO_x, SO_x, VOC, CO and particulates. The emission factors are computed by VIA-RWTH: they are fuel, car size, occupancy rate and speed specific. For each pollutant a monetary value is assigned, representing its social cost.

The impact of CO_2 is of a global nature, thus it is only valued at the federal level. The valuation uses an indirect method, interpreting the energy-carbon tax of $10 per barrel of oil as the marginal willingness of the EC to pay for decreases in CO_2 emissions.

The valuation of NO_x, SO_x and VOC at the federal level is performed in an indirect way as well. Belgium has committed itself to certain reductions of the emissions of these pollutants in international agreements. Starting from these reduction objectives, the avoided abatement costs are calculated.[5] Through their contribution to ozone formation, NO_x and VOC also have a local impact. The damage of NO_x and VOC (mainly related to health and materials) has been estimated by Small and Kazimi (1994). As most of the emissions generated in Brussels are exported, only a small fraction of this damage estimate is applied for the urban valuation and a somewhat larger fraction for the interregional valuation.

Particulates and CO can be very harmful for human health, but their impact is very limited in place and time. Therefore, they are only taken into account for the urban region. The damage estimate used is again based on Small and Kazimi (1994).

Table 9.2 Transport externalities and their valuation at the different levels of decision-making

Type of externality impact	Urban region	Peripheral region	Federation
Noise Local	car[1] peak: –0.00841 ECU/carkm off-peak: 0.0082 ECU/carkm bus[2] peak: 0.0305 ECU/buskm off-peak: 0.076 ECU/buskm	Not included	Same valuation as the urban region
Accidents Local	0.0945 ECU/carkm and 0.1516 ECU/ pub transp. vehkm	0.07825 ECU/carkm 0.06 ECU /truckkm	Same valuation as the regions
Road Depreciation Local	No	0.03 ECU/truckkm	Same valuation as the regions
CO_2 emissions (contribution to climate change) Global	Valuation = 0	Valuation = 0	0.000018125 ECU/g
NO_x emissions (contribution to acidification and to ozone) National/global	0.0006894 ECU/g	0.0013788 ECU/g	0.002225 ECU/g
SO_x emissions (contribution to acidification) National/global	Valuation = 0	Valuation = 0	0.000325 ECU/g
VOC emissions (contribution to ozone) National/global	0.000266 ECU/g	0.000532 ECU/g	0.004565 ECU/g
CO emissions Local	0.000266875 ECU/g	Valuation = 0	Idem regions
Particulates (PM_{10}) Local	0.0079808 ECU/g	Valuation = 0	Idem regions

Notes:
1. From Mayeres (1993)[8] b.
2. The figures computed in Boniver and Thiry (1993) are used here.

Accident costs were assumed constant per vehicle-km. They take into account both the material and physical damages. Finally, consistent with Newberry (1990), road depreciation was fully attributed to trucks.

The objective function
In the TRENEN model, the government is assumed to maximize an objective function which reflects its concern for consumer welfare, producer surpluses, tax revenues and external costs. It consists of the sum of the representative consumer's indirect utility, normalized by the marginal utility of income, and the appropriate government's tax revenues and public transport surpluses weighted by the shadow cost of public funds, minus the monetary value of total external costs other than congestion. As previously mentioned, congestion is directly captured in the consumer's indirect utility through the use of generalized prices.

Operation of the model
The solution of the model runs in two steps. First, using a minimum of data for a reference situation (this can be the observed equilibrium), all remaining model parameters are calibrated (utility function parameters, cost function parameters in the interregional model, and so on) using default values for substitution elasticities and other mode data. The reference situation can then be interpreted as reflecting an initial market equilibrium. Once the model parameters have been determined, alternative regulated equilibria are constructed by optimizing the regulators' objective function under other constraints on the sets of instruments (different taxes, and so on).

Policy preferences of the urban government

The reference solution
The transport flows in the urban region of Brussels consist of the trips of its 0.9 million inhabitants and 0.5 million commuters. The urban region has three problems in the reference situation (this corresponds to the 1990 situation): excessive congestion, high public transport deficits and local air pollution. In the reference situation, the only instrument the urban government really uses is the public transport prices which are kept far below the average costs and below the marginal costs. The urban government does not use tolls (they may use parking fees, but these are still rather low and parking restrictions are not well enforced). The main sources of revenue for the urban region are lump-sum grants and revenue sharing of VAT and income taxes.

In Table 9.3[6] the reference solution is represented in the first column. The policy instruments to be discussed are the different types of taxes

Table 9.3 Policy preferences of the urban government: summary

	Reference		Local optimal toll + pub. tr. prices only tax rev: cars Bxl received			Local optimal toll + pub. tr. prices total tax rev: cars received			Local optimal public transp. prices		Federal optim. toll + pub. prices fuel tax at reference level			Federal optim. toll + pub. prices fuel tax harmonized		
	Total tax /pass-km	Ext. cost* /pass-km	Toll /pass-km	Total tax /pass-km	Ext. cost* /pass-km	Toll /pass-km	Total tax /pass-km	Ext. cost* /pass-km	Total tax /pass-km	Ext. cost* /pass-km	Toll /pass-km	Total tax /pass-km	Ext. cost* /pass-km	Toll /pass-km	Total tax /pass-km	Ext. cost* /pass-km
Peak big gas	0.1200	0.4048	0.3178	0.4380	0.1433	0.2434	0.3636	0.1618	0.1200	0.3859	0.1598	0.2800	0.2049	0.1973	0.2632	0.2052
Peak big die	0.0838	0.4043	0.3178	0.4016	0.1427	0.2434	0.3272	0.1613	0.0838	0.3853	0.1598	0.2436	0.2016	0.1973	0.2460	0.2020
Peak bus and tram	0.0395	0.0207		0.0802	0.0077		0.0819	0.0086	-0.0105	0.0198		0.0156	0.0114		0.0149	0.0114
Peak metro	0.0558	0.0039		0.0622	0.0039		0.0618	0.0039	-0.0049	0.0039		0.0065	0.0047		0.0060	0.0047
Off-peak big gas	0.1238	0.1071	0.2248	0.3486	0.1069	0.1239	0.2477	0.1070	0.1238	0.1071	0.0421	0.1659	0.1189	0.0809	0.1446	0.1189
Off-peak big die	0.0856	0.1068	0.2248	0.3104	0.1067	0.1239	0.2095	0.1067	0.0856	0.1068	0.0421	0.1277	0.1161	0.0809	0.1287	0.1161
Off-peak bus and tram	-0.1511	0.0275		0.1254	0.0274		0.1290	0.0275	-0.0491	0.0275		0.0404	0.0333		0.0364	0.0333
Off-peak metro	-0.0944	0.0171		0.1015	0.0171		0.1042	0.0171	-0.0312	0.0171		0.0281	0.0209		0.0252	0.0209
	MECU /day		MECU /day	% change wrt refer.		MECU /day	% change wrt refer.		MECU /day	% change	MECU /day	% change wrt refer.		MECU /day	% change wrt refer.	
CSinhabitants	82.0332		81.4618	-0.70		81.6309	-0.49		82.0703	0.05	81.8592	-0.21		81.8701	-0.20	
CSnonresidents	47.1540		46.6968	0.97		46.8244	-0.70		47.2057	0.11	47.0185	-0.29		47.0268	-0.27	
Total taxrev cars	0.3666		1.2357	237.07		1.0078	174.91		0.3667	0.03	0.7442	103.00		0.7290	98.86	
Taxrev cars Bxl	0.0000		0.9429			0.6932			0.0000		0.4102			0.5618		
Taxrev pub transp	-0.3283		-0.2312	-29.58		-0.2370	-27.83		-0.3934	19.82	-0.3469	5.64		-0.3485	6.13	
Tot. ext. air poll.c. **	0.0601		0.0480	-20.07		0.0511	-14.91		0.0599	-0.35	0.0545	-9.25		0.0549	-8.57	
Tot. ext. accid. cost	0.4266		0.3329	-21.96		0.3586	-15.93		0.4264	-0.04	0.3843	-9.91		0.3847	-9.82	
Welfare federal	128.7426		128.7837	0.03		128.8175	0.06		128.7665	0.02	128.8370	0.07		128.8387	0.07	
Welfare Bxl	118.9893		119.1868	0.17		119.1756	0.16		119.0026	0.01	119.1395	0.13		119.3066	0.27	

Notes: * External cost per passenger km valued from the local point of view for the first four exercises and from the federal point of view.
         ** Total external air pollution cost valued from the federal point of view.

233

and public transport prices. If the government is a welfare optimizer, if there are no distribution problems and if the marginal cost of public funds is 1, taxes equal to marginal external costs would be optimal. In the table we shall therefore systematically indicate the total tax level and the marginal external cost for some categories of transport. In comparing marginal external costs across equilibria, one needs to remember that marginal external costs (mainly congestion) are endogenous in the model. Moreover, the welfare levels of residents and nonresidents, the total tax revenue collected on cars (by the urban government and by the federal government), and the net deficit of local public transport are shown. In the table the other externality costs are also listed: air pollution and accidents. These were defined in Table 9.2 and the values reported here are the definitions of the federal government. Recall that the congestion costs are implicitly taken into account in the higher generalized prices and thus in the lower consumer welfare. The different effects are summed up in two political welfare measures: one used by the federal government (equal weights for residents and nonresidents, all tax revenue is taken into account and external costs are defined on a federal level); and one used as the objective function by the urban government (lower weights for the non-residents, only its own tax revenue counts and external costs only cover local damages).

In the reference solution the differentiation of the taxes levied by the federal government (mainly on fuel but also on vehicles) overestimates the differentiation in external air pollution costs, and does not cover the external congestion costs of the peak period. During the peak period, the total tax on car use is only 25 per cent of marginal external costs. There are high taxes on gasoline, although this is not well linked to external costs.

During the peak period, public transport prices are higher than total social marginal costs per pass-km[7] (resource costs + marginal external costs) but lower in the off-peak. In total, there is a substantial subsidy for public transport as there are also important fixed costs. Finally, it is important to take into account the relative magnitude of the different external costs. Congestion dominates, followed by accidents and finally by air and noise pollution. These factors will drive the policy measures.

The potential of readjusting two instruments will be examined here: local tolls and public transport pricing. By local road tolls is meant here electronic road pricing that can discriminate taxes in function of the level of congestion (peak versus off-peak), although not in function of the type of car and the fuel used. The public transport prices can be differentiated between peak and off-peak periods. It is assumed that in setting the prices the regional government cannot discriminate between residents and commuters.

Note that a rather restricted set of instruments is considered here. It might be different in other countries, but in the Belgian context it is unfeasible to have different car regulations or fuel prices in the urban and non-urban areas because of huge regional tax competition.

Five alternative sets of instruments will be discussed. The results are all reported in Table 9.3. The first three alternative equilibria correspond to the preferences of the urban government under different sets of restrictions on their policy instruments.

Optimal choice of a toll and public transport prices
In a first exercise, the urban government optimally chooses public transport fares and a toll system. The results are summarized in the second part of Table 9.3. It should be noted that the tolls and public transport prices are fixed at a very high level. In fact, the outcome is such that the total tax (which also contains the fixed fuel taxes and other taxes levied at the federal level) paid per pass-km is multiplied by a factor two to four. Clearly, the full tax by far exceeds the marginal external cost, contrary to the usual Pigouvian solution.

The explanation for this finding is obvious in the light of the structure of the problem. There are four 'distortions' that induce deviations from Pigouvian taxation: fiscal externalities, tax exporting, the difference between local and global externalities, and the use of imperfect instruments.

1. *Fiscal externalities.* Since it has been assumed that the revenues of the federal (fuel and vehicle) taxes remain at the federal level and do not automatically return to the urban region, federal taxes are considered to be extra resource costs by the local authority. These national taxes create a fiscal externality that is ignored by the local government. The only way in which existing federal taxes[8] are instrumental in solving the externality is by driving down demand, thereby lowering the marginal external costs. Of course, this solution is highly inefficient: there will be a large gap between the real total marginal social cost and the consumer prices. The urban government considers the other existing taxes as resource costs and will levy additional Pigouvian taxes:

   Consumer price = marginal external cost + federal tax + resource costs

2. The *tax exporting distortion.* The urban government gives a lower welfare weight to the non-residents commuting to the urban area. This will result in tax exporting by driving all prices up in order to exploit the possibility of tax exporting to non-residents.[9] There will be higher mark-ups for those types of trips that are more intensively used by non-residents and that have a low price elasticity.

3. The *global externalities distortion*. The urban region takes into account only the externalities that affect its residents. This means that congestion (with, however, a lower weight for the commuters from the peripheral region), local air and noise pollution and accidents will be taken into account. More global externalities, such as tropospheric ozone, acid rain and climate change, are only taken into account in so far as there is local damage. This results in too low taxes from a federal or international efficiency viewpoint.

4. The *use of imperfect instruments*. The urban region can only use a toll (identical for all cars) and public transport pricing to bring the consumer prices in line with the marginal external costs. Tolls can be efficient to reduce congestion but are less efficient to address pollution problems.

Two final remarks conclude the discussion related to this first exercise. First, note that, in comparison to the reference scenario, the welfare of the regional government improves. This was to be expected as an extra instrument (namely tolls) was available, and the government was allowed to optimize this instrument in function of local preferences. Interestingly, the welfare as defined by the federal government improves slightly as well. Apparently, even an additional instrument controlled by a regional government with biased preferences increases federal welfare here. Second, pollution damages decrease almost in proportion to the reduction of traffic (−20 per cent).

Correcting the revenue-sharing distortion
In the third group of columns in Table 9.3, the revenue-sharing distortion was corrected by assuming that the federal government would use a grant system that allows a correction for the fiscal externalities. The urban government now receives all the tax revenue generated from the use of cars in its territory. It can be seen that the solution implies much lower tax rates and that this improves the federal measure of urban welfare strongly at only a small cost for the urban government objective function.

There are still very high tax rates compared to the marginal external costs. There are two reasons for this: first, the tax exporting effect is still present; second and more importantly, the existing high fuel taxes imply that the off-peak prices are far too high. The second-best way for the urban government (which takes these fuel prices as given) to correct for this is to levy an extra toll on peak transport.

Limiting the instruments of the urban government
Tolls are an important, but relatively new, instrument and it can take some time before they are politically and socially accepted. Meanwhile, urban

public transport pricing, which is a politically less controversial instrument, can be used to partially correct inefficiencies. The results of allowing this instrument only are given in the fourth group of columns in Table 9.3. The results indicate that there are subsidies (defined as the difference between the marginal cost and the consumer price) in both the peak and the off-peak periods. This is a traditional second-best way of correcting for insufficient taxes on peak car use (De Borger et al. 1996). However, the total welfare gain of this instrument is very limited. The major reason is the limited importance of public transport in total urban passenger transport.

Policy preferences of the peripheral region

The reference situation in the peripheral region
The main elements characterizing the reference situation in the peripheral region are summarized in the first columns of Table 9.4. As far as passenger transport is concerned, the same modes as those used in the urban model are considered here. Thus the same comments apply. However, public transport can also occur by train, a typical interregional mode. Moreover, the peripheral region also faces important domestic and transit freight transport flows. Domestic and transit freight transport taxation differ.

It has been assumed that taxes (that is, not only fuel taxes but also traffic taxes, and so on) on domestic freight transport go entirely to the regional government. All these taxes are also paid by transit freight transport users, but part of the revenue goes to the foreign governments, for example, annual circulation taxes. Consequently, it was assumed that the regional authority only receives the revenue of fuel taxes from transit freight transport. Note that transit demand was assumed to be quite price elastic, consistent with the position of a small country such as Belgium, which is well connected to the rest of Europe.

The first rows in Table 9.4 provide information on the different welfare components (consumer surplus, tax revenue, pollution, and so on) and two measures of regional welfare: one based on regional preferences (using evaluations of externalities relevant from the regional perspective) and one based on federal preferences (using evaluations of all nationally relevant externalities).

The preferred solutions of the peripheral region
In this subsection the tax solutions preferred by the peripheral region are described. Note that the model contains both passenger and freight transport. The latter consists of domestic traffic as well as transit. In order to avoid the possibility that transit traffic would be severely taxed because of

Table 9.4 Reference situation and optimal taxes of the peripheral region

		Regional point of view			Federal point of view		
	Reference	With toll		No toll	With toll		No toll
Passenger	pass-tax/km	pass-toll/km	pass-tax/km	pass-tax/km	pass-toll/km	pass-tax/km	pass-tax/km
Peak big gas	0.119	0.160	0.247	0.193	0.168	0.254	0.203
Peak big die	0.084	0.160	0.229	0.186	0.171	0.233	0.193
Peak bus	−0.029		0.019	0.014		0.021	0.016
Peak train	−0.054		0.005	0.002		0.006	0.001
Off-peak big gas	0.119	0.051	0.137	0.195	0.060	0.146	0.205
Off-peak big die	0.084	0.051	0.120	0.193	0.060	0.126	0.201
Off-peak bus	0.023		0.012	0.015		0.014	0.016
Off-peak train	−0.005		0.004	0.005		0.005	0.007
Domestic freight	tax/ton-km	tax/ton-km		tax/ton-km	tax/ton-km		tax/ton-km
Peak road	0.043	0.181		0.193	0.192		0.203
Off-peak road	0.043	0.111		0.112	0.124		0.124
Waterways	0.023	0.057		0.058	0.057		0.058
Rail	0.004	0.029		0.030	0.033		0.033
Transit freight	tax/ton-km	tax/ton-km		tax/ton-km	tax/ton-km		tax/tonkm
Peak road	0.008	0.146		0.158	0.157		0.169
Off-peak road	0.008	0.077		0.077	0.089		0.090
Waterways	0.002	0.036		0.037	0.036		0.037
Rail	0.000	0.026		0.026	0.029		0.029
Welfare components (million ECU/day)							
Consumer surplus	910.000	895.211		894.811	893.623		893.150
Tax inc.passenger transport	9.841	18.986		18.731	19.749		19.553
Tax in. freight transport	3.056	9.234		9.407	9.942		10.130
Poll national	2.536				2.301		2.281
Poll regional	0.848	0.779		0.772			
Accidents	10.649	9.762		9.725	9.669		9.635
Road depreciation	0.443	0.393		0.393	0.386		0.386
Total welfare							
National	909.269				910.958		910.531
Regional	910.957	912.497		912.059			

tax exporting behaviour by the regional government, price discrimination between domestic and transit freight transport is not allowed.

In a first exercise, it is assumed that the regional government can use both a fuel tax and a toll system to optimally price transport services. The results of this analysis are summarized in the second column of Table 9.4. The most important findings are easily reviewed. First, it is clear that all transport services become more expensive, with the exception of bus traffic in the off-peak period. Use of the toll allows differences in external effects between periods to be captured. Price increases are largest for relatively small cars and for both bus and train travel during the peak. All freight transport prices substantially increase as well: peak prices for road traffic more than double. Both rail and inland waterway transport become more expensive as well. Of course, the increase in freight transport taxes is, in part, due to the possibility of partial tax exporting associated with transit traffic. Second, note that the toll captures most of the external costs of transport. The optimal fuel tax only serves to correct for the fuel-specific differences in pollution: the optimal fuel tax on gasoline is zero and the tax on diesel amounts to 0.105 ECU per litre. Third, all external costs have been reduced in the optimum as compared to the reference situation. Finally, implementation of the optimal policy would imply a welfare gain of approximately 1.54 million ECU per day.

A second exercise is based on the assumption that the regional government does not use a toll system for some reason, so that its instruments are limited to public transport prices and a fuel tax. Results are shown in the third column of Table 9.4. Although the general trends are similar to those of the first exercise, there are some obvious differences. The absence of a toll no longer permits the fine-tuning of the tax system according to temporal and spatial externality differences. The fuel tax now serves as a very imperfect instrument to correct for both congestion and environmental concerns. All prices rise, but differences between periods (and car types) are much less pronounced. Total tax revenues and reductions in external effects are comparable to those of the previous exercise. However, the additional restriction on available tax instruments implies a welfare loss relative to the case where a toll could be implemented. The impossibility of having a toll system available leads to a reduction in welfare gain relative to the reference situation from 1.54 million ECU per day to 1.10 million ECU per day. In other words, the absence of the toll reduces the welfare gain by approximately 30 per cent.

The federal solution

In this section, what could be called a 'federal' solution is considered. However, instead of using a third model representing all urban and inter-regional traffic simultaneously, the models for the urban region and the peripheral region are optimized separately, in each case using the objective function describing federal preferences. For reasons that will become obvious, the peripheral solution is considered first, followed by the outcome for the urban region.

The 'federal' solution for the peripheral region amounts to taking the viewpoint of the federal government in determining optimal prices. In other words, all external effects relevant from the federal viewpoint are taken into account. In the fourth column of Table 9.4, the results of this exercise in the case where use is made of public transport pricing, a fuel tax and a toll system are presented. The fifth column contains the findings when a toll is not available. Since the external effects relevant from the federal viewpoint differ only slightly from those relevant from the peripheral region's viewpoint, it is not surprising to find that the results do not differ substantially (see Table 9.1). Effectively, the only difference is in the valuation of pollution costs. As these costs count for only a small part of the total external costs, this will result in optimal prices being nearly the same from both points of view. External costs of transport consist mainly of congestion costs and accident costs, both of which are given the same weights by the two government levels. Consequently, if columns 2 and 4 from Table 9.4 are compared, it is clear that all transport modes are being taxed more heavily by the federal government than by the authority of the peripheral region, as the former is more sensitive to all pollution effects. This results in only minor differences, though. Identical conclusions can be drawn from a comparison of columns 3 and 5 of Table 9.4.

For the urban model, the 'federal solution' requires corrections in the fiscal externality (by having the revenue of all taxes go to the federal treasury), the tax export distortion (because residents and non-residents are given the same weight) and the global externalities distortion.

If both the toll and public transport prices can be optimally selected, it is evident from the fifth group of columns in Table 9.3 that the taxes approximate the marginal external cost quite well. Because the fuel taxes (and the other car taxes) are kept at their initial level, the 'imperfect instrument distortion' is still present and prevents pure Pigouvian taxation. The reductions in consumer surplus are more moderate and are borne more equally by residents and commuters than in the local optimum with the same instruments (first column). The welfare from a federal point of view has, of course, increased even more than in the local optimum. According to the local preferences there is a welfare gain as well, but this gain is slightly less than in the case where Brussels can itself decide on tolls and public transport fares.

Comparing this 'federal' solution with the preferred combination of the urban government under perfect revenue sharing demonstrates the importance of the tax exporting effect and the global externalities distortion. It can be seen that the tax exporting effect dominates, as the total tax rate is now on average about 0.04 ECU/pass-km less than in the solution preferred by the urban government.

Fuel taxes are an important tax instrument in current Belgian policies, but, as mentioned above, it does not make much sense to let urban governments choose a city-specific fuel tax. On the other hand, previous results pointed to the superiority of a toll in fighting congestion problems, implementation costs being ignored. Therefore, in a final exercise related to the urban region, the tolls were optimally determined assuming that the fuel tax is fixed at the optimal values resulting from application of the interregional model with federal preferences. Actually, there are two options available here, namely the case where the peripheral region uses only fuel taxes as an instrument, and the case where both a fuel tax and toll are possible. In the first case, as discussed previously, the fuel taxes are very high. This option is not very appealing because of intense tax competition at the European level. Moreover, high fuel taxes will induce shifts to more fuel-efficient vehicles (this effect is not included in the model) and thus mitigate the reduction of car use and congestion. In the second situation the fuel taxes are very low, because the toll already captures all common externalities of gasoline and diesel cars. The fuel taxes will be harmonized at this level, namely, zero tax on gasoline and 0.0645 ECU/litre on diesel.

The result of this harmonized tax solution is summarized in the last group of columns of Table 9.3. Compared with the previous federal solution, taxes are now nearer to the marginal external costs thanks to the reduction of the imperfect instrument distortion. Not only federal welfare, but also local welfare, are increased compared to all previous cases. This reveals that maintaining the currently prevailing high fuel taxes moves each solution far from the first-best solution. The fact that local welfare is also higher than in the local optimum is due principally to the larger share of the tax revenue coming from tolls and thus accruing to the local authorities.

Conclusion

In this chapter a first attempt has been made to empirically study questions related to decision-making in the domain of transport and the environment when there are regional and federal authorities with different interests and concerns. Use was made of the TRENEN model, which was shown to provide a flexible tool to analyse the welfare economics associated with transport and environmental policies. The approach assumes that the government maximizes an objective function that takes into account consumer welfare, tax revenues, and all relevant external costs. Moreover, it allows for a very disaggregated representation of the transport market.

In the simulation analyses, the problem faced by the governments of an urban and a peripheral region that together form a federation was considered. The urban government was assumed to use public transport prices and/or a toll; the peripheral region was allowed to use fuel taxes in addition to tolls and public transport prices. The results suggested that even in the simple set-up considered in this chapter, optimal taxation of transport services is quite complicated, because of tax exporting, fiscal externalities, restrictions on instruments and divergences in environmental preferences between regional and federal governments. It was clearly observed that, in the absence of revenue-sharing mechanisms, the existence of federal taxes implies a fiscal externality that is ignored by the urban government. This leads to urban tolls that largely exceed marginal external costs. Even correcting this externality yielded inefficiently high tolls, mainly because of tax exporting and the level of federally fixed fuel taxes. With respect to the regional authorities, it was found that a toll system, supplemented by a low fuel tax, is far more efficient than a fuel tax alone in improving welfare.

In a final set of simulations, a 'federal' solution was approximated by using federal preferences and eliminating fiscal externalities. Moreover, the fuel taxes were federally determined and imposed on the regional governments. For the peripheral region, the results were close to the peripheral optimum and yielded a substantial toll supplemented by a small fuel tax. At the urban level an identical fuel tax was imposed and optimally supplemented by a local toll.

This chapter should be viewed as a modest first step towards the development of a full-scale model to study the economics of price setting for transport services in a federal state. Such a model should ultimately consider the strategic interactions among the members of the federation (for example, tax competition) and capture in a more explicit way the spill overs implied by particular externalities. This remains a difficult task, both in theory and in view of data requirements (for example, information is needed on proportions of air pollution exported and imported).

Notes

1. TRENEN is a model developed in the framework of the JOULE–II programme (1994–1995) of DGXII by a consortium composed of CES – KUL Leuven (coordinator S. Proost), SESO – UFSIA Antwerp, GRETA – Venice, TCD – Dublin and VIA – RWTH Aachen.
2. The congestion costs are thus included via the consumer surplus. For the valuation of time, the study of Hague Consulting Group (1990) is used.
3. In the exercises performed in this chapter, however, this is not taken into account. The shadow price of local public funds is assumed to equal 1.
4. A car is equal to one PCU, whereas buses and trucks are both equal to two PCUs.
5. This method is described in detail in Mayeres (1992).
6. For the sake of convenience, not all modes and all variables are shown. A complete picture is available upon request from the authors.
7. The occupancy rates of public transport are fixed at 40 passengers per vehicle during the peak period and 9 passengers per vehicle during the off-peak period.
8. Recall that the federal taxes remain fixed when the policy preferences of the urban government are considered. In reality, the federal government can anticipate the behaviour of the regional governments and vice versa.
9. In the model, all urban taxes imposed on commuters are fully borne by commuters as there is no feedback via increased wages or reduced land rents.

References

Boniver, V. and B. Thiry (1993), 'Les coûts marginaux externes du transport public de personnes en milieu urbain, Estimation chiffrée pour la Belgique', *Cahiers Economiques de Bruxelles,* **142**, 203–40.

De Borger, B., I. Mayeres, S. Proost and S. Wouters (1996), 'Optimal pricing of urban passenger transport', *Journal of Transport Economics and Policy*, **30**, 31–54.

Hague Consulting Group (1990), *The Netherlands' 'Value of Time' Study: Final Report*, The Hague: Hague Consulting Group.

Keller, W.J. (1976), 'A nested CES-type utility function and its demand and price-index functions', *European Economic Review*, **7**, 175–86.

Kirwan K.J., M.M. O'Mahony, and D. O'Sullivan (1995), 'Speed–flow relationships for use in an urban transport policy assessment model', working paper, Trinity College, Dublin.

Laffont, J.J. and J. Tirole (1993), *A Theory of Incentives in Procurement and Regulation*, Cambridge, MA: MIT Press.

Mayeres, I. (1992), 'The social cost of transport: air pollution', working paper CES, Leuven.

Mayeres, I. (1993a), 'The private car user costs', working paper, CES, Leuven.

Mayeres, I. (1993b), 'The marginal external costs of car use – with an application to Belgium', *Tijdschrift voor Economie en Management*, **XXXVIII**, 225–58.

Mayeres, I. (1994), 'The marginal external costs of trucks', working paper, CES, Leuven.

Mayeres, I. and S. Proost (1997), 'Optimal taxes for congestion type of externalities', forthcoming in *Scandinavian Journal of Economics*, **99** (2), 255–73.

Newberry, D.M.G (1990), 'Road user charges in Britain', *Economic Journal*, **98**, 161–76.

Small K. and C. Kazimi (1995), 'On the costs of air pollution from motor vehicles', *Journal of Transport Economics and Policy*, **29**, 7–32.

Wildasin, D.E. (1988), 'Nash equilibria in models of fiscal competition', *Journal of Public Economics*, **35**, 229–40.

Appendix Table 9AI.1 Computation of the marginal external costs valuation

Type of externality Impact	Urban region	Peripheral region	Federation
Noise Local	Effect on noise of an extra carkm:function of speed, distance and traffic flow Valuation: hedonic housing: urban car: peak: –0.00841 ECU/carkm; off-peak: 0.0082ECU carkm; for urban bus: peak: 0.0305 ECU/buskm; off-peak:	Not included 0.076	Same valuation as the urban region
Accidents Local	Mayeres (1993b): urban and other roads: 0.0945 ECU/carkm and 0.1516 ECU/pub transp. vehkm	Mayeres (1993b): highways: 0.07825 ECU/ Carkm; Mayeres (1994): 0.06 ECU/truckkm	Same valuation as the regions
Road Depreciation Local	No	Mayeres (1994) and Newberry (1990): 0.03 ECU/truckkm	
CO_2 emissions (contribution to climate change) global	Emissions: function of urban traffic and speed Valuation= 0	Emissions: function of interregional traffic and and speed Valuation = 0	Valuation: EC energy-carbon tax: 725 BF/ton CO_2 (= 0.000018125 EC)
NO_x emissions (contribution to acidification and to ozone) National/global	Emissions: function of urban traffic and speed Valuation= Small (1995): nationwide damage= 7879 $ per ton NO_x, we use 1/10 of this estimate for urban damage: 0.0006894 ECU/g	Emissions: function of interregional traffic and speed Valuation = Small (1994): nationwide damage = 7879 $ per ton NO_x, we use 2/10 of this for interregional ozone damage: 0.0013788 ECU/g	International agreements, avoided abatement cost (Mayeres 1993b): 0.002225 ECU/g NO_x
SO_x emissions (contribution to acidification) National/global	Emissions: function of urban traffic and speed Valuation = 0	Emissions: function of interregional traffic and speed Valuation = 0	International agreements, avoided abatement cost (Mayeres 1993b): 0.000325 ECU/g SO_x
VOC emissions (contribution to ozone) National/global	Emissions: function of urban traffic and speed Valuation =Small(1995): nationwide damage 3040 $ per ton HC, we use 1/10 $ of this estimate for urban ozone damage: 0.000266 ECU/g	Emissions: function of interregional traffic and speed; Valuation = Small: nationwide damage 3040 $ per ton HC, we use 2/10 of this for interregional ozone damage: 0.000532 ECU/g	International agreements, avoided abatement cost (Mayeres 1993b):0.004565 ECU/HC
CO emissions Local	Emissions: VIA Valuation: Small (1995): 305 $/ton (=0.000266875 ECU/g)	Valuation = 0	Idem regions
Particulates (PM_{10}) Local	Emissions: Small (1995) Valuation: Small: 9121 $/ton (=0.0079808 ECU/g)	Valuation = 0	Idem regions

Index

abatement strategies, economic considerations 214
acid rain, Canada 5
acidification 49, 206, 211
AEA, Technology Consultancy Services 184, 185
aggregation and benchmark data 28–32
air pollution
  regulation 215–17
  in TRENEN model 230
  US 132
air quality
  objectives, regional measures 163–4
  problems, defined 160–64
  regional variations 159
  standards
    in European cities, computational results 187–94
    policy instruments in EU 158–202
Alberini, A. 145
Alcamo, J. 184
Almost Ideal Demand System (AIDS) 88
Ando, A. 108
Ando–Modigliani formula 108
AOT90, ozone concentrations 161, 167–8
Armington assumption 10
Armington model 20–24, 30, 36–43
  energy goods in 44–5
Armington, P.S. 108
Aroesty, J. 149
Arrow–Debreu general equilibrium 21
Athens
  air quality standards 187, 191
  car scrapping scheme 195
  NO_x emissions 197
auctioned permits 33–4, 38–43, 45
Auto/Oil Programme 159, 162, 200
automobile emissions, central versus local regulation 203–20

Baldwin, R. 101
Barker, T. 79

Baron, D. 5
Baumol, W.J. 214
Beaton, S.P. 149
Belgium 9
  environmental and transport policy 221–44
benchmark data and aggregation 28–32
Bergman, L. 107
Berlin conference 6, 16
Bishop, G.A. 149
Blanchard, O. 101
Bohm, P. 19
Böhringer, C. 7, 8–11, 19, 30
Boniver, V. 231
Boone, L. 101
Bourguignon, F. 107
Bovenberg, L. 78, 79, 101, 117
Braden, J. 2
Brunello, G. 91
Burniaux, J.-M. 18
butane, in gasoline 212

Cairo conference 6, 16
California 152
  vehicle emission standards 11–13, 131–3, 136–7, 140–41
    costs and benefits of adoption 142–6
California Air Resources Board 152
Calvert, J.B. 151
Calvert, J.G. 208, 210
Canada, acid rain 5
capital, in GEM–E3 model 108
Capros, P. 6, 7, 8, 11, 48, 76, 79, 107, 117
car emissions
  central versus local regulation 203–220
  reduction benefits 143
car scrapping schemes 162, 182–3, 195
car tax 13–14
CARB (Californian Air Resources Board) 209, 211
carbon dioxide *see* CO_2